THE GOOD
WAGNER OPERA
GUIDE

THE GOOD
WAGNER
OPERA
GUIDE

Denis Forman

Weidenfeld & Nicolson

LONDON

Chapters on *The Flying Dutchman, Tannhäuser, Tristan and Isolde, Meistersinger, The Ring* and *Parsifal* first published in Great Britain in 1994 by Weidenfeld & Nicolson

A CIP catalogue record for this book is available from the British Library.

ISBN 0 297 64401 7

Typeset by Deltatype Ltd, Birkenhead, Merseyside
Printed in Great Britain by Clays Ltd, St Ives plc

Weidenfeld & Nicolson
The Orion Publishing Group Ltd
Orion House
5 Upper Saint Martin's Lane
London, WC2H 9EA

Contents

Note

The Good Wagner Opera Guide gives the story of each of his operas, a guide to the music (Look Out For) with stars given for the best passages, some background information (News and Gossip) and a critical comment. The material covering the later operas is largely reproduced from *The Good Opera Guide* (Denis Forman, Weidenfeld & Nicolson 1994). To these the three early operas (*Die Feen, Das Liebesverbot* and *Rienzi*) are added, also *Lohengrin*. The title most commonly used for each opera is adopted, e.g. *Meistersinger, The Flying Dutchman*. There is also a brief account of Wagner's life, of his music and personality and an appendix tracing his creative path.

Wagner conducting Wagner

About Wagner (1822–1880)

During his long and controversial life many people must have called Wagner a bastard. This may have been closer to the truth than they imagined. Wagner's official father was a police actuary, Carl Friederich Wagner, but his real father may well have been one Ludwig Geyer, whom his mother married soon after her husband's death and Richard Wagner's birth on 22 May 1822. Geyer was an artistic type of no settled employment and would seem a more likely father for a musical son than a stolid Leipzig policeman.

Wagner's mother, Johanna, had been the mistress of the local mini-royal, Prince Constantin of Saxe-Weimar-Eisenach, but as the years went on her income from that source must have dwindled. Thus Wagner's claim in his autobiography *Mein Liebe* that he grew up in poverty as a ragged-arsed lad may well be true, although his claim that he was entirely self-taught in music is not. During his teens he had two tutors in musical theory and spent a year or more as a music student at Leipzig University. His early compositions have no whiff of genius, but they prove that by the age of nineteen he had mastered the basic principles of harmony and composition. He then became a poverty-stricken, unsuccessful musician bumming his way around the theatres and opera houses of north Germany until at last he landed a decent but pretty dim job as musical director of a theatre in remotest Riga. Here he shared a very small apartment with one Minna Planer whom he had just married, her sister and a wolf cub. He was soon seriously in hock. He avoided paying his debts by means of a secret midnight exodus to Paris, where he started to get into debt again. By this time he had written two operas, *Die Feen* (never performed) and *Das Liebesverbot*, whose one and only attempted performance was a disaster. In Paris he was met by Meyerbeer who was frightfully decent to him, though why he should have taken pains over a bankrupt musician from the Baltic it is hard to know. Meyerbeer tried to help Wagner get *Rienzi* put on at the Opéra but failed. So Wagner wrote music criticism for the public prints including several pieces telling the Opéra management why they were doing everything wrong, which must have done wonders for his chances of getting a commission. Nevertheless he sold them the idea of the *Dutchman* for a few hundred francs but they wouldn't let him develop it.

Just as it seemed he would be jailed for debt (for the second time) Meyerbeer helped to get *Rienzi* accepted by the Dresden Opera (which kindness Wagner repaid in later life by writing vitriolic anti-Semitic attacks on poor Meyerbeer). *Rienzi* turned out to be a wow and the *Dutchman* followed a year later. Dresdeners were not so wild about this one but Wagner (now aged thirty) got the job of number two to the Dresden Intendant.

During his Dresden years Wagner began to brood on the subjects of the operas that were going to occupy him for the rest of his life. In politics he was a leftie and incautiously let this be known pretty widely. As a result, when the 1848 Revolution broke out he had to skip out pretty fast, being a marked man (one of the Dresden Ten). He escaped to Switzerland where he lived on money he had managed to mesmerize out of two rich women. Minna was giving him a hard time and he had chronic constipation (a fact not sufficiently taken into account when discussing his music), but despite this he managed to force out *Lohengrin* which his fan and pen-pal Liszt put on in Weimar. It went down well. Wagner was now working himself into a frenzy over *The Ring* and also his huge debts (third time) when he persuaded an admirer, one Wesendonck, to pay off his debts in exchange for all future income from his works. Wesendonck also gave him a home next to his own and Wagner promptly fell in love with his wife which stopped him dead in his tracks in the matter of working on *The Ring* and switched him on to *Tristan* instead. Meanwhile, he managed to engineer a production of *Tannhäuser* at the Opéra in Paris, but it ended in disaster.

Wagner was allowed back into Germany in 1860 but within a few years he was under threat of being jailed for debt once again, this time in Vienna (fourth time). In the nick of time an angel appeared. Rich, royal and mad, this teenage (eighteen) fan bailed Wagner out. Ludwig II, the newly crowned King of Bavaria, paid his debts and gave him a luxury mansion in Munich and then set about building a jumbo-sized opera house fit for the production of the Master's masterpieces. But this was too much for the taxpayers to stomach. The Treasury put a stop to the opera house and now both Wagner and Ludwig became really unpopular. Wagner was sent off to compose in Switzerland whilst things cooled down.

Ludwig mounted *Tristan* and *Meistersinger* (a success) in the run-of-the-mill royal theatre in Munich (1868) and *Rhinegold*

(1869) and *Valkyrie* (1870). Wagner grumbled about the standards of the production but the first two helpings of the mighty *Ring* set all operatic Europe agog. Now people could see the stature of Wagner's work and the process of deification began (not that there weren't plenty of antis too). Wagner had by now taken up with Cosima, the wife of his friend the conductor Von Bülow, and he tried with a smokescreen of mendacity to conceal this scandalous matter from Ludwig. He needn't have bothered. When it did come out Ludwig just went on listening to bits of *The Ring* and didn't turn a hair.

Wagner's big idea was to set up a Festival Theatre in his own honour, built by him, at a place of his choosing and dedicated to the performance of his works and not the works of anyone else. This megalomaniac scheme actually came about in the chosen town of Bayreuth in 1872. It took four years to get the theatre built and to get the first *Ring* cycle going and by then, of course, Wagner had run out of money. In a pathetic attempt to raise funds he gave some concerts in the Royal Albert Hall in London, but the net profit was £700, about enough to pay for the costumes of a couple of Valkyries. Once again Ludwig saw him right and from then on it should have been all gas and gaiters chez the Wagners (he had married Cosima by now), what with world-wide fame and the success of his last opera *Parsifal*, but it wasn't. In Bayreuth Wagner did not produce or conduct himself but he couldn't leave a production alone. He therefore made the lives of the producers and the music directors and everyone else on the picture pretty well unbearable. Also his megalomania led him to think that he would do for the human race in general what he had done for opera – namely reform it root and branch. So he set to work writing out his plans for the salvation of mankind, which included quite a lot of Nietzsche's notions plus vegetarianism, anti-Semitism and a good deal about Christ's blood. He died in the grand manner at the age of seventy.

As a composer Wagner was a genius. As a man he was distinctly unpleasant, being an egomaniac who believed that as a great artist he had a divine right to do anything, say anything, follow any whim regardless. He took no thought for anyone else unless they could further his concerns or were women he wanted to go to bed with. He was anti-Semitic. He was a con man. His philosophizing was a load of bunk. He was a liar. He was a congenital debtor. But here, strangely enough, his musical genius saved him from prison at least four times, for on each occasion he was bailed out by one or other of his admirers. Some people find it hard to separate the Dr Jekyll Wagner from Wagner the Mr Hyde, and rubbish his music because the man was such a horror. This is a mistake because his music is very very good.

THE MUSIC

Wagner's story really begins with the *Dutchman* and ends with *Parsifal*, ten huge steps in taking opera from where she used to be to where he wanted to put her. His aim was music drama, a seamless robe of music and words woven together to make a work of high art which was the noblest aim in life. High art should be produced not just for the rich and clever, but for all mankind to whom if it were good enough, it would have an instant appeal. (So those persons fidgeting at the back of the hall whilst Wotan is doing his stuff must either be suffering from original sin or Jewish).

None of this theorizing (Wagner must be the only composer who during his lifetime wrote almost as many words as notes) prevented him from getting on with his work on the operas; his revolutionary theories proved to be practical. He did change the face of opera. He did make his vision come alive. The way he did it – the whole business of Wagner's methods of composing, leitmotifs (mottos), word setting, orchestration and all is fully discussed in the *General Hello to The Ring* (page 123).

If one takes an overall view of the Wagnerian saga one can see that the *Dutchman* was still pretty well a numbers opera (Senta's Ballad, the Sailors' Chorus). Some of the bits between numbers were a kind of souped-up recitatif but others were moving towards the vintage Wagner (the Dutchman's long solos in partnership with an active orchestra). This is what the later bel cantos would call arioso, but it is high-powered arioso with a continuous drive. There are mottos, not many, all unmistakable and often used like the bell on an ice-cream cart to let you know what vehicle is coming down the road. Wagner took great pains to make the overture into a concert piece and it turned out to be the best tone poem of its day, catching both the smell of the sea and the spookiness of the phantom ship wonderfully well.

There is no huge advance in the technique for *Tannhäuser*. Still there are numbers ('O Star of Eve'). There are a lot of good tunes and the mottos are used more widely than in the *Dutchman*. *Lohengrin* is a great step forward. A few seams still show in the set pieces (The Bridal Chorus, Elsa's Dream) but these aside the whole piece flows steadily along from start to finish and in particular the chorus is magnificently integrated into the drama. *Meistersinger* is the most friendly of the later operas. It meets us on our own ground. Everyone is a human being, everything is real life, no Nibelungers, no sprouting staves. It has its set numbers but now they come only when there is a song required by the plot (the Trial Song, the Schusterlied, the Prize Song). There are mottos, but limited in number and very precise in what they mean (Apprentices, Masters, Cobbling). It is a huge work.

With *Tristan* Wagner moves into a new and dreamy world also into a new harmonic field which is a million miles away from the four-square diatonic *Dutchman* of twenty years before. Mottos stand for feelings, not things, and they are used with greater subtlety. The climaxes are emotional, not physical. No Ride of the Valkyries here and no terminal flames shooting up from Valhalla, but a lovers' duet and a lovers' death.

So to the mighty *Ring*. Now all Wagner's theories were put into practice with results that have amazed the world. The motto-work in itself is immensely complex, both from the musical and the psychological point of view. There is practically nothing in the field of human industry, including the building of the Great Wall of China, that so stuns the imagination as the amount of toil that went into the creation of *The Ring*. But at last there it was, the new thing, over a dozen hours of music drama, something quite different from what we used to call opera.

With *Parsifal* there was some retreat from the system of mickey-mouse mottos. Now mottos are even more general, they stand for concepts and ideas rather than specific things or feelings, e.g. the idea of the holiness of the Grail rather than for the jug itself, the idea of a holy wound rather than the hole in Amfortas's side. The secular bits of *Parsifal* have as much zest and zing as anything in *The Ring* but the music of the holy parts drifts upwards onto Cloud Nine, where it is sometimes very beautiful and sometimes just a little nauseating when you consider the nature and characteristics of its creator.

It is impossible to imagine a world in which Wagner never happened. If we had lost either of the other two 'greats' they would have left a devastating gap in the repertoire, but opera would have gone on. Mozart, at the time, was seen as one of many. Verdi carried Italian opera to glorious heights, but had there been no Verdi Puccini would no doubt have picked up the baton just the same. But without Wagner we would be missing the second act of all opera. In no other art did one man make such an impact. It is as if in the world of the visual arts the post-Impressionists had all been one man. He was at the same time a horror, a phenomenon and a genius. But he was Wagner, and he has left us some of the greatest work ever created by the human imagination.

Die Feen
(The Fairies)

Fairytale fantasy

The one where a doe hunted by a king is transformed into a fairy princess and subsequently, because he asks a forbidden question, encased in stone.

CAST

Arindal, King of Tramund	Tenor
Ada, a fairy princess and Arindal's wife	Soprano
Lora, Arindal's sister	Soprano
Morald, Arindal's friend, Lora's good friend	Baritone
Gernot, Arindal's gamekeeper	Bass
Drolla, Lora's maid	Soprano
Gunther, courtier to Arindal	Tenor
King of the Fairies	Bass
Harald, Arindal's C-in-C	Bass
Fairies, a messenger, the voice of Gruma	

3 acts: running time 2 hrs 45 mins

STORY

Before we begin

Prince Arindal whilst engaging in blood sports with his hunter Gernot pursued a singularly beautiful doe into fairyland. Here, in proper fairy fashion, the doe was transmogrified into Ada, a fairy princess. Naturally there was love at first sight followed by marriage and two children. But marriage was conditional on Arindal never, but never, asking Ada who she was. After seven years Arindal gets the seven-year itch and pops the forbidden question. Bang! Crash! Thunder! He and the faithful Gernot (who has asked no questions at all) are magicked out of fairyland into a nasty rocky desert.

Back in fairyland Ada pines for Arindal and decides she will rejoin him on earth and become a mortal. But her dad, the King of the fairies, a hard man, lays down a number of sufferings Arindal must endure if she joins him on earth. [Probably heard about Hercules: Ed.]

Act I Sc 1

We are in fairyland, indeed a fairy garden with female fairies in considerable numbers. Two leading fairies say that silly Ada may want to follow that no-good Arindal back to earth. We must not lose her girls! We must stop it! Kindly use your best endeavours, they sing.

Sc 2

Gernot mooning about on his own in the rocky place suddenly meets two old mates from Arindal's court, Morald and Gunther. He tells them Arindal has married into fairyland. We must get the lad back home, they say. Arindal comes on moaning about the loss of Ada. The three chaps hide until he has finished his rather long aria. They then try a number of tricks (disguising themselves as a priest and – God help us – as Arindal's dead father etc.) which fail. But when Morald tells Arindal his kingdom lies in ruins he suddenly and surprisingly agrees to go quietly. Meanwhile he takes a nap.

Sc 3

Back in fairyland: Ada's palace. I am very miserable, she sings. Then Arindal wakes up not in the rocky place but right here in Ada's palace. The men from earth are there too. What a smashing bird, says Morald, I can see why he wants to stay. Two leading fairies enter. Ada, they say, your dad, the King, is dead and now you are our Queen. Oh my God, says Ada, I can't go down to earth now. Maybe I can come later but only if you swear you will never curse me (for some reason she is forbidden to tell him about the sufferings ahead). Curse you? Of course not. No, never, says the somewhat confused Arindal. I swear.

Act II Sc 1

Back on earth Arindal's sister Lora (a ringer for Boadicea) tries to hype up the spirits of her cowardly troops who are scared to death by the enemy at their gates. She is, however, fearful on another account – that her brother Arindal will never return. But no, a herald announces that he is on the way and no sooner is he announced than he arrives along with Morald and soon after Gunther and Gernot. Joy! Bliss! Gernot is reunited with his girlfriend Drolla and for some strange reason they both volunteer that they have been sleeping around during their time apart. So we have a comedy quarrel and reconciliation. Now Ada appears, having decided to come to earth and take the risk of Arindal cursing her. She tells us at great length that the King has told her to do terrible things to Arindal to induce him to curse her. If and when he curses she will be turned into stone.

The enemy at the gates who have kept quiet to allow for the comedy scene now start to carry on something dreadful. Come on Arindal, lead us out into battle says Morald. Not in the mood, says Arindal, lead them out yourself. Suddenly Ada is in our midst with the two kids. Nice to see you again children, says Arindal. Give them back to me, says Ada, seizing them and chucking them over a nearby cliff. That was a nasty thing to do, Ada, says Arindal. Now the army is back, quickly beaten and in disarray, Morald dead. Harald the C-in-C comes in. You win? asks everyone. Nope, says Harald. A woman called Ada came and dispersed my troops, (spotting Ada) ah, there she is. This is a terrible woman also my wife says Arindal. Ada, I curse you. Two fairies appear to reclaim Ada for fairyland. O Lord now I'll be encased in stone for a hundred years says she. But you killed my children, says Arindal (the children rush in, alive and well); and dispersed Harald's troops (they were enemy troops, Harald is a traitor, says Ada); and killed Morald (Morald enters shouting that he has won the war). I'm confused, says Arindal [No wonder: Ed.] Well anyway we have victory, say the troops. Sorry Ada. I misjudged you, says Arindal. Will you please take me back? I can't, says Ada, anyway I'm just about to be encased in stone.

Act III Sc 1

We are in a room in Arindal's palace but the poor fellow has gone potty. Morald and Lora have been appointed King and Queen. The people rejoice and exit. The mad Arindal stumbles on. He hears Ada's distant voice. I'm encased in stone, she says, and not very comfortable. But now he hears another voice, the voice of Gruma, the family sage, now deceased. Get moving Arindal, says Gruma's voice, you can still save Ada; here are the necessary props – a shield, a sword and a lyre. They appear by magic.

The two leading fairies enter. Let's encourage Arindal to try to liberate Ada, they say (a nasty plot: they are certain he will be killed in the attempt). Wakey wakey, Arindal, they cry. We'll lead you to rescue Ada.

Sc 2

Now we are in a gruesome underground cavern where Ada's stone coffin is defended by a small army of sprites. Arindal attacks them and is about to be licked when Gruma's voice cues him: THE SHIELD it says. Arindal grabs the shield. Instantly the sprites disappear.

Suddenly we are at another mouth of the cavern guarded by a platoon of bronze men. Arindal takes them on, but this time the shield doesn't work. Gruma cues him again: THE SWORD. Arindal defeats them. A rock splits open and lo and behold there is Ada's stone coffin. Arindal gets his third cue: THE LYRE. Arindal sings an extempore song. The stone melts away. Ada and Arindal embrace.

Sc 3

Now we are at the court of the King of the fairies. [Risen from the dead? Or former reports of his death greatly exaggerated? Ed] You done well Arindal, says the King. I have decided to make you an immortal. Morald, Lora and Co. are led up (from earth). OK you lot you can rule over my earthly kingdom. I'm immortal now, says Arindal. Just see what the power of love can do, sing the fairy chorus. Yes indeed.

LOOK OUT FOR
MINUTES FROM START
Overture

This is a lively concert piece with a Weber-like whirl amongst the strings as its first tune and a pert little march (which lives long in the ear) in its second. The construction and carpentry are again modelled on Weber, but Weber on an off day, for the joins and links sound like apprentice work. There are some generous helpings of noisy bluster that mean little, and the thumping at the end seems interminable.

Act I Sc 1

Fairy music for two solo fairies and chorus. All

agreeable but in no way arresting.

Act I Sc 2

This long scene for the four men keeps interest alive throughout. The recitatif is easy on the ear and the song passages if not exactly tuneful, flow pleasantly. Arindal's first number, although too long, has style. There is mickey-mousing for thunder, the ghost trick etc. but for the rest the music does not always follow the sense of the words as when, for instance, Arindal learns of doom and disaster in his kingdom in the course of a jolly bar-room trio.

27: *Doch trug sie einen ring*

27

Act I Sc 3

Ada's opening Cavatina is one of the two best pieces in the opera.* It has a quaint engaging melody – quite unlike the later Wagner we know and love – and is simple, elegant and moving.

42: *Wie muss ich doch*

42

The ensuing Arindal/Ada duet is written in a mixture of quasi-recitatif and mini-aria and it runs along well enough. This is followed by the long concerted finale in which the plot develops at break-neck speed with huge emphasis on the forbidden curse and lots of fortissimo singing by the fairies as they hail their new queen.

Act II

Lora's exhortation to her cavalry troops and their choral response make up a pretty high-class opening scene. Her solo lamenting the absence of Arindal is quite striking, and when she swings from recitatif into aria it has pathos and charm.* The return of Arindal and the Morald/Lora duet hold up well and then we plunge deep into Weber-land with a lengthy (and it must be confessed clumsy) buffo duet between Gernot and Drolla turning on the topic of mutual infidelity.

6: *O Mosst du Hoffnung*

6

Some standard fairy recitatif introduces Ada's great Act II solo. This is long (eleven minutes), powerful, and when it switches from recitatif to aria it turns into something of a test piece for budding Wagnerian sopranos, and judging from the response to it on the only available CD, a

25: *Weh mir*

25

live recording, it can clearly bring an audience to its feet. The long Weber tune from the overture reappears during its later stages.*

In the again long finale (seventeen minutes) climax is piled upon climax as the plot bounds along from one astonishing event to the next. There are occasional lulls, as when an over-sweet flute accompanies the children's arrival on stage and moments of hush after they have been chucked into the abyss, when the traitor Harald enters and after Arindal has given vent to the dreaded curse, but otherwise it is pretty well turmoil all the way including a frenzied outburst from Ada herself. There is a much quieter duet between Ada and Arindal as everything comes right – children alive, Morald victorious, Harald unmasked – but then the act ends with a welter of noisy and somewhat banal choral rejoicing.

Act III Sc 1

In the first scene of Act III the opera moves up a gear. The opening chorus is dramatic yet restrained, the following sextet a big success, with a sotto voce chorus deferentially supporting the six in their prayer and the crazy Arindal putting on a fine vocal display of madness – much demented recitatif with a touching central aria and mellifluous short interludes by the woodwind.

10: *Mein gatte Arindal*

So it goes on. When the sleeping Arindal hears the absent Ada's aria it is a good one and the offstage voice of the mysterious Gruma has the appropriate resonance and solemnity. Arindal's exchange with the two fairies keeps up the standard and the trio that closes the scene is lively and catches Arindal's mood of fresh determination. Altogether quite the best scene in the opera.*

10

Act III Sc 2

Now we enter that part of the story that lies dangerously near pantomime. The action is rapid, the plot races forward from one piece of fairy business to the next and the music – alas –

33: *Oh ihr Des busens*
Act III Sc 3

has to do what it can to add to the melodrama. This it does manfully with one or two decent short choruses from gnomes, sprites and armed men. Arindal's lyre song is tuneful and appealing though scarcely, perhaps, powerful enough to melt a concrete coffin.

33

This very short scene (six minutes) ends the opera with the fairy king singing his blessing in a kingly way, the chorus going through the standard reactions of rejoicing, hailing etc. But it is scrappy and by no means up to the quality of the music of Scene 1. The perky tune from the overture pops up again at the end, but in a much less sexy form.

NOTES

Die Feen   Wagner's first completed opera
First night   Munich Königliches Hof-und Nationaltheater June 1888
Reception   Not known, but it caused no stir
Libretto   Wagner
Source   *La Donna Serpente*, a fairytale by Gozzi

NEWS AND GOSSIP

Wagner's first two attempts at opera were snuffed out by the disapproval of his family. For the very first (*Shäferoper*) he wrote no music at all; for the second (*Die Hoenzeit*) he got as far as the overture and an opening chorus before his sister Rosalin made him tear them up. But when emancipated from his family as an apprentice chorus master at Wurzburg he set to on *Die Feen* without interference. He picked the story from the writings of one Carlo Gozzi, whose form of transformation for the heroine was not into stone but into a snake and wrote the 'poem' himself. He started work on *Die Feen* early in 1833 and finished it a year later. Not bad for a lad of twenty with a full-time job as chorus master. Alas, no one would put it on; and as yet he had no muscle in musical politics and no friends to hassle for him. *Die Feen* was not performed in Germany until five years after Wagner's death and not in England until 1969, when it was put on in Birmingham by the concisely titled Midland Music Makers Grand Opera Society.

COMMENT

There is not much in *Die Feen* to have us think that Wagner was going to be a great, great opera composer. The young Rossini had had seven operas produced at the same age (twenty-one) but for Wagner this was clearly an exercise in learning. Yet it does have a few positive indicators. It shows that Wagner can orchestrate, can build a climax, and above all can write a tune. There are many promising tunes in *Die Feen* which slip by almost unnoticed and undeveloped and this is in sharp contrast to his later work where every scrap of melody is made to work to the full and some of the mottos or motifs are hammered nearly to death.

If *Die Feen* were revived today – and it should be – it would come off as a pleasant evening of simple opera going. Arindal and Ada have a top-class aria each, there is one complete scene (Act III Sc 1) which would bear comparison with what the Italians did in the same style and although longish for its weight ($2\frac{3}{4}$ hours) it is seldom boring. The ludicrous plot is a heavy disadvantage. The final verdict must in honesty be between a beta and a gamma.

Das Liebesverbot
(The Ban On Love)

Sexual Comedy

Shakespeare's *Measure for Measure* (well, more or less) set to music in old-time Palermo.

CAST

Frederick, Viceroy of Palermo		Bass
Isabella, Novice in a convent		Soprano
Claudio, Isabella's brother		Tenor
Mariana, Frederick's ex-wife, now co-novice with Isabella		Soprano
Lucio, a man about town		Tenor
Antonio	Sicilian gents	Tenor
Angelo		Bass
Dorella, once Isabella's servant, now a barmaid		Soprano
Pontius Pilate, a ruffian, later a gaoler		Tenor
Danielli, bar owner		Bass

2 acts: running time 2 hrs 30 mins

STORY

Act I Sc 1

We are in a fairground in sunny Sicily, some five hundred years ago. The King is taking a long holiday in the Bahamas, so he has appointed Frederick, an unpopular German and a fanatical moralist as his Regent. Brighella, the chief of police and his boys in blue are breaking up liquor stores and arresting folks right and left and centre. What's all this about? cry the citizens. Orders from the boss, says Brighella. Anyone boozing or indulging in sexual hanky-panky will be punished by death. Amongst the prisoners taken are aristocrat Claudio, who is known to have had it off with a high-born lady Julia, and a barmaid Dorella, one-time lady's maid to Claudio's sister Isabella. Luckily for Claudio his man-about-town friend Lucio comes on unarrested and says he will ask Claudio's sister Isabella, a person of influence, now a novice in a convent, to plead for his life.

Sc 2

The courtyard of a convent. Isabella is chatting to a new recruit, her old friend Mariana. They let their hair down. I came in because all my family (except surely brother Claudio) died, says Isabella. I came because I was secretly married to that ghastly regent Frederick and he dumped me because I was too common and might have spoiled his chances of getting the top job, says Mariana. She exits. Lucio comes on and says Isabella you must save your brother Claudio's life by pleading, and anyway I fancy you. Will you be my wife? Not on your life, says Isabella, you are known to be in the habit of sleeping around quite a lot.

Sc 3

A courtroom. The court awaits the arrival of Regent Frederick. Brighella decides to take on the role of magistrate and tries a common person with the unlikely name of Pontius Pilate. He sentences him to exile for pimping. Next he tries Dorella for serving liquor but finds her extremely sexy and makes a pass at her instead. The Regent arrives and gives Brighella a severe reprimand for his presumption. Business proceeds. A delegation presents a petition to hold a carnival. Not on your life, says Frederick, and tears it up. Next Claudio, whom he condemns to death along with his girlfriend Julia. Isabella arrives and asks for a private word. The court is cleared. She pleads for Claudio. Frederick begins to feel very sexy. He lusts for her. He offers a deal: Claudio will be spared if she agrees to go to bed with him. The gob-smacked Isabella says she will expose his hypocrisy to all the citizens of Palermo who immediately and obligingly rush into the courtroom. Frederick tells her that if he says she is lying everyone will believe him, not her. Isabella has a brainwave. She accepts the deal but will send a proxy, Mariana, disguised, to have sex with the wicked Frederick, her one-time husband.

Act II Sc 1

We are in the garden of the prison where Claudio is held. Isabella, a prison visitor, tells him that Frederick will release him but only if she agrees to have sex with him. No! Never! Your virtue is more important than my life, cries Claudio. But then as he thinks about it, well, perhaps not. After all it's only for one night. Go on, Sister, do it, he begs. Shut your eyes and think of Palermo. You cowardly bastard, she says, and decides not to tell him of her scheme for Mariana to act as her sex-substitute. She will intercept Claudio's reprieve and let the dirty dog sweat for a while. Exit Claudio, enter Dorella. Isabella –

1) Gives her a letter to Frederick arranging the meeting.
2) Also a letter to Mariana giving her her marching orders.
3) Tells her to get Brighella, who is crazy about her, to intercept the pardon.

Isabella then chats Dorella up about Lucio, a well-known man-about-town, whom she clearly fancies. Dorella says his reputation is simply terrible, he had propositioned every nubile woman in Palermo including herself. Lucio comes in to see how it is going for his friend Claudio. Dorella says how about all that hanky-panky and your promise to marry me, eh? Lucio brushes her off. Isabella tells Lucio of Frederick's proposition. I'll kill the bastard, yells Lucio, and rants and raves in a state of considerable outrage for quite a long time. Isabella is impressed. Pontius Pilate comes in and says he has been promoted from being a criminal to become a screw. Isabella offers him a hundred bucks to hand over Claudio's reprieve to her as soon as he gets it. [In case her message to Pontius's boss Brighella didn't work? Ed.]

Sc 2

Frederick broods: on the one hand his high moral principles, on the other sex with Isabella. A difficult time for him and he is quite upset. Dorella comes in and hands him Isabella's note saying OK, I'm on, let's meet at the Corso, but masked. Frederick is chuffed and gloats prospectively. Brighella asks Dorella to meet him on the Corso, and she says yes, but masked.

Sc 3

An illegal carnival is starting up on the Corso despite Frederick's veto. Brighella and his boys put on a show of trying to stop it. Things get rough and Lucio comes on to referee. The Corso clears and Brighella goes off (masked) to find Dorella. Isabella and Mariana come on (masked). Mariana goes to the rendezvous with Frederick as set up by Isabella.

Now things happen quickly [and confusingly: Ed.] Frederick comes in (masked) but Lucio has recognized him and follows saying what a ghastly hypocrite this Frederick is, trying to stop our fun while trying to get into bed with Isabella and making other nasty anti-Frederick remarks. When Frederick meets Mariana (masked) both men take her for Isabella. Lucio lurks. He is jealous. But Dorella rushes on and get physical with Lucio saying she will not let him go unless they have a little hanky-panky together. Isabella and Brighella, both lurking, both masked, see all this. Brighella is not pleased and emerges. Dorella runs away from him. Lucio follows Frederick and Mariana offstage.

Pontius comes on and dutifully gives Isabella Claudio's reprieve. She opens it and finds that Frederick has double-crossed her. It is no reprieve; Claudio is to die. A furious Isabella calls the citizens on to the Corso and publicly exposes Frederick as a womanizer, a hypocrite and a double-crosser. The citizens are aghast: Frederick says OK it's a fair cop; I'm ready for the chop: the citizens surprisingly decide to forgive him. Isabella takes up with Lucio, Brighella with Dorella (no news about poor Mariana) and they all go off joyfully to the docks to greet the King disembarking, greatly refreshed as one hopes by his trip to the Bahamas, and fortunate not to have landed a couple of hours earlier.

LOOK OUT FOR
MINUTES FROM START
Overture

> The overture is a lively piece with two main tunes and one motif or motto. The first tune could be mistaken for Offenbach at his most theatrical, although it is in fact very close to the theme twice used by Rossini in the early stages of both *Comte D'Ory* and *Voyage à Rheims*. Each time it is interrupted by the dark brooding Puritan motto (slow, emphatic strings in unison). After the Offenbach tune has died a natural death we have a sweet legato melody from the strings (represents the power of love and will be heard again, – not quite a motto), which picks up in pace to reach a slightly clumsy climax. Next a minor Offenbach tune, a second helping of both Rossini and the sweet melody, some trumpeting and a gallop to the finish still based on Rossini. Carnival-like castanets and tambourines

abound throughout. Delightful, and never performed.

Act I Sc 1

The opera opens with a lengthy musically confused carnival scuffle whilst Brighella does his police work. From time to time solo lines swing out of the somewhat confused texture as each principal develops his part of the story. When the crowd ask who is responsible for the new law Brighella does not sing but reads Frederick's decree aloud. This is greeted by what can only be called the Ha Ha Chorus. Claudio now takes the stage with a new and catchy tune which works together with Offenbach until we reach Claudio's cavatina in which he begs Lucio to persuade Isabella to plead for his life. A very lengthy choral scene ensues which eventually concludes this very lively first scene.

15: *Du kennst Jenen*

15

Act I Sc 2

Scene two opens with holy bells and a reference to the Dresden Amen, (to reappear much later more importantly in *Parsifal*). Then we have a brief but agreeable chorus of nuns who walk off to leave the stage clear for a duet between Mariana and Isabella. This opens with a dryish recitatif but flowers dramatically as Mariana tells all. Isabella reacts with a powerful outburst of outrage and this leads to Mariana's first aria, tuneful and easy on the ear. The two together then express sisterly feelings in a long but never dull duet.* Bells again, exit Mariana, enter Lucio with a Sousa-like flourish. After an inappropriately jaunty recitatif and a pleasant cavatina Lucio and Isabella launch into a lengthy duet at first declamatory but moving into a lyrical mode as Lucio starts to fancy Isabella. After his proposal of marriage this speeds up into hurry music as Lucio pleads eagerly and Isabella takes flight into coloratura passages of high virtuosity. All very fine and thoroughly satisfactory.*

20: *Las mir Die träner*

20

22: *Göttlicher frieden*

22

25: *Er fület réu und will*

25

Act I Sc 3

At the outset we hear the Puritan motto but soon we are off into a buffo scene as Brighella 'tries' Pontius Pilate. Some recitatif, some oom-pah tunes and nothing distinguished except for the lively and original orchestral accompaniment. Brighella's scene with Dorella, which follows (still Italian-style buffo), is much more fun and full of catchy snatches of song and laced with ironical references to the Puritan motto. It ends with the seduction duet.

A confused chorus number marks the entry of the crowd and continues until Frederick enters, not very impressively. Some jolly stuff as Antonio (a minor figure) presents the carnival petition which Frederick turns down with a strong negative (the Puritan motto again). The following duet with Claudio is the high spot of this scene – it is melodious, inventive and garnished with a number of catchy side-tunes

58: *Ha, ihr seid Claudio*

from the orchestra.** So to the run-of-the-mill chorus and ensemble that greets Isabella's arrival. 58

A charming woodwind introduction leads to the first part of Isabella's big aria (all right but no stunner). After some interruptions by Frederick she moves into the much better second

72: *Kennst du das lied*

part with a grand climax in part three, powerful, effective and a winner.** 72

Frederick then puts his disgraceful proposition in agitato recitatif and, reeling from shock, Isabella calls in the citizens for yet another chorus, intending to expose his villainy. In an almost jaunty side exchange over a walking bass Frederick convinces Isabella (rather quickly) that no one will believe her if she accuses him. As she stands irresolute she is given sympathetic support first from a gentle and sweet trio of Angelino, Dorella and Brighella, and then the full chorus. But when she has the bright idea of substituting Mariana for herself the musical mood changes in a recitatif which is all dash and

86: *Maria wie o gotterlicht*

go. This is followed by an incongruously cheery duet between Frederick and Isabella (He: I must have her. She: Revenge) leading to a chorus of confusion [no wonder: Ed.] Now begins a race towards the end of the act – the plot unwinding at incomprehensible speed with duets, solos but mainly the chorus with frequent interjections from the principals. All very jolly.

Act II Sc 1

A gloomy but fortunately short prelude leads us to Claudio lamenting his plight in a wimpish cavatina of no great merit. Things look up when Isabella arrives and tells him of Frederick's villainy in melodramatic style. The long duet that follows is not notable so long as Claudio remains noble but when he stoops to plead that his sister trades her virtue for his life things liven up considerably and the scene ends with brio.

9: *Ha feiger*

    Claudio is taken off by the gaolers as Isabella rehearses her plan in pedestrian recitatif again interspersed with short bursts of melody from the orchestra, the first of which will reach its full and final form in the grand march in *Tannhäuser*. This is followed by a spell of even more banal recitatif (optionally spoken, not sung) as Dorella gets her marching orders. Now, as Lucio the philanderer is exposed, we have a lively trio with two Donizetti-like tunes in quick succession. This gathers pace as Frederick's proposition is unfolded and Claudio responds with outrage. A good number. Another batch of seemingly unnecessary spoken dialogue ends the scene.

16: *Sei's so*

Act II Sc 2

So now it's Frederick with a dark and broody recitatif about being guilty and then a somewhat soppy aria as his mind turns to his love/desire/lust for Isabella. But when he gets her letter he breaks into a splendid triumphal piece of gloating,* tamped down only slightly by residual thoughts of guilt and the decision not to

5: *Von Isabella diese Nacht*

Act II Sc 3

free Claudio. Another bout of spoken dialogue (this time more relevant) ends the scene.

A prelude and chorus such as you would expect at a carnival. Everyone urges everyone else to be jolly and Lucio sings a ditty. Then there is a wild Sicilian dance to the Rossini tune first heard in the overture [omitted in the only CD recording of the opera: Ed.] The attempt by the officious Brighella to stop everything, the crowd's angry reaction and Lucio's pacification are all dealt with quickly and efficiently. And

47: *Verweile hier*

now we have a little miracle – a duet between the apprehensive Mariana and the determined Isabella. A sweet woodwind phrase leads into a lyrical dialogue between the two with many hints of the Wagner to come both in its melodic

50: *Welch wunderbar*

line and in some bold harmonic shifts.** Isabella leaves and Mariana gives her big number, again slow, sweet and beautiful.

47

50

The encounters between Frederick and Lucio and Lucio and Dorella pass off well enough with the only real interest lying once again in some adventurous work by the orchestra. But now Wagner seems to have exhausted his powers of invention and the temperature drops – even Isabella's shock solo when she discovers the pardon is no pardon at all is not up to snuff. The last bout of plot-unwinding is made up of a combination of solos (explaining) and chorus (exclaiming). Some earlier tunes are called back for duty, a stage band heralds the return of the king and the closing choruses are predictable, repetitious but (for once) not too long.

NOTES

Das Liebesverbot	Wagner's second opera.
First Night	Magdeburg Stadttheater March 1836
Libretto	Wagner
Source	Shakespeare's *Measure for Measure*

NEWS AND GOSSIP

In 1834 at the age of twenty-one Wagner was on a walking tour in Bohemia with a friend when he read two books that set his pulse racing. They were *Ardinghello* by Wilhelm Heinze and *Das Junge Europa* by Heinrich Lauve, both advocating free love and declaring war on Puritanism. So Wagner embarked on an opera about sexual liberation, based on Shakespeare's *Measure for Measure* (which is not about sexual liberation at all). He also decided that he would make it a comedy. Work started on the libretto in June 1834 and the opera was completed in July 1836.

The first and only attempted performance of *Das Liebesverbot* in Wagner's lifetime was a fiasco. A back stage row aborted the performance just after the overture. A planned second performance never happened and after that Wagner seems to have given up and never tried to get it afloat again.

Years later he presented the score to his patron and bank-roller King Ludwig of Bavaria with an inscription worthy of Uriah Heap which has been translated (badly) as follows:

> I know that in my youth I went astray
> And now that error I would fain repair.
> The child of sin at your feet let me lay
> Hoping that it may find forgiveness there.

Das Liebesverbot was not given again in Germany until 1923 (in Munich) and in England in an abridged form at University College London in 1965. There was a top-class revival at the Munich Opera Festival in 1982 but aside from that no known professional production.

COMMENT

There are many operas, some by famous composers, which lie on the shelf in well-deserved obscurity. *Liebesverbot* is not one of them. It is almost incredible that in these days of adventurous opera impresarios that there has never been a revival. There is little doubt that it would give the average opera goer an evening in the theatre perhaps less weighty but every bit as enjoyable as *Tannhäuser*. Although Wagner had not yet found his true persona as an opera composer it is an accomplished piece, with several really good numbers, and it is full of delights. Unlike all the later operas it has no pretensions to grandeur, holiness, mythology of the sublime power of love.

Its strengths lie in its set-piece numbers, in particular the big arias for Isabella and Mariana, in the several duets and trios of which the duet between Frederick and Claudio in Act I and the trio with Isabella, Dorella and Lucio in Act II are outstanding, in its musical architecture and in the racy buffo encounters between the characters in the sub-plots. The orchestral writing throughout is inventive and constantly livens up events with an astonishingly prolific supply of catchy side-tunes which go far beyond the range of the orchestral accompaniment supplied by Donizetti, Bellini and Co. who are, of course, the models from which *Liebesverbot* derives.

Its weakness lies in the spoken dialogue, which is pedestrian, in the recitatifs which are often drab and in some of the seemingly interminable choruses. Also Wagner has not yet learnt how to tell a story in operatic form. The Italians moved the plot forward in recitatif, less often in discourse amongst the principals, reserving the ensembles and finales only for great dramatic strokes. But in *Liebesverbot* Wagner often develops a plot of great complexity, by means of high-speed interjections by principals in the midst of huge choruses, thereby ensuring that the audience can have no hope of grasping what is going on.

Liebesverbot is pastiche, but well-digested pastiche, and it has its own integrity within a borrowed style. Surprisingly, the German influence of Weber and others, so dominant in *Die Feen*, has completely disappeared.

So two cheers for *Liebesverbot*, Wagner's surprise package, and a clear B+ and please, opera directors all, let us have a revival as soon as you can fit this lively piece into your repertory.

Rienzi

The one about the last tribune of Rome who becomes the people's
Führer but not for long.

CAST

Rienzi, tribune of Rome	Tenor
Irene, his sister	Soprano
Colonna, a nobleman	Bass
Adriano, Colonna's son	Mezzo-Soprano
Orsini, another nobleman	Bass
Raimundo, the Pope's man in Rome	Bass
Barroncelli ⎫ Roman citizens	Tenor
Cecco ⎭	Bass

Ambassadors of Peace, nobles, priests, monks, soldiers, messengers and citizens.
5 acts: running time 3 hrs 45 mins (with cuts, see NEWS AND
GOSSIP).

STORY

Act 1 Sc 1

It is ancient Rome but not so very ancient – fifth century AD – and
the Roman noblemen are behaving badly. One lot, the Orsinis, are
trying to abduct Rienzi's sister Irene by means of an expanding
ladder. Another lot, the Colonnas, try to stop them and the result
is a good old inter-family fracas. The Pope's man, Cardinal
Raimundo, tells them to give over. They tell him to get lost. Enter
Rienzi. You miserable scruffs, he says, this lawless behaviour is
dreadfully bad form and has brought Rome into disrepute. Stop it.
The citizens cheer. Good man, Rienzi, they cry. Listen to these
sweaty nightcaps telling us what to do, say the nobles, but OK,
owing to the strength of public opinion, we will take an
intermission now and resume battle outside the city gates at 06 30
tomorrow morning.

Aha, thinks Rienzi, aha, I will shut the gates whilst they are out
there fighting. He puts it to the citizens and asks if they will
support him. Sure thing, Rienzi, they cry, you are our only hope.
Right, says Rienzi, when, tomorrow morning, you hear a trumpet
sound turn out on parade in full battle order and we will fall on

them outside the walls. And God is on your side too, says the Pope's man, Raimundo.

Sc 2

Rienzi, Irene and Adriano Colonna, son of Colonna, are on stage. How is it with you Sis? asks Rienzi. This Adriano here saved me from abduction, says she. Thanks Adriano, says Rienzi, in this shindig with the nobles are you on my side or your family's side? Difficult decision, says Adriano. On the one hand I greatly admired your speech about freeing Rome from the nobles. On the other hand my dad is one of the nobles and I don't want to fight against him. Chicken, says Rienzi. Did you know that my young brother was killed in one of your noblemen's brawls and the murderer was a Colonna? Terribly sorry about that, says Adriano. How can I make up for it? Support me in the class struggle, says Rienzi. OK, I will, says Adriano. Good man, says Rienzi. Good man, says Irene. Great, says Rienzi, I must be off to organize the people's rising. Would you kindly look after Irene for me? (Exits)

Sc 3

Do you trust me, Irene, says Adriano. You know I am a Colonna. Sure I trust you, says Irene. What if the nobles lick Rienzi and his mob, what then? says Adriano. Don't be so damn gloomy, says Irene, and by the way I love you. I love you too, says Adriano, and what is that sound I hear? [It is the alarum trumpet: the night has passed very quickly: Ed.]

Sc 4

The citizens swarm on. The nobles have been licked. Hey ho for freedom, they shout. Dawn breaks and a large choir (the Pope's) processes from backstage singing Freedom At Last. Raimundo and Rienzi come on. Rienzi makes a rabble-rousing speech on the topic of freeing Rome from the tyranny of the frightful nobles. Rienzi is good, cry the people, Rienzi is great. Would you like to be our king, Rienzi? says a spokesperson. Perish the thought, says Rienzi. Let Rome become a social democracy and I will be a Tribune of the People, nothing more. Hail Rienzi, our saviour and our tribune, sing the people, loudly. (Meanwhile the nobles, realizing the game is up, give up fighting and set about plotting to assassinate Rienzi.)

Act II Sc 1

A great hall in the Capitol. The stage is empty. A chorus of peace envoys is heard. They enter singing that everything is wonderful throughout the region, the sheep wax fat, the crops are green and everyone is behaving nicely. As they sing Rienzi, now in fancy dress as a Tribune, senators, praetors, foreign ambassadors and the now apparently tamed nobles, process. Well done Rienzi, cry all. Rienzi makes a statesmanlike speech. The nobles grovel and swear allegiance.

Sc 2

All exit except the nobles, who plot. Adriano comes on and hides. He hears the nobles, including his father, plotting to assassinate Rienzi. He jumps out. You double-crossing toads, he cries, you have just sworn allegiance to Rienzi and now you are going to kill him. Be quiet, my boy, says father Colonna. What has to be done has to be done. They ignore him and exit. Adriano decides to stick by Rienzi.

Sc 3

It is festival time and there are processions, again. Citizens, senators, nobles, priests and ambassadors etc. Rejoice. Hooray, etc. sings everyone. Rienzi and Irene appear. Rienzi is great, Rienzi is good, they shout. Rienzi welcomes a number of ambassadors and tells them that now Rome is free it will need to have a vote in the appointment of the German Emperor's man in Rome. He can no longer do it himself. Meanwhile Adriano pulls his sleeve. The nobles plan to rub you out, Rienzi, he says. There are then a number of bizarre and allegorical dances performed during which the nobles attempt to assassinate Rienzi. No good. He is wearing a dagger-proof vest and the dagger fails to penetrate. You are a bunch of double-crossing hoodlums, says Rienzi. Kill them, kill them cry the crowd. Well hardly that, says Rienzi. Yes. Yes. Kill Kill they shout. Well OK if you insist, says Rienzi. The nobles are marched off to the death cells. (A back-drop falls and we are in a room. Rienzi is alone. Enter Adriano and Irene). Rienzi, you can't kill my Dad, cries Adriano. Spare him or else I will avenge him by killing you. (Offstage we hear monks chanting the last rites). Come on, brother, show some mercy, says Irene. The backdrop goes up showing the citizens are still shouting Kill Kill. See what I mean? says Rienzi. But all right. I am a clement fellow and will reprieve them. [A bit sudden: Ed.] You must be mad, shout the crowd. No, no, says Rienzi, clemency above all. The nobles are brought up from the cells. You must all swear a fresh oath of allegiance, says Rienzi. We swear, says the nobles. (Swear away chaps, says Colonna, when this pantomime is over we can still kill him). He will live to regret this, say two citizens (Barroncelli and Cecco). Well, well, sing the citizens, what a wonderfully clement tribune we have. Rienzi is great, Rienzi is good, and Rienzi is also clement.

Act III Sc 1

A square near the Forum. The nobles have gathered an army in the provinces and are preparing to march on Rome. What now, Rienzi? say the citizens. The nobles are on the march. Sorry, I made a mistake, says Rienzi, I overdid the clemency. To arms everyone. OK – arms it is, say the citizens.

Sc 2

The indeterminate Adriano agonizes. Should he fight for his father or for Rienzi? He makes a meal of this dilemma and remains indeterminate.

Sc 3

Swarms of armed persons cross the stage. More processions, this time military. Let's sing a battle hymn, says Rienzi. They sing a battle hymn. Adriano comes on and seizes the bridle of Rienzi's horse. Hold on, Rienzi, he cries, what about clemency now? Send me to see my father and I will do a deal. Clemency is out, says Rienzi. To battle everyone. They exit singing the battle hymn again.

Adriano is left with Irene and a number of Roman women. They agonize. Then they hear the battle hymn in the distance. Rienzi and the citizens have won a very quick victory and return on stage triumphant. We won folks, sings Rienzi, bring on the corpses. Adriano falls on the body of his dead father. Rienzi, he cries, you killed my dad. I'll get you for this. Idiot boy, says

Rienzi, get the triumphal marches going. Everyone processes, jubilates and rejoices.

Act IV Sc 1

A square in Rome. Night. The citizens assemble at the bidding of an anonymous person (agents of the still-plotting nobles). Barroncelli and Cecco start discussing the latest news:

1) The German Emperor has severed diplomatic relations because he sees Rienzi as a dangerous left-winger, trying to challenge his power.
2) The Pope has withdrawn his cardinal from Rome. He had been told Rienzi is a heretic and has severed diplomatic relations.
3) Pope and Emperor are considering joint actions against Rienzi.

Remember all that clemency stuff? says Barroncelli. It was no more than a front. Rienzi let the nobles off because he wanted to join forces with them by marrying his sister to Colonna's son. Good Lord and all that bloodshed too, say the citizens. Is this really true? Yes it is, cries Adriano, jumping out of the woodwork. I am Colonna's son and I will avenge his death. Rienzi is a no good, ambitious adventurer. He has let you down. Rienzi is a traitor, say the mob. Vengeance! Revenge. Let's get after him during these big festival processions he has planned for today.

Just then a procession comes on stage with Raimundo the cardinal at its head. Great Scott, say the conspirators, the Pope's man is still here after all. [The story about the Pope recalling him just a rumour: Ed.] The church is supporting Rienzi. We can't go ahead now. God is still with him. Chicken! says Adriano. All right. I'll kill Rienzi myself when he is kneeling at the altar.

Sc 2

The procession reaches the church. The conspirators and the citizens hang around. Rienzi and Irene come in. Not joining in? Rienzi asks the citizens, you should be ashamed of yourselves. Sorry, Rienzi, they say, of course we will. They do. The monks are chanting what should have been a victory Te Deum but isn't. It is something very ominous. Raimundo steps forward and excommunicates Rienzi. Everyone disappears except Rienzi and Irene. Good gracious, says Rienzi, what a nasty surprise. Adriano springs out. Irene, fly with me, he says. No I'm sticking with brother Rienzi, says she.

Act V Sc 1

A hall in the Capitol. Rienzi prays at an altar for a long time.

Sc 2

Irene comes in. I chucked Adriano for you and I could have been his bride, she says. Thanks sister, says Rienzi. Rome is my bride and she done me wrong. There's still time for you to pop off with Adriano, says Rienzi. Never, says Irene. They embrace. Rienzi exits.

Sc 3

Adriano comes on. Fly with me, Irene, he cries. Negative, says Irene. I've pretty well gone mad, says Adriano, and I'm going to kill your brother you know. Meanwhile the citizens have set fire to the Capitol. So you'll be burnt alive if you stay here, says Adriano. I'm staying, says Irene.

Sc 4

A square in front of the Capitol. The citizens run on carrying stones. Rienzi appears on a balcony. Pack it in, shouts Rienzi. Peace! Peace! Remember I am the guy who saved you! Rome will be great again! Stone him, cry the mob. (They stone him). The burning building collapses, neatly winding up the plot by killing Rienzi, Irene and Adriano all at one blow.

LOOK OUT FOR

MINUTES FROM START

Overture

The overture has three tunes, a good quantity of brassy bombast, a motto and a recurrent trumpet note. This last forecasts the trumpet call which will summon the citizens to arms, and it casts an eerie shadow over the piece. After the trumpet call we have Rienzi's prayer, quite the best tune in the opera, and between its first outing (piano) and the second (forte) we have the motto Rienzi's Fate floating around. It recurs from time to time in the opera but not significantly. Next the second tune, later heard in one of the choruses with awkwardly rising semitones, quite the worst in the opera, and finally the third, a sprightly item which could have been written by any one of half a dozen of the Italians. (Returns in the finale to Act II). A decent concert piece, but no star.

Act I Sc 1

The attempted seduction and the bustling squabble between the Orsinis and the Colonnas is all lively, operatic and tuneful, the tunes coming mainly from the orchestra. Rienzi's first recitatif is nicely paced and verges on nobility, but is longer than required by the plot or by the audience. The nobles react with a scoffing chorus, the citizens with praise for Rienzi, and the two work well together until the nobles exit to do their Tweedledum and Tweedledee act outside the walls.

Rienzi tells his freedom-fighters to go home but to rally when the trumpet sounds. This cavatina, the first set piece in the opera, is stirring and melodious * and the ensuing dispersal chorus comes off really well, as indeed do all the choruses so far.

21: *Doch hörret ihr der trompete*   21

Act I Sc 2

The first part of the scene where Rienzi, Adriano and Irene do their stint of plot-clearing runs along well enough but when all three sing together in their long trio things improve greatly. Look out especially for Irene's elegant decorative top line, not quite coloratura, more a descant.

31: *Rienzi du bist*   31

Act I Sc 3

A humdrum stretch of recitatif opens this scene when Adriano and Irene come to an accommodation but then their sung-together duet races away to a happy finish – until, in the distance –

Act I Sc 4

the spooky trumpet rings out.

A buzz and a flourish takes us into another good crowd chorus, capped by an organ voluntary from the Lateran church so poor as to sound like a village organist extemporizing because he had

36: *Ja eine Welt*

forgotten his music. A double chorus by the two choirs within the church fares better although choirs do not seem able to decide in which century they are singing, for there are hints both of plainsong and *Tristan* – Rienzi does another macho piece (the Freedom Song) much as he had done before and the chorus acclaim him as they always do. All of this is stirring stuff, but the offer and rejection of position of monarch and the final chorus (Great Rome) are definitely ornery.

36

Act II Sc 1

The prelude is brief and dreamy, the opening unaccompanied chorus of the messengers of

2: *Ihr Römwe hört die Kunde*

peace is a great success. The reception of the nuns by Rienzi and friends is agreeably joyful and the second chorus by the peace persons, this time unaccompanied, fades away sweetly as they disappear from view – all in all quite the best piece of the opera so far, and well worth a star.* Now some pretty boring recitatif from Rienzi and the hypocritical nobles as they congratulate him on his success.

2

Act II Sc 2

Things perk up as the plotters begin to plot in 3/4 time, a blessed relief from the pounding 4/4 march rhythms that have dominated the opera since the start. This short scene ends with good dramatic exchanges between Adriano and his father and a final agonized recitatif as Adriano faces the choice of becoming a traitor either to his father or to Rienzi and Rome.

Act II Sc 3

A catchy march tune brings on the procession of senators, citizens etc. and stays with us through a good deal of chorus rejoicing and gloating by

Rienzi over his political and military success. Then a stretch of pompous musical rhetoric covering the processing, ambassadorial greetings and the like which is not much affected by Rienzi dropping his bombshell (Rome to challenge the power of Germany). Adriano's warning of treachery gives us a welcome lull but soon the orchestra are at it again and we get another dose of processional music, some of it not far from the March of the Toy Soldiers. The ballets continue in boisterous blustering mode until we get to the Entrance of the Virgins – a pleasant, calm piece, if a little soppy. The final ballet takes us back for more bluster, this time with a couple of good tunes fighting to get out and some fancy trumpet solos. The assassination attempt misfires musically and we get little drama until death comes to our aid in the form of the chorus of condemned nobles and the monks, all appropriately solemn. From then on as Adriano pleads for the life of his father and Rienzi, turning merciful, reprieves the whole lot of conspirators, we have the best scene in the opera, the several parties well characterized, the public agog, and all leading to a fine solo by

35: *O labt der Gnade*

Rienzi* followed by an intricate and wholly 35 successful final ensemble where noise and triumphalism give way to sentiments variously held and clearly expressed, the people holding an anchor role in subdued chorus. Rienzi meditative, Adriano and Irene supplying an elegant descant and the plotters bumbling on in the bass. An undoubted star.*

Act III Sc 1

Rome in turmoil. Wave after wave of musical rhetoric, most of it empty, but improving towards the end as Rienzi makes his brisk call to arms and the citizens respond with spirit.

Act III Sc 2

15: *In seiner Blüte*

Adriano's long recitatif is all right, no more, but the aria that follows is something special. In the 15 first section the music has real feeling for the poor fellow's plight and makes its simple appeal with good effect. Then the tocsin sounds and a more animated Adriano decides that a return to dad is the best option. Lots of bravura.

Act III Sc 3

Offstage bells are always evocative but here they fail to do their work as well as in *Boris* or *Tosca*, and anyway they are soon drowned by yet another outburst of trumpeting and military bombast. This goes on for a very long time (seven minutes) and is finally reinforced by Rienzi and chorus singing their Battle Hymn. There is some relief in the exchanges between the pleading Adriano and Rienzi, but not for long. At last the hordes exit and a highly

33: *Unsel ger sieh* dramatic duet between Adriano and Irene lightens the texture as does a gentle female chorus wishing their warriors well. But alas, victory bring the whole pack back on stage again amidst much shouting and cheering. In the middle of all this the bodies of Orsini and Colonna are brought on to the stage and the trumpet sounds out above heavy rolls on the drums. Adriano swears vengeance on Rienzi (more high dramatic recitatif). The final chorus of rejoicing pretty well tops everything that has gone before, and that is saying something.   33

Act IV Sc 1

Sinister drumbeats and a gloomy downward scale introduce the conspirators' march. They assemble and converse at first in a guilty sotto voce manner. But as they warm to their work they get louder and faster. Adriano's mob-stirring

7: *Colonnas Sohn!* aria is a really good piece* and the citizens' angry reaction to it does well too.   7

Act IV Sc 2

Another procession but this time (although there are still trumpets) it is holier, quieter and more dignified. Rienzi's orations to the craven citizens is high-class recitatif and ends mel-

14: *Wie oder ist* odiously.* The ominous chanting of monks   14
der Mut is appropriately spooky and Raimundo's

excommunication act (lots of trombones) awesome. Now everything is working well, a tremulous hush, more chanting and the agitato tussle duet between Adriano and Irene. Rienzi comes out of his trance with a shout of confidence in Rome and we finish with a bout of chanting, very piano. Quite the best act in the opera.*

Act V Sc 1

5: *Stärk test du mich*

The trumpet again, but softly and now sounding even more spooky, some harp arpeggios, and then the prelude launches into Rienzi's prayer. Rienzi starts his prayer in quasi recitatif but soon we have the great melody tout simple and very affecting it is. The prayer builds to a climax. We hear the great tune again and a quiet prayerful finish to what is one of Wagner's really successful set pieces.** 5

Act V Sc 2

13: *Ich liebe glühend*

Irene enters. She greets Rienzi tenderly, mainly in recitatif until Rienzi launches into his passionate declaration of love for his bride – Rome. The ensuing duet starts with a soft appeal from Irene but soon emotions run high and we have a series of dramatic exchanges ending with a sung-together piece of great verve.* A good scene. 13

Act V Sc 3

Adriano and Irene, now both pretty hysterical, confront each other. Fly with me, your only chance, says he. Never, says she. Then suddenly Adriano calms down, sinks to his knees and sings a rather beautiful aria. Irene responds, still firm, and as the Capitol is set on fire they depart.

Act V Sc 4

Tumult. The citizens are out. The Capitol burns. Remember me? sings Rienzi. Let's have some peace. But there is only more tumult as they begin to stone him. Adriano rushes on to save Irene. Now Wagner seems to run out of steam, for instead of a great climactic chorus we have sudden death, not only for the three principals, but for the opera itself. A poor finish.

NOTES

Rienzi   Wagner's third opera
First night   Dresden, Königlich Sächsisches Hoftheater October
              1842
Reception   A wow
Libretto   Wagner
Source   Edward Bulwar-Lytton's novel *Rienzi, the Last of the Roman Tribunes*

NEWS AND GOSSIP

In the summer of 1937 when Wager was staying in Blasewitz near Dresden, he read Bulwar-Lytton's novel *Rienzi, The Last of the Roman Tribunes*. He had already been steered towards *Rienzi* as a subject for an opera by his friend Apel and now he was convinced that it would make a stirring opera of the grandest kind and one which could only be performed in a major house (hopefully the Paris Opéra) and thus escape the fate of *Liebesverbot* which had sunk without trace.

Wagner sketched a prose draft then a verse draft and completed the first two acts by the summer of 1839. After a gap of nearly a year (during which he escaped from Riga and arrived in Paris) he completed a draft of Acts III–V by October 1840. The overture was written last.

Rienzi was first put on in Dresden in October 1842. It was a smash hit. Suddenly the unknown Wagner had made it and this despite the fact that the performance lasted (with intervals) for over six hours. Realizing, no doubt reluctantly, that this was a bit over the top, Wagner then cut it in half and put it on on two successive nights. This didn't work, so he produced a cut version which ran for a mere four and three quarter hours and this was no doubt the version that was soon to be performed triumphantly all over Germany, being put on in Dresden above a hundred times by 1873 and two hundred times by 1908. But for some unknown reason Rienzi did not hit New York until 1879, nor London until one year later. But early in the twentieth century spectacle opera was out and *Rienzi* quietly died the death. Nobody really knows what the original *Rienzi* score was like. Hitler, who was stunned when he first saw the opera in 1908 (no surprise) appropriated the original manuscript and it died with him. Wagner's own cut score is lost and has since been cut and cut again by many hands. But there is no reason to believe that what we have now does not do reasonable justice to Wagner's monster venture into Grand Opera.

In later life Wagner was ashamed of *Rienzi*. Wagnerites did not mention it much and amongst the brotherhood it became the opera that dared not speak its name. It was never put on at Bayreuth. Today it rarely appears. To muster such huge resources for what is regarded as a second-rate piece does not appeal to opera managements. *Lohengrin* is cheaper and has a better reputation.

COMMENT

There are plenty of views as to which is Wagner's best opera but unanimity over which is his worst – *Rienzi*. Ernest Newman, music's great scribe of the last generation, could find nothing bad enough to say about it – the 'pretentious poverty' of its musical invention, its 'intolerable prolixity' and plenty more. Today's universal Wagnerian, Barry Millington, finds it an embarrassment and every modern music critic treats it as something between a bad joke and a folie de grandeur. And yet within the mountainous bulk of *Rienzi* there is a good opera trying to get out, and at its heart we can find some of the best music Wagner wrote and in Rienzi's Prayer, certainly one of his best tunes.

Wagner wrote *Rienzi* as a Grand Opera for the Paris stage. Five acts, loads of spectacle, an army of extras, ballets – the full works. About *Rienzi* he wrote: 'Grand Opera with all its scenic and musical splendour ... stood before me; my artistic ambition demanded not merely that I should imitate it but that I should outdo all previous examples with sumptuous extravagance.' And, O boy, didn't he do just that. *Rienzi* is a case of operatic overkill, which made it a huge success in his lifetime but a dog for audiences today.

Volumes have been written about *Rienzi*'s role in inspiring the Fascist movement in inter-war Germany. It is true that Hitler took a great shine to *Rienzi* when he first heard it and later appropriated the score but it would seem this was because it is about the power of demagoguery rather than because it presents a blueprint for any deep-seated political theory. After all, the opera follows Bulwar-Lytton's novel pretty closely and it is unlikely that this mild-mannered English gentleman would want to plant the seeds of Fascism in his simple tale of Roman folk. Most of the theorizing must surely be baloney.

The plot, as Wagner treats it, is as sound as a bell except perhaps for the hurried and confused account of why the people so suddenly turned against their hero. Excommunication yes, his challenge to the German Emperor surely no – a popular vote-catcher if ever there was one – a secret alliance with the nobles? But second time around he killed them all. So how come his sudden drop in the polls? Mobs may be fickle but they must have something to be fickle about.

In his approach to *Rienzi* it seems that Wagner forgot his aspirations towards opera as a pure music-drama. There are few mottos it is true, but no more than Verdi used, say, in *The Force of Destiny*. More than one third of the opera is bang bang, shout shout, marches, ballets, choruses.

Several scholarly scribes have detected a difference in style between Acts I and II (influenced by Meyerbeer and other French Grand Operatics) and the later Acts (Wagner moving towards his own music-drama philosophy), but you would have to search very hard to make anything of this one. To this author it all sounds much the same, the noisy parts all blatantly noisy, the lyrical bits equally lyrical, not many mottos and not a single dissonant chord.

It is strange that so far as I know none of *Rienzi*'s scribes has mentioned Wagner's bizarre decision to make Adriano a trouser role. After the Castrati, poor things, had disappeared their roles were sometimes taken by women (more often by tenors) and there are a few leading breeches roles in Italian opera but none for adults after 1840 although pages, Tsarevitches, and other teenagers were still sung by women. So Wagner's female Adriano remains a mystery, and no one seems to have noticed it.

Rienzi remains an untapped quarry of good music. Amongst choruses, many of them pretty ghastly, there is one gem – the report of the Peace Delegation in Act II but the main joys lie in the solos, duets and trios – for instance Adriano pleading for his father's life in Act II. Act IV is high-class stuff throughout with Rienzi's address to the citizens working really well and his hymn to the greatness of Rome giving it a resounding climax. Finally Rienzi's prayer itself is a great set piece and one which would transfer well to the concert hall but unlike *Tannhäuser*'s Star of Eve it is seldom heard. So *Rienzi* remains an opera for the selective CD listener who can with a little expertise gouge at least an hour or two of pure pleasure out of its mountainous bulk. A patchy B.

The Flying Dutchman
(Der Fliegende Holländer)

Nautical fantasy

A waterborne Dutchman seeks a good woman to release him from sailing the high seas for ever: he finds one who jumps off a cliff and they ascend to heaven together.

CAST

Daland, a Norwegian skipper	Bass
Senta, his daughter	Soprano
Mary, Senta's old nurse	Contralto
Erik, a young Norwegian in love with Senta	Tenor
Smith, Daland's helmsman	Tenor
The Dutchman	Bass—baritone

3 acts: running time 2 hrs 30 mins

STORY

Act I A harbour in a rocky bay: cliffs beetle

We are in the Norwegian fiord of Sandwigen at some unspecified date and the weather is bad. Skipper Daland has brought his ship in for shelter: he is vexed because he has seen his home but missed making a landfall at his home port by seven miles owing to a mighty storm. Relax lads he says to the crew and stop singing that halloyoho stuff for Chrissake: the storm is dying out. Go below. Smith, he says, you take helmsman's watch. See and keep awake. Exits.

Smith sings soppily about his girlfriend. He requests the south wind to propel the ship in her direction. He goes to sleep. The Dutchman's ship sails in alongside. Smith wakes up. The Dutchman goes ashore. Smith nods off again. The Dutchman says Heigho so that's another seven years gone: I am permitted by my curse contract with the superior powers one landing each septaquennium to try to negotiate my release from perpetual sea voyaging: boy am I sick of this compulsory touring. I tried suicide but the conditions of the curse contract forbid it. Roll on Judgement Day. And you can say that again sing the Dutchman's crew (invisible ghosts).

Daland comes up: You asleep again Smith? he says. Nothing happened Boss honest says Smith. Then how about this bloody great ship lying alongside? says Daland. Sorry Boss it escaped my attention says Smith. He shouts ahoy. The Dutchman appears. You all right old boy? asks Daland. Ship and tackle OK says the Dutchman: just one thing do you take paying guests at your nearby home? I have large quantities of loot aboard. What kind of stuff? asks Daland. Gold bars, pearls, specie, diamonds, platinum and heavy water says the Dutchman – you can have the contents of chest 67 in return for one night's lodging (he opens chest 67 and displays contents). Cripes! says Daland be my guest. I always admired the Dutch.

Have you a young girl preferably a daughter about the home? asks the Dutchman. Indeed I have an excellent daughter says Daland. May I marry her? asks the Dutchman. Of course of course of course you can says Daland. The terms of my curse contract are stringent says the Dutchman. I must travel perpetually so wealth is of no value to me. If I marry your daughter you can take the lot. My daughter is sexy virtuous industrious honest and beautiful says Daland. OK it's a deal says the Dutchman can I take her over today? As soon as we get clearance for take off from Met. says Daland.

Will this marriage meet the conditions of the escape clause in my curse contract? thinks the Dutchman, if so goody. Lucky old storm, lucky encounter, lucky old me thinks Daland. Fax in from Met. Captain sir says Smith: South wind force 5 about to commence. Fine great OK says Daland. You go first I follow says the Dutchman. Daland's sailors (after a rest of only 45 minutes) cheerfully rig for departure.

Act II The spinning room in Daland's house

Mary supervises the midday shift of spinning operatives working in Daland's house for West Norwegian Home Industries. All the girls sing as they spin except Senta who gazes at the portrait of a romantic-looking but pasty-faced man. Get spinning Senta says Mary, looking at that pin-up all day is disgraceful. She's acting funny because she's in love with Erik the Animal Conservation Officer say the girls. Sing us the ballad of the Flying Dutchman Mary please says Senta. Negative says Mary. Then I'll sing it myself she says: gather round girls.

Yohohojehohijaho she sings to put them in the mood there was this ship with blood-red sails in serious need of maintenance owing to endless voyaging round and round the world. The skipper was a gaunt man from Amsterdam who once uttered a blasphemous four-letter word when in extreme nautical difficulties rounding Cape Horn in a force 12 gale. The tetchy superior powers laid a curse contract on him namely he must sail the seas for ever until he finds good woman who is eternally faithful to him. He is permitted access to dry land once every seven years to contact marriage bureaux etc. How interesting, say the girls.

Hey hey girls shouts Erik, I've seen Senta's Dad's ship coming in. Oo! Oo! The men will be home any minute say the girls. And what was that rubbish you were going on with? says Erik to Senta. You know your Dad could give permission for our wedding this visit? I can't talk now I'm busy says Senta. I am upset Senta, says Erik your Dad wants a rich son-in-law and my pay as an Animal Conservation Officer is not good. Also you seem to have gone potty about that pin-up picture guy who looks like a corpse. Listen: I dreamed a dream that I saw a strange ship and two men came ashore one your Dad the other the guy in that picture. You fell at his knees and then you gave him a big kiss and the two of you went off together.

The door opens: Daland and the Dutchman enter. Senta is stunned. It is he! Hello Senta I brought this bloke along with me – do you mind if he stays the night? says Daland: by the way he wants to marry you and I've agreed. He's very rich. Now I'll leave you both to get on with it. Exits.

Good Lord! This is the girl of my dreams thinks the Dutchman. Good Lord! This is the man in the picture thinks Senta. Will you do what your father wants? asks he. I always do what my father wants says she. You may be the means of activating the escape route clause 17B in my curse contract says he. I will do my utmost to oblige says she. Actually I am overwhelmed by romantic passion and will be true to you unto death. Sounds like pretty good news says he. 'Scuse me says Daland popping in I can't hold up the end-of-trip party any longer the crew are battering on the door for booze: have you two fixed up that marriage? Yea, fixed it says Senta. I confirm that says Dutchman.

Act III A cove: the two boats moored alongside each other, Daland's with the crew on deck, the Dutchman's deserted. Daland's house visible, also a steep cliff. Night

The sailors on board Daland's ship rollick on deck singing nautical rhubarb. A bevy of local girls arrive with picnic baskets alcoholic refreshments etc. They approach the Dutchman's ship. Hey there you lot they shout: like a snack? No response. You asleep or something? say girls. No response. Must be dead say sailors. Funny they say this ship is very similar to the legendary vessel of the Flying Dutchman. The girls leave the Dutchman's ship and present their picnic baskets to Daland's crew: exit.

Daland's crew dance and sing nautical rhubarb once again. Blue fireworks explode round the Dutchman's ship. The sea seethes and the wind howls in a very localized storm which is confined to the immediate area around the Dutch ship. The Dutchman's crew come to life and sing a ghostly chorus. Let's hope the skipper really is fixed up they say then our endless voyages are over. We can't see a soul say Daland's crew. They must be ghosts. They start off on rhubarb again. The Dutchman's crew interrupt Daland's crew with cries and shrieks of ghostly rhubarb. A choral contest develops Daland's versus Dutchman's. The Dutchman's wins. The localized storm stops.

Senta runs on Erik in pursuit. It can't be true says Erik. You are dumping me for this total stranger? It's my duty says Senta also destiny also father's instructions. Hold on Senta says Erik remember when we went fell-walking together? When cuddling you said 'I love you' over and over. The Dutchman eavesdropping in the rocks jumps out. That's torn it! he cries. Unfaithful! Goodbye Senta! Hold on, says Senta where are you going? To sea for ever says the Dutchman. Right boys get ready to sail. No need! Stop! A mistake! I am faithful! says Senta. Not so says the Dutchman you are proven to be unfaithful. If you had claimed faithfulness on oath you would have suffered eternal damnation. A lot of women have gone down that way. You have had a lucky escape.

He jumps on to his boat and sails off to sea. I can prove I am faithful unto death shouts Senta. She jumps off a cliff and kills herself. The Dutchman's ship sinks instantly. The sun rises. The Dutchman and Senta, hand in hand, float heavenwards no doubt to sort out his release from clause 17B of the contract with superior powers.

LOOK OUT FOR

MINUTES FROM START

o	The overture,*** full of salt and spray, is a splendid concert piece. Mainly stormy, up to	o

force 9, it has patches of calm when the redemption motto and the Sailors' Chorus from Act III break in.

Act I

17: *Mit Gewitter und Sturm*

A heavily skittish figure featuring the bassoons introduces the steersman's song to his absent girlfriend* but his thoughts about her are not exciting enough to keep him awake. After the first stanza of agreeable tenor music he comes out with a sort of seaman's yodel which HOJOHOHOs around for some time. As he drops off we hear the approaching Dutchman's boat playing his motif on its foghorns.

17

23: *Die Frist ist um*

The Dutchman is gloomy, and not without reason.**

23

1. He talks to the sea (for which he has formed an intense dislike) for a while in recitatif and then launches into:

2. A vigorous account of his roving life which we have already heard instrumentally in the overture. The sea swirls and washes about in the strings in a wonderfully pictorial fashion. This is quite the best bit of the Dutchman's rather long message about himself and his problems.

3. A quieter piece follows where he asks to be let off from eternal wandering. (But he must know it's no good.)

4. Then more ranting against fate: he looks forward to Judgement Day when it will surely be curtains for everyone. Look out for the very loud Last Trump – three heavy blows delivered by the brass. He ends noisily: an unhappy man.

The second half of this act is made up of a duet between Daland and the Dutchman:

43: *All' meinen Reichtum*

1. This suddenly gets animated when the Dutchman offers all his treasure in exchange for a wife and a good home.** Romance is in the air: we can't smell the sea any longer, it's all roses and waltz time as the men gyrate with delight at the thought of (a) riches and (b) a fixed abode. This section ends with a neat little symphony.

43

47: *Wohl Fremdling*

2. It's still springtime but now we move on to more practical matters.* Pretty four-square phrases: a deal is done: and there is metaphorically a very long handshake: everything most melodious, and wholly harmonious.   47

49: *Wenn aus der Qualen*

3. Still they go on:** what great luck, I'm rich says Daland (but the Dutchman can't hear him). Hope for me at last says the Dutchman (and it doesn't matter whether Daland can hear him or not). The pair of them swing and sway together in rounded lyrical lines urged on by the strings and towards the end what sounds like a battalion of horns.   49

Action! The south wind gets up (so what wind was blowing the hell out of everything twenty minutes ago?). Daland decides to get moving to the steersman's skittish figures, now

54: *Du siehst, das Glück*

transformed into a strange little circus dance* and we move into a sailors' choral version of the steersman's song. Although they have only had a very short rest the crew are keen to get to their girlfriends. If it weren't Wagner one might say some of the progressions in the sailors' music were definitely ornery. The concluding symphony fades away to a bit of the Spinning Chorus – to be continued in the next act.   54

Act II

The spinning wheels hum and buzz along in the strings: an oboe sings out a tune you can't forget although after its tenth repetition, you will

0: *Summ' und brumm'*

probably want to. The girls take up the tune*** to its treadmill accompaniment. There is an interruption by Mary. Then they sing it all over again. For some reason the girls seem to think that a good bout of spinning will hasten their lovers' return. Wagner does an immaculate job here – the spinning sound picture, the tune, the choral and orchestral writing all neat, precise and satisfactory. A winner in its own class.   0

9: *Johohohe!*

Senta's ballad** is introduced by the Dutchman's motto swinging about in the orchestra. She opens with a touch of the JOHOHOs like   9 the sailors in Act I but soon settles into a conventional three-stanza ballad, each one with the same three-part structure.

1. Opening strain repeated four times telling the story of the Dutchman and his curse.

2. Sea music accompaniment as in the overture and the Dutchman's first big piece. Continuing the story but with the interesting exclamation HOOEY! popped in at the head of each of the three phrases.

3. A sort of holy calm with a simple tune (three blind mice, the third one with a hiccup: the Redemption motto) doubled in the woodwind. Hopes of redemption. At the end of stanza 2 the chorus whisper along with the end bars and in stanza 3 they take over the redemption section completely until Senta bursts out in a wild free-ranging coda (quite a relief after the straightjacket of the ballad form) 'I'll do it myself' she cries 'I'll be his woman'. This stretches credibility a bit because she hasn't yet met him, but if you can accept that Satan would condemn the poor fellow to a wandering life for ever just for using a four-letter word in bad weather, then you can believe anything.

17: *Ach! Wie viel hab' ich*

The girls' exit chorus.* Suddenly we have a 17 scuttering scampering piece of theatre music that might have been lifted straight from an Offenbach opera. Bizarre.

After a lyrical duet in which Erik tells Senta at some length that he loves her in an agreeable but rather ornery fashion we come to Erik's

26: *Senta hass dir vertrau'n*

Dream.* Spooky music: hushed tones: a 26 stranger comes to take her away (Dutchman's motto: no doubt who it is): she went with him: she never came back (Redemption motto). This is more like the later Wagner we know and admire: not desperately exciting and with not much tune, but moving freely into new ways of writing continuous dramatic music without stop—starts, without recitatif, without set numbers.

Senta finishes off the piece thoughtfully, with more Redemption.

As Daland introduces the Dutchman something happens in the strings* – a new kind of music with a yearning sweet-water tune, quite different from the salt-and-spray stuff or anything else we have heard so far. It never gets into the main action but stays in the accompaniment surfacing from time to time as Daland sings his very four-square four-lines-at-a-time stanzas. He recommends Senta as a suitable marriage prospect.

Senta takes the Dutchman aboard, a big set-piece duet in three parts:

1.*** Both in a dream. The Dutchman starts slowly almost unaccompanied (This is the girl of my dreams) but when Senta comes in (This is the man of my dreams) things warm up considerably and as they sing together we have the first great love duet climax in Wagner. Very fine. (A whiff of the Redemption motto at the end.)

2.** Now down to practicalities. Will you have me? he asks. I always do what Dad tells me, she replies. Hope I can redeem him she thinks aloud (actually very loud). What an angel says he (Redemption motto) but you must be always faithful says he, if not (amidst a lot of the sea music) I'm off on the trail again. It will be my pleasure says she.

3.** Together they exult: bliss: joyful union: the curse is off. Another good climax.

The short trio that ends the act is made rather special by the conviction of Senta's promise to be faithful sung in a high soprano line.** She gives her fidelity bond.

Act III

Between the acts there is one of those musical transformation scenes at which Wagner was going to be so frightfully good. As the musical mood changes so imperceptibly do the mottos. From the high emotion of the last trio to

---

33: *Mögst du, mein Kind*   33

40: *Wie aus der Ferne*   40

45: *Wirst du des Vaters Wahl*   45

51: *Ein heil'ger Balsam*   51

55: *Hier meine Hand!*   55

carousel on deck in about fourteen stealthily taken steps.

The sailors' chorus – the orchestra does it

2: *Steuermann, lass'* first so it is no surprise – is rousing.** There are 2
die Wacht! in fact two associated mottos around in here, the second a variation of the first sung by the girls. The scene ploughs on as the male and female choruses duet and marvel at the Dutchman's ghostly ship lying alongside. Daland's crew try to reassure themselves with a full repeat of the opening chorus.

11: *Yohohoeh!* A sort of choral contest* between the Dutch- 11
man's ghostly crew and Daland's robust Norwegians. The ghosts win. Powerful stuff, mottos flying around, perhaps a little crude, but effective.

A mildish reproof for Senta from Erik in a

17: *Willst jenes* low voltage but agreeable tenor aria.* He 17
Tag's reminds her he used to risk his life climbing cliffs to get her flowers – and she said she loved him.

As the Dutchman gives orders to hoist sail we have an impassioned trio from three tortured

23: *Segel auf!* people,* the Dutchman (She broke her word: 23
Anker los! back to sea), Senta (You're wrong, I'm very reliable: stay!), Erik (Senta! That's an evil fellow). There is real urgency and bite in this stormy section which fades into something more ornery as we get nearer and nearer to the melodrama of the last scene, when the music finally becomes the sort of stuff used to support a D. W. Griffith silent movie, but a grand one, let's say *Intolerance*.

NOTES

The Flying Dutchman	Wagner's fourth opera
First night	Königliches Sächsiscles Hoftheater, Dresden, 2 January 1843
Reception	Mixed, which means pretty bad
Libretto	Wagner

Source   Several: Sir Walter Scott, Captain
                                    Marryat, Fenimore Cooper, but
                                    mainly a book of fictional memoirs by
                                    Hein

NEWS AND GOSSIP

In 1839 Wagner made a sea crossing to London which should have
taken eight days but lasted three and a half weeks. Storms drove
the boat – the *Thetis* – into a Norwegian fiord where Wagner was
deeply impressed by the sounds of the crews' shouts echoing
around the rocks. The experience he said, unreliably, led to the
concept of the *Dutchman*, but there is no evidence that he started
work on it until eighteen months later. He wrote the libretto (the
'poem') in Paris and because he was broke sold a prose version to
the management of the Paris Opéra where an opera called *Le
Vaisseau fantôme* was developed and put on by people of whom we
now know little, and which was a total flop. Wagner then
completed his own version and sent it to Berlin. No takers there.
Meanwhile, his *Rienzi* had been a big success and as a result he got
the *Dutchman* staged in Dresden. He had dickered around with a
Scottish setting (in which Daland was called Donald!) before
settling for Norway and had written the opera as a continuous
piece without act breaks, which must have posed an impossible
problem for the technical staff. By the time it was ready to put on
it was pretty well in its present shape, but after a rough first night
it had only three performances before it was withdrawn. The
Dutchman then lay around for a decade or so until Wagner had
made his name with *Tannhäuser* and *Lohengrin*, when it was put on
in Zurich. Wagner kept tinkering with the score and a later version
reached London and America in the 1870s and spread to all those
operatic parts of the world where Wagner was OK. The *Dutchman*
came to be reckoned as a true Wagner opera, which it probably
isn't (*Rienzi* was thought to be a Wagner opera written before
Wagnerization set in). The set pieces have a concert life equal to
any in Wagner partly because they are not 'bleeding chunks' but
self-contained pieces of the sort that well-balanced operas had
offered to the concert hall ever since opera began. The *Dutchman*
is now an occasional piece in the rep of any major opera house and
is enjoying a healthy life.

COMMENT

With the *Dutchman* we find Wagner moving down the road towards a new kind of opera, but he hasn't got far. What is best about the *Dutchman* is the stand-alone traditional numbers – the overture, the Spinning Chorus, Senta's Ballad, Erik's Dream. There are stop—start items with quite a lot of old-fashioned recitatif around them. Then we have the sailors' choruses, the last act with quite a lot of dramatic ding-dong and big free solos for the Dutchman and Daland – all of which are fine. But to present the old thing as a continuous music drama, even with the act breaks rubbed out and musical links played through the scene changes, is going too far. We don't find Wagner's mesmeric power in the *Dutchman* as we do in the *Ring*. We don't get sucked in. No spell lies across the whole opera, and although the good bits are very good, the gear changes are obvious and jolt us from one mood to another almost like a roll on the drums between music hall acts.

The story is strong in its central idea of the Dutchman condemned to sail the seas for ever in his phantom ship until redeemed, but weak in detail, not to say ludicrous. Why should Satan, presumably in favour of sin and bad behaviour, take exception to blasphemy? Anyone who blasphemed, one would have thought, was batting on his side. And if all blaspheming sailors were treated like the Dutchman the seas of the world would be teeming with nautical peripatetics. Senta's fixation on the man in the picture is incredible but permissible under the normal operatic ground rules. But for the Dutchman to shy off her like a terrified mustang because she had a teenage cuddle and kiss with the boy scout Erik seems strange; also his requirement that faithfulness should be retrospective into a time before any two parties meet seems against reason and certainly against common law, otherwise nearly everyone would enter the state of marriage with grounds for divorce already established. Finally, the heavenly assumption of the Dutchman and Senta is risible because the opera is simply not grand enough to carry this sort of supernatural happening – *Götterdämmerung* perhaps, but not this simpler saga of seafaring folk.

But when all is said and done, the *Dutchman* has a top-class overture and patches of splendid music where Wagner demonstrates that he can not only write a good tune but make it work for him dramatically in a way no one else knew how. An alpha.

Tannhäuser

The one where the Pilgrims sing their Chorus, where Venus loses her man, and where runner beans start to sprout from the Pope's staff.

CAST

Heinrich Tannhäuser, errant knight and minstrel		Tenor
Venus, the goddess in person		Soprano
Hermann, Landgrave (ruler) of Thuringia		Bass
Elisabeth, his niece		Soprano
Wolfram, knight, minstrel and former friend of Tannhäuser		Baritone
Walther		Tenor
Biterolf	Thuringian knights and	Bass
Heinrich	minstrels (Minisingers)	Tenor
Reinmar		Bass
A shepherd's boy		Treble

3 acts: running time 3 hrs plus

STORY

Act I Sc 1 Venusberg

We are in Venus's country place: rocks, cascades, lakes, bowers and all that stuff. The time is the thirteenth century (Venus herself aged at least 6000 but wearing well). A variety of classical wildlife is on view including fauns, satyrs, nymphs, bacchantes, all revelling. Sexy dancing all round leads to a terrific orgy but before anyone can really orge the Three Graces call in Cupids to clean things up. They discharge volleys of arrows which drive the revellers offstage. Now we see in the clouds sexy visions from Greek mythology, Europa and the Bull, Leda and the Swan.

But soon all activity ceases. Tannhäuser is having a nap centre stage. He disentangles himself from Venus stretches yawns. What's up with you? asks Venus. Homesick says Tannhäuser. You must be mad says Venus. There's nothing like this life: top-class porn available free and you can have it off whenever you feel inclined. Cheer up Tan give us a song do.

Tan sings that it's all lovely, super, sexy and dreamy in Venus's place but he wants out. Ungrateful beast says Venus stay on and I'll give you a specially nice time. Must go says Tan I miss green grass, bells, birdsong. OK get out you puritanical pig says Venus but come back. Shan't says Tan. This debate continues until Tan invokes the name of the Blessed Virgin Mary. Venus (who knows when she is licked) disappears.

Act I Sc 2 A green valley in the Wartburg. A shrine to the Virgin visible

Tan kneels at prayer. A traditional operatic shepherd's boy plays his customary pipe and sings a conventional rhubarb song about spring. Enter Landgrave Hermann with flock of hunting Minisingers at his back. Hey! Who is that praying guy? he asks. The Minisingers approach Tan. Why if it isn't Harry Tannhäuser! says Wolfram. Are you all right old boy? What have you bin up to? I prefer not to tell says Tan. But I'm glad to be back. Welcome, come with us say Minisingers. No: I prefer to go it alone says Tan. Remember that female Elisabeth? asks Wolfram. After you left she pined and went solitary. If you come back she will socialize again. OK I'll come says Tan. Jolly good show say all the Minisingers. Hunting recommences to the inevitable outbreak of horns.

Act II The Festival Hall, Wartburg

Hello hall! Elisabeth says: this is the venue where Tan used to sing so nicely and now he's coming back! Tan and Wolfram enter. Long time no see says Elisabeth what have you bin up to? Can't remember says Tan I had a blackout. I had a nervous collapse says Elisabeth. Nice to have you back Harry. Nice to be back says Tan. (Bang goes my chance of making it with Elisabeth thinks dejected Wolfram.) Exit Tan and Wolfram.

Enter Hermann. What were you and Harry saying? he asks. Private matters says Elisabeth. OK says Hermann remember this song contest I mentioned? It's starting now and you are president. There is a big parade with lots of noisy brass band music. The hall fills. Hermann explains the rules and hints coyly that Elisabeth can give the winner any prize including herself in marriage.

The first competitor Wolfram sings a standard song contest number about romantic love employing terms such as enraptured, sublime, virtuous, radiant, dazzled etc. Pretty good say the lords and ladies. Bloody rubbish says Tan. Nuts to pure love – copulation is the thing. Nothing like it. Shock horror! How can you be so disgusting and in front of ladies too? says Biterolf. You horrible depraved vulgar man get your sword out I challenge you. Me too cry several Minisingers unfurling swords. You sex-starved sparrow Biterolf, says Tan, you've never even done it. You're not worth stabbing.

Steady lads steady says Hermann. Let our Miniclub shun all this beastliness and stick to sublime love says Wolfram. Nuts to sublime love give me the real stuff like I got in the Venusberg massage parlour says Tan. Gawd! they cry in shock he's been to the Venusberg massage parlour! All females leave in disgust.

The Minisingers crowd Tan with prodding swords. Elisabeth interposes. Stand back she cries. Give poor Tan a chance to repent before death. Crumbs! she must be an angel of God say the lords and ladies. We'd better treat her with respect. Elisabeth influences me greatly says Tan. Now I see I am a sinner and really should repent. Get off the premises you loathsome toad says Hermann: get on a pilgrimage at once with them there pilgrims. Yes good idea says everyone get in there with the pilgrims. Some pilgrims with treble voices are heard outside (either very young or not entire). OK says Tan – to Rome! To Rome! shouts everyone else. Curtain.

Act III Green valley, as Act I Sc 2. It is getting dark

The prelude offers a tone poem of Tannhäuser's pilgrimage to Rome. Elisabeth prays at the shrine of the Virgin. Wolfram watches. He thinks: she's praying for Tan to return with a clearance certificate from the Pope. The pilgrims are heard offstage. We got our chits they sing. Good news we can all repatriate. Elisabeth watches but sees no Tan. Hail BVM says she I'm coming to join you. Pardon me says Wolfram might I have a word before you go? Negative signals Elisabeth who then slowly disappears up a path to heaven.

Wolfram pulls out his harp and requests the evening star to pay its respects to her as she passes en route to becoming an angel. It gets dark. Tan enters in rags. Why if it isn't Harry Tannhäuser again says Wolfram what now? I'm looking for Venusberg says Tan. Didn't you get to Rome? says Wolfram. Got to Rome says Tan. Did you attend the holy feast? asks Wolfram. Attended holy feast says Tan. Got your clearance certificate? says Wolfram. No clearance certificate says Tan. Why? asks Wolfram. Well there is this Pope, says Tan, pardoning thousands all around but when it comes to Joe Soap not a word. Not an if or a maybe. If you've had it off with Venus in person says this Pope then nothing doing. No certificate unless my staff sprouts with runner beans. It's very disappointing. So I say to myself this holy lark's a dead loss I'm off to Venusberg again. Funny: I can't seem to find the way: it was easy enough last time.

You're mad to go there says Wolfram: Aha! Venusberg approaches cries Tan as a pink mist plus the aroma of cheap scent engulfs the stage. Venus appears in person: welcome back old thing she says. 'Swounds how could a decent chap like me get mixed up in such goings-on says Wolfram. Leave her Harry leave her. Let me be says Tan. Remember Elisabeth says Wolfram.

Darkness suddenly falls as a chorus of Minisingers is heard offstage. Elisabeth − now an angel − is praying for you on high says Wolfram: Harry you're saved. (Zut! Lost another says Venus: she disappears.) A funeral cortège enters bearing Elisabeth's corpse: Pray for me Elisabeth cries Tan: he falls down dead. It gets light. Soprano pilgrims march on carrying the Pope's staff now sprouting runner beans. Here's salvation for all they sing. Including our Tannhäuser (but it's too late). Curtain.

LOOK OUT FOR

MINUTES FROM START

Act I Sc 1

0

Some of the best music in the opera lies in the first twenty minutes, made up of the overture*** followed by the ballet music of the Orgy. In the overture, which is a sort of reader's digest of the whole opera, we have first the Pilgrims' Chorus reverently presented by the brass choir and answered by a sad string tune: this section builds to a very loud restatement of the Pilgrims with the trombones doing their nuts. It fades away and we are into something naughty − wild arpeggios in the strings, flutters in the woodwind and more pretty sexy stuff. Then the clear statement of Tannhäuser's plea to be let off the chain (coming shortly), more mildly orgiastic stuff, then a window for a brief glimpse of the blue skies of the good life (quiet, in the woodwind): more orgy: a big statement of Tannhäuser's plea and so into the orgy proper, and a pretty good orgy it is.** Wagner uses four

0

10

10

main themes to whip up a mighty turmoil of excitement, although, as always in orgiastic ballets, there is a lot of delirious foreplay but no actual consummation. Judging by the crashing and thwacking by the percussion there is a certain amount of sado-masochism about too. The Three Graces restore order. After all this excitement there is a rather long patch of calm with visions in the sky and the Sirens calling OO-AH before the mists clear away.

22 Tannhäuser and Venus begin a sometimes acrimonious dialogue that is to run for the rest of the scene: at first it is mainly recitatif under another name, striking, powerful recitatif with a rich accompaniment and much modulation, but recitatif just the same, ending with a spirited burst from Venus as she asks Tannhäuser for a song. His song** is a set piece in two stanzas to a harp accompaniment and to the tune we have already heard in the overture (Tannhäuser's plea). It sounds a bit strenuous for the boudoir. Maybe it is telling us that Tannhäuser was a great sexual athlete. As well as praising Venus for being the tops in bed he has another message – I want to go home. **22**

27: *Dir töne Lob!* **27**

32: *Geliebter, komm!* Venus wheedles. A seductive ramble* around Tannhäuser's ego amidst a sensual welter of strings and woodwind with harps later plus, alas, a reprehensible solo violin. Tannhäuser rebuffs her with stanza 3 of the song above. **32**

Venus lets him have it. Get lost! she cries to an absolutely furious orchestral accompaniment (strings really angry; downward staccato scales). Then she goes soft again. Then another outburst. Then a bit of sweet self-pity** (What have I done wrong?) wrapped in a cloud of ravishing accompanying sound with the woodwind working some effective magic. But she gets cranky again and the duet finishes with the two of them definitely at cross purposes. Finally Tannhäuser cheekily quotes the Virgin Mary as his sponsor, at which Venus disappears in a puff

44: *Wie hätt'ich das erworben* **44**

of holy smoke with an immense orchestral crash.

Act I Sc 2

A pretty rum old scene, this one. First we have the Shepherd's Boy and his pipe (with a range of four octaves) with a song which is pretty ornery stuff (surely Wagner could have done better). Then the pilgrims creep up on us 51: *Zu dir wall ich* chorusing away mighty impressively** and finally Tannhäuser gets in there amongst the pipe and the pilgrims. 51

No composer can resist a hunting horn but here Wagner goes mad and bombards us with horns to the right of us, horns to the left of us, 55 horns solo and horns in chorus.* (In Paris he wanted twenty-four horns but only got sixteen. Short commons.) For those listeners who like horns it's great. (But today you usually get only twelve.) 55

Suddenly, as happens so often in Wagner, we strike a patch of sparkling water in the middle of a fairly turgid run. Wolfram welcomes Tann- 58: *Gegrüsst sei uns* häuser back to the ranch.* Tannhäuser's interest picks up when he hears the name Elisabeth. The Minisingers come in one by one, we have a happy ensemble, soothing, melodious and, as it should be, welcoming. 58

Wolfram recalls Tannhäuser's days as No. 1 62: *Als du in* in the charts.** A formal piece, the second *kühnem* stanza holding what emerges as the tune. This is introduced by a really fetching few bars of strings and woodwind but the tune itself (which has to do a lot of work before the scene ends) has an unfortunate whiff of schmaltz about it. The ensemble which follows is very satisfactory up to a sudden and coarse change of key just before Tannhäuser's final capitulation. The finale speeds up a little jerkily towards the end (the Maestro can help greatly here) but it is joyful, enjoyable and ends with another abso- lutely frenzied outbreak of horns. 62

Act II

3: *Wie jetzt mein Busen*

12: *Gepriesen sei die Stunde*

20

34: *Blick ich umher*

43: *Dir, Göttin der Liebe*

Elisabeth's greeting. After a short prelude (agreeable woodwind solos) with tantalizing snatches of a big string tune and eight lines of recitatif (I was really sad when Tannhäuser left) we are into the clear straight line of Elisabeth's aria.** And at the end, at last, we get a full statement of the big tune. But even now it is elusive.   3

The duet* that follows the Greeting warms   12
up as it goes along. Elisabeth, the simple soul, is pretty well thrown by Tannhäuser's return, she doesn't know why, but perks up when she recalls the songs of the sixties. A series of excited flourishes in the violins move them into an exultant mood,** the duet takes off and races to a brilliant finish as our two carol away happily over the gloomy asides from Wolfram.

This time it's trumpets, simply bursting out all over the place. Introductory of course, for trumpets in large numbers are nearly always used fanfarishly. What they introduce here is the Grand March,*** three catchy tunes one   20
after the other at first orchestral and then, as American academics would say, choralized. Grows in volume to become quite deafening. Marvellous: vulgar: irresistible, especially the third tune over the I'VE-GOT-FOUR-NOTES accompaniment.

The song contest begins.* Wolfram first, a   34
rather limp recitatif-ish entry, but then he's only allotted harps and then violas and cellos. His song is well liked in the Hall of Song but no prizes from us. Tannhäuser's contribution is sung in something of a sexual trauma, and is more interesting but Biterolf's shocked response lowers the temperature again. Now we sail into the fourth stanza of Tannhäuser's address to Venus from Act I.** But this time the accompani-   43
ment is full of naughty Venusberg music and the message is reversed: instead of wanting out he's wanting to get back. At this point, incidentally,

the song contest finally gets lost in an argument about sexual morality. And it's very heated stuff because in those days a Minisinger found in Venusberg was the equivalent of discovering a bishop in a massage parlour today.

And now for something much more substantial, perhaps the best sequence in the opera. After the dramatics of the drawn swords, Elisabeth makes her plea for Tannhäuser to be spared** so that he may repent. There is no great Wagnerian tune here nor any musical excitement but suddenly the scene becomes serious and moving. We respond to Elisabeth's courage, nobly expressed, and so do Landgrave Hermann and the Minisingers in a profound, reflective chorus*** which anticipates the melody of Elisabeth's prayer in the next act: Tannhäuser sings in an anguished tenor line amidst this and Elisabeth soars above in a radiant descant.

46: *Zurück!*

51: *Ein Engel stieg*

A very decent recitatif from Hermann which keeps up the high tone of what has gone before: it breaks into a trot (in the accompaniment) and becomes arioso if not an aria.* He tells Tannhäuser to get in there amongst the pilgrims.

61: *Versammelt sind aus meinen Landen*

62: *Mit ihnen sollst du wallen*

The final chorus:** still on the same elevated plane. The burden of the melody (a long winding one) is taken first by the tenors, then by Elisabeth solo. Everyone is saying roughly the same thing: it's a good idea for Tannhäuser to turn pilgrim. There is a lot of counterpoint about with busy voices all around: everything stops dead whilst we hear teeny teenage pilgrims warbling in the valley. A good idea, but Wagner lacked Verdi's certainty of touch with offstagers, and it sounds a bit Hollywood. Melodramatic shouts of Roma! Roma! Here I Come! from Tannhäuser. Curtain.

Act III

0

Prelude.* Solemn and rather aimless chording in the wind begins to take the shape of part of the Pilgrims' Chorus, but we lose it, get a

46

51

61

62

0

cascade of descending notes in the strings plus the sad string tune (which we have heard in the overture) for the redemption of Tannhäuser, which goes on both loud and soft for some time.

After Wolfram's uninspired comments about Elisabeth at prayer, we hear the Pilgrims' Chorus*** swelling up proper (all grown-up pilgrims and entire, no trebles) and very fine it is: the final burst with the full orchestral treatment sounds more secular than holy, but it would still stun a priest at fifty yards. Then it fades. Tannhäuser is not amongst them.

11: *Begluckt darf nun dich*   11

Elisabeth's prayer.** Calm, intense and again with a firm outline. The woodwind embellish and accompany the vocal part ingeniously but do tend to slow things up towards the end where they become aimless. Rather like the stuff which the organist plays when he has run off all the music billed for the voluntary and has to fill in time until the bride arrives. Meanwhile Elisabeth is ascending to heaven, but very slowly.

16: *Allmächt'ge Jungfrau*   16

O star of eve** (not of Eve as some have mistakenly thought). Well! Arresting, certainly, popular, very, but isn't it just a little too much? Those scoopy chromatic bits? Isn't that snatch of throbbing cello pretty ghastly?

26: *O du mein holder Abendstern*   26

Tannhäuser's long narration.* We start with two stanzas accompanied by the winding string figure that was in the Prelude to Act III. This takes the lead and dominates the scene as Tannhäuser tells us what a hard time he gave himself on the road to Rome. Then a long stretch of unremarkable recitatif. Things chirp up with the entry of the Venusberg music and the piece ends strongly.

34: *Inbrunst im Herzen*   34

(After the formal opening this nine-minute stretch of narrative is freely written in Wagner's new style and hence is generally thought to be a step forward to greater things. One wishes however he had taken shorter steps or walked a bit faster, or both.)

The final stages. Tannhäuser's narrative is followed by a lively argument** between Wolfram (You would be mad to go back to Venus) and Tannhäuser (I'm going just the same) which becomes engulfed in an orgy of Venusberg music coming to a climax as Venus appears in person, pink fog and all, very ready to have Tannhäuser back. Now we have an exciting tug of war between the forces of good (Wolfram) and evil (Venus) for the soul of Tannhäuser, by now one would have thought not a particularly desirable item. Wolfram scores an easy win by just invoking the name of Elisabeth. Tannhäuser echoes 'Elisabeth!' as he did in Act I and this appears to have much the same effect on Venus as did the introduction of the BVM into the conversation in Act I. Now we hear male offstagers approaching and singing a magnificent chorus** about Elisabeth's soul. This is the *coup de grâce*: Venus concedes, fades away into the pink and Elisabeth's funeral cortège comes on to centre stage, her corpse prominent on a bier. 'She's praying for Tannhäuser' sing the pilgrims, knights and Minisingers, making a wild guess in order to be as helpful as possible to the plot. 'O Elisabeth, pray for me' sings Tannhäuser, and expires, (cause of death unknown). Meanwhile the teenage pilgrims strike up a much weaker chorus reporting the issue of runner beans from the Pope's staff, which means that pretty well everyone is pardoned, including Tannhäuser. The musical situation is saved by a final sonorous rendering of the Pilgrims' Chorus and the curtain falls with everyone really pleased that Tannhäuser's soul, thanks either to the love of a good woman or to the greenery sprouting from the Pope's staff, or both, has safely gone aloft.

43: *Halt ein! Halt ein!*

48: *Ihr ward der Engel*

43

48

NOTES

Tannhäuser	Wagner's fifth opera
First night	1. Königliches Sächsiscles Hoftheater, Dresden, 19 October 1845
	2. Opéra, Paris, 13 March 1861
Reception	1. Uncomprehending. 2. Fiasco
Libretto	Wagner
Source	Two unrelated mediaeval legends

NEWS AND GOSSIP

In 1843 Wagner went to the Dresden court as assistant Intendant, musically a young lion and politically a revolutionary. He had already done quite a lot of work on *Tannhäuser* and, now an insider, he persuaded the management to put it on. It didn't go down well. The singers found it too tough and neither the Tannhäuser nor the Elisabeth had the vocal stamina to last out the evening. Also the Dresdeners were somewhat stunned by this new kind of music. Four years later Wagner was involved in the Dresden uprising. It failed and he pushed off to Paris where in 1860 (he was by now quite famous) the Emperor Napoleon III invited him to put on *Tannhäuser* at the Opéra. There were two snags:

1) All operas at the Opéra had to be in French.
2) A ballet in Act II was a must.

Wagner said OK to the translation but insisted the opening Venusberg stuff should serve as the ballet and set about expanding and rewriting it. He was warned this would not do and it didn't. The first night was a disaster. Not from lack of rehearsal – there were 163 of them – nor from any skimping on production values – an outsize orchestra: sixteen horns, six horses and ten dogs on stage in the hunting scene – but because of the Jockey Club. The young aristos of the Club were apt to stroll into the opera after dinner to look over the girls in the second-act ballet and then to stroll out again. They did not expect to stroll in on something like a Pilgrims' Chorus and took steps to teach the management a lesson by turning up in huge numbers at the point where the ballet should have been and by whistling, catcalling, booing and carrying on as high-spirited young gentlemen will do when indulging in tribal customs. There was also a conspiracy theory, namely that the whole débâcle was staged to spite the politically unpopular

Princess Metternick, who had persuaded Napoleon to have the opera put on. After three nights of hooliganism the opera was taken off and no doubt there was a second-act ballet in every show for the rest of the season. Even before the Paris débâcle, *Tannhäuser* had played in some sixty German houses and now with this scandal behind it, it spread even faster and quicker. Early this century, along with the *Dutchman* and *Lohengrin*, it was amongst the most popular Wagners, but as taste swung towards late Wagner *Tannhäuser* probably suffered most. Opera managements now think of it as something of a curiosity and as a wasteful use of that rare commodity – a Wagner tenor.

COMMENT

Anyone seeking proof that Wagner had no sense of humour need look no further than *Tannhäuser*. It begins with the spectacle of a well-built Wagnerian soprano lying on a couch with a Wagnerian tenor, likely to be no sparrow either, in a rosy-pink brothel-like light, both of them in a post-coital trance, whilst an orgy rages around in which a large number of the sex-mad throng are half animals. Later we have the spectacle of the bodily assumption of Elisabeth to heaven, although today she is generally spared the hike up the rainbow staircase to the skies. There is also the bodily return of Venus to the Thuringian countryside – although even Wagner became queasy about this and in later productions Venus was heard but not seen. If Wagner's pompous solemnity about Tannhäuser's moral welfare were good for a laugh and no more, we could sit back and enjoy the good things in the show. But enjoyment fades as his false religiosity becomes more and more nauseating. Wagner was not a believer and wrongly thought that the spirituality which had inspired Bach's B minor Mass, the painting of the Florentines and Dante's *Inferno* could be used by any good pro. as a mechanism to wheel out a holy plot. Which it can't, because when false piety is rumbled it is seen to be humbug. That is why the pilgrims trudging to and from Rome are cardboard figures, why Elisabeth is no more than a nutcase, why the Minisingers are a comical band of prefects at a pious public school and why Tannhäuser himself is a ludicrous figure. The other great plot motivator, the belief that an evil man can be saved by the love of a good woman, already one of Wagner's obsessions, is not so silly. But here it doesn't work so well as in the *Dutchman*, because he was a wild romantic figure who gripped the imagination whereas Tannhäuser, although maybe a good singer, is an unattractive man who is making a terrible mess of his life. Not worth praying for, much less dying for.

So what's good about *Tannhäuser*? Well, certainly the tunes and the orchestration. The tunes are striking and memorable, but not all of them pass muster. The Pilgrims' Chorus, although noble and holy when sung offstage, loses its solemn charm as it gets louder and when brayed out fortissimo by the trombones it tends to parody its own quiet and more decent self. Tannhäuser's first act aria is vigorous, Elisabeth's two big numbers effective, the Venusberg music – later Wagner grafted on to earlier Wagner – is wonderfully sparky and the big climax a real banger. O Star of Eve has a sort of ghastly attraction. But then secretly many of us relish a bit of a wallow in music which is not in the best of taste, rather like the two old ladies on holiday in the Riviera who would say to each other 'Let's go down to the beach and be scandalized'. The three best bits are the overture, which Wagner worked over and over to make it an effective concert piece, the Grand March in Act II Scene 2, and the finale to this scene (from the point of Elisabeth's plea to save Tannhäuser to the final ensemble) when for a moment real values and true feeling take over.

Musically *Tannhäuser* is still made up of a succession of striking musical numbers linked together by recitatif-type material of a much lower voltage. It is still a long way away from the seamless musical flow that Wagner was aiming for and finally achieved in *Tristan* and *The Ring*. On the credit side there is not much that is dull: Tannhäuser's narrative in Act III, although hailed by the musicos as a great leap forward in Wagnerian technique, is dreary listening: the Minisingers tend to go on a bit and the song contest could have been organized with more pace and better songs, but on the whole, although you may not be delighted by *Tannhäuser*, you are unlikely to be bored. A beta.

Lohengrin

Mythological drama

The one about a knight, a swan, and a woman who asks a forbidden question which results in disaster and death.

CAST

Heinrich, King of Germany	Bass
Lohengrin, a holy knight	Tenor
Elsa of Brabant	Soprano
Friederich of Telramund	Baritone
Ortrud, his wife	Mezzo-Soprano
Heralds, nobles, ladies of honour etc.	

3 acts: running time 3 hrs 50 mins

STORY

Act I The banks of the River Scheldt in Holland

Under a mighty oak – The Judgement Oak – sits the great Führer of all Germany, Heinrich, with massed SS troops at his back, and facing them the fighting men of Brabant, as Holland was quaintly known in ancient days, with the top people in front. Topmost and foremost are Friederich Telramund and his wicked wife Ortrud. The air is full of pageantry, heraldry, chivalry and trumpet fanfares. After a burst of heraldic activity Heinrich makes his recruiting speech. I soundly thrashed those frightful Hungarians some years ago and built a Maginot line to keep them out, he sings, but believe it or nor they are at it again. Infiltrating. The Empire needs you men of Brabant to join my army double quick. Certainly, say the men of Brabant, only too happy to oblige. And while I am in Brabant, says the King, I would like to sort out the matter of succession. I gather there has been a lot of feuding and bickering and there is no clear winner. Speak up the first contender, Friederich.

Well, M'Lud, says Friederich, you see it was this way. When the old ruler died he left his son and daughter as my wards. The girl, Elsa, grew up nicely and I proposed marriage but she turned me down flat. Shortly after that she went for a walk with her brother, Gottfried, in the woods and murdered him so that she could queen it alone over Brabant. So then I married this Ortrud here. My God, what a terrible story, say the assembled company.

This is a serious matter, says the King. I must make a

judgement. Call Elsa. Elsa steps up in a dreamy state. What is your defence Elsa, asks the King. Well I had a dream, says Elsa, about this Knight in shining armour. He will shortly arrive to defend me, wait and see. OK, says the King, that means ordeal by battle. Do you agree Friederich? Sure thing, says Friederich. And you, Elsa, do you agree? Yes I do, says Elsa. And what is the name of your champion, asks the King. Don't know, says Elsa, he'll be along shortly. You heralds, ask the champion of Elsa to stand forth, says the King. Everybody waits, breathlessly. No one appears. Looks dicey for Elsa, say the crowd. Try again heralds, says the King. Another long wait. Then a swan is espied dragging a rubber dingy with a shining knight standing in it, holding the reins. Mother of God, cry the crowd, did you ever see the like of this? The knight disembarks and politely thanks the swan for a safe and comfortable trip.

Hello, King, says Lohengrin (for it is he). I'm Elsa's champion. Is it OK with you, Elsa? Oo yes says Elsa. And if I win will you marry me, the knight asks. Oo yes says Elsa. Just one little thing before we start Elsa, says Lohengrin, you must never ask me my name. Never will, says Elsa. Not now, not at all, not ever, says Lohengrin. Gottit? Gottit, says Elsa. What an amazing carry-on say the crowd. Be careful, Friederich, there is magic around and he may be protected by God or something. Stuff that, says Friederich.

Can we get going King, asks Lohengrin. I declare this swordfight open, says the King. They fight. Walkover for Lohengrin. He (unwisely) spares Friederich's life. What a fighter, says everyone, also seems to be pure, good, virtuous, protector of the meek and fond of animals. I won because Elsa is innocent, says Lohengrin. Great result, says Elsa. Who is this bastard who has ruined my life, says Ortrud. I've lost my dukedom, my glory and my honour to this guy who is clearly a magicman, says Friederich, and passes out. Lohengrin is held aloft on a platform of shields by the King's men, Elsa ditto by the Brabantians. Everyone rejoices except the awful Ortrud and Friederich.

Act II Outside Antwerp Castle

Friederich and Ortrud are lying on some steps. They are dressed in rags. (Why? Ed) There is revelry within. No point in hanging around here, says Friederich. Let's move on. Can't, says Ortrud, I'm bound here by a spell. I've got a good mind to dump you and shove off, says Friederich. Look what you've done to me, I've lost my sword, my good reputation, my honour, my kingdom – everything. If I still had my sword I'd carve you up. Why so hostile? asks Ortrud. Because it was you who told me that whole pack of lies about Elsa killing Gottfried and got me into this mess, says Friederich. It's God's judgement on us. God, says Ortrud (a devout heathen). Pshaw! Shut up and listen to me. Do you know that if Elsa forces this flaming knight to say who he is his magic power will disappear? Pouf! Like that. So: says Friederich, very interesting. We must sow the seeds of suspicion in Elsa and get her to pop the question, says Ortrud. And even if that fails there is a second line of attack – brute force. If you cut off his little finger that would do it too. No finger, no magic. [How does she know this? Ed.] If only you'd cut off any bit of him during the fight, you incompetent sod, you would have won. Now I know it really was magic and not God that licked me I feel much better, says Friederich. Let's set about plotting right away.

Elsa appears on a nearby balcony. O happy me, she says, I love him and he loves me. Get off, Friederich, says Ortrud, leave this scene to me. He gets off and hides. Hey Elsa, shouts Ortrud, you see here an unhappy woman. How's that? says Elsa. After you had given that ghastly Friederich the heave-ho, he married me and made up all those fibs about you. He's sorry enough for it now. How awful, says Elsa, how can I help you? Hold on. I'll come down. (She disappears). Come on you heathen gods, especially Woden and Freya, cries Ortrud. Revenge!

Elsa reappears at ground level. What a pitiful sight, she says. Ortrud, I forgive you everything and tomorrow I will ask my knight to show mercy to you and to Friederich too. That's really nice of you, says Ortrud, but before you do that there is something you should know. Beware! Your knight came to you by magic and at any moment he may go by magic. Surely not, says Elsa, but be my guest, come inside. They disappear into the castle. Friederich reappears. Oho, he says, Revenge! It's going well. Revenge! (He hides again).

Dawn breaks, rather quickly. The stage fills first with servants, then with noblemen and soldiers (the same old lot as in Act I). Dawn chorus of soldiers etc. Trumpets. A herald proclaims Friederich to be an outlaw. What a nasty man, sing the chorus. The King has proclaimed Elsa's knight to be Lord of Brabant, says the herald, and he orders an immediate wedding, after which the knight will lead you to fight against the Hungarians. Very good.

We're on, sing the soldiers. Absolutely. Steady on, say four Friederich-loyal nobles, why should we go and fight for this bastard from out of town against an enemy who is no threat to us? Can no one stop this madness? I can, cries Friederich revealing himself. Good Lord, it's old Friederich, say the nobles, but you can't do it, you're outlawed. Wait and see, says Friederich.

With a blast of pageantry Elsa enters in her wedding dress with a crowd of subservient women at her back. God bless Elsa, say all. Ortrud pushes to the front, now dressed fit to kill. Pshaw! Elsa, she shouts. Pshaw! My man Friederich was known and respected throughout the land. Who is this guy who is carrying on as your champion? No pedigree, no identity, no C.V. He was smart enough to tell you not to ask any questions. It's not good enough. You dirty double-crosser, says Elsa. You came crawling to me for mercy and now you challenge the bona fides of my champion, who is good, pure, noble, licked your man in combat, and is fond of animals. Yes, by magic, says Ortrud. I appeal to you assembled people, cries Elsa, which of the two men is in the right? Your man, Elsa, shout the crowd, no doubt about it.

The King and Lohengrin make their way through the crowd. Now now now what's all this, asks the King. It's this terrible Ortrud, says Elsa. I took pity on her and let her into the palace and now she says I can't trust my knight because of lack of identity. Do you believe her, or do you trust me? asks Lohengrin. I trust you, says Elsa. Now Friederich springs up. Hey, listen to me, he cries. Shame on him, he's a certified outlaw, shouts everyone. Chuck him out! No, says Friederich, listen to me. I have been terribly wronged. This so-called knight won by magic and trickery. Who is he anyway? I put it to him now: WHO THE HELL ARE YOU? I will only answer the question if it is put to me by Elsa, replies Lohengrin.

Suddenly there is a buzz of doubt throughout the crowd. Elsa's worried, you can see that, they say. Knight, why not tell all, says the King. We'll stand by you, whoever you may be, sing the soldiers. And another thing, Elsa, says Friederich, if I cut off his little finger his magic is rubbed out. Pouf! Like that. Let me have a go at him tonight and I'll prove it. Never, says Elsa. Get away from her you nasty man, says Lohengrin. Now Elsa, do you trust me or do you want to put the question. Yes or no? Well, they had me worried for a while, says she, but on the whole I trust you. Good girl Elsa, says Lohengrin. Let's get married. Hail Elsa, hail Sir Anon. Hail and hail again, sing the crowd joyfully. But Ortrud is not licked – she makes a rude gesture indicating (rightly) that Elsa has got it coming to her.

Act III Sc 1 The Bridal Chamber

Something on the scale of a royal wedding is afoot [set up in less than 24 hours? Ed.] Scores of courtiers, retainers etc. process through the bridal chamber without a thought about the bride's personal privacy. God bless Elsa, they say, at length. At last they leave the happy couple alone. I love you, says Elsa, and I love you, says Lohengrin. Are you happy, says Lohengrin. Yes very, says Elsa, but she begins to get another fit of the worries. Pity I can't address my lover by name, she says. Not that it would make any difference, of course. But it would be quite safe to confide in me: no one would ever get the secret out of *me*. Shut up Elsa, says Lohengrin. O come on – tell, she says. Remember your oath Elsa, says he, you swore you'd never ask. But it's no good: she gets into a frenzy, thinks she sees the swan coming to take him away and puts the identity question to him point blank. Now you've blown it, says Lohengrin, and meanwhile kills Friederich (who has crept into the bedroom to murder him) rather quickly. I'll give you an answer, but it will have to be done proper, in front of the King and nobles.

Sc 2 Back on the banks of the Scheldt

The multitude assembles. Well, here we are again, says King Heinrich, and you are all going to fight for me like anything, led by this amazing knight. Four of Friederich's men come in. What are you doing here? asks the King. You'll find out, they reply. (They are carrying Friederich's concealed corpse). Elsa comes on. You look a bit droopy, love, says the King. Everything all right?

Lohengrin comes on. Hail Leader, shout the soldiers. Not your leader, says Lohengrin. First I killed this man (uncovers the corpse) because he tried to murder me. That's all right, isn't it? Second, Elsa has let me down. How's that, cry the multitude. She swore not to ask my name, says Lohengrin, but she did. So I will have to tell all. Listen to me. I'm one of those very special knights who was detailed for Holy Grail guard duty. We guards are a brotherhood, rather like the masons but more so. My Dad is Parsifal [Parsifal a family man? Ed.] the boss of the Holy Grail elite corps, and I have all manner of extrasensory powers, but only so long as I remain anonymous. Now because of Elsa I have to tell you that my name is – LOHENGRIN.

Good Lord, how amazing, says everyone. Oh dear, how dreadfully silly I have been, says Elsa. So now I must leave you, says Lohengrin. No, no, cried Elsa. Afraid so, says Lohengrin. Stay, be our leader, shout the soldiers. Can't says Lohengrin. The swan appears. Hello swan, good to see you again, says Lohengrin. Here Elsa, take this ring for yourself and keep this horn and this sword for your brother Gottfried. He is not dead and will return.

Hooray, good riddance, shouts Ortrud. I and my heathen gods have won. That ain't no swan. See the chain round his neck? It's the one I took off Gottfried. Then I magicked him into a swan. But Lohengrin is not licked. He pushes the swan down under the water and pulls out a shining knight in its place – Gottfried. Behold your leader, he cries. Meanwhile a hovering dove has appeared (sent by the grail) and despite its puny pulling power it draws Lohengrin and his boat slowly away into the sunset.

The Main Mottos

In Lohengrin Wagner was developing his theory of Leitmotifs or mottos (which he took to the limit, some would say to excess, in *The Ring*, to represent a character or an idea). There are several subsidiary mottos, for instance a cluster of sweet woodwind phrases that make up much of the music surrounding Elsa, but only three main mottos that will strike the ear of even the least motto-prone listener.

1.	The Grail	A slow, shining tune played in slightly uncomfortable close harmony by high violins. Opens the prelude to Act I. Unmistakable.
2.	The Forbidden Question	Rather like Tchaikovsky's big tune for *Swan Lake* (perhaps its origin?). High – down to four quick notes – rising to the starting note again with a dotted note, or hiccup.
3.	The Evil Ortrud	Often played loudly and menacingly by the brass. First heard when Lohengrin tells Elsa never to ask his name. Two long downward sweeps, most clearly heard on the cellos at the beginning of the prelude to Act II. Melodramatic.

LOOK OUT FOR

MINUTES FROM START

Act I Prelude

After a long sustained high chord – but not so long as the opening chord of *Rhinegold* – we hear the Grail music, high violins in stressful close harmony. This carries on in its own style for quite a time until a new ponderous theme slowly emerges beneath it and gradually builds up to a crashing climax then tails off until it reaches once again a vigorous close. There is a parting touch of the Grail. Admired by many but no star in this guide.

Act I Sc 1

Minutes from the start we are confronted by a rumbustious sea of sound to match the great gathering of military men on the stage – hearty choruses, declamatory heralds, trumpet fanfares busting out all over. King Heinrich's recruiting speech is delivered in vigorous quasi-recitatif but tones down a notch or two when he returns to the delicate matter of the disputed leadership.

Friederich makes his case against Elsa in a superior style of recitatif, at first seemingly saddened by her quite appalling behaviour then growing more animated, driven on by explosive interventions from the lower strings. The military men react to such terrible accusations in a suitably hushed manner but, as Elsa is summonsed to appear, we have a welcome patch of blue sky – a calm interlude from the orchestra followed, as she enters, by a gentle un-military chorus from the serried ranks who are instantly smitten by her beauty and innocence.

When the King asks her to answer the charges, she fails to react and, as if in a trance, she recounts her dream of a knight in shining 25: *Einsam in trüben* armour who will be her saviour. This, Elsa's 25 *tagen* Dream, is not so formal as Senta's ballad in the *Dutchman* but it is not far from being a set piece aria. There are two stanzas – Wagner at his lyrical best – the second introduced by a touch of Grail. After all the macho bustle of the previous twenty minutes Elsa's Dream has a stunning effect – quiet, calm and quite lovely.** And from now on Wagner raises his game, the appeal (in vain) for Friederich to think again, the decision for ordeal by combat, the repeated summons for Elsa's champion to step forward, her fevered pleas to her knight to appear, all pass off with pace and panache, leading to a wonderful stretch of sustained anticipation until, at last, the swan and Knight are sighted. This is greeted by one of Wagner's great choruses rising from a susurration of wonder and gradually **37: *Seht! Seht!*** blazing into a triumphant climax of welcome.** 37 (Arrival of The Swan).

And now it must be admitted, the temperature drops. Lohengrin's prissy little vote of thanks to the Swan (lots of Grail) not quite the thing expected of a hero's arrival (but the chorus continues to work well). Things pick up a bit with Lohengrin's greeting to the King and in his pompous but emphatic mission statement. But **46: *Elsa soll ich dien*** with the ensuing duet with Elsa (first outing of 46 the Forbidden Question) we have something superior, for it conveys a sense of tenderness and wonder which is one of the specialities of this opera.* Now Lohengrin turns belligerent and the run-up to the duel is all good vigorous stuff, including a striking orchestral piece as the battleground is prepared and an impressive request to God by the King to make sure the best man wins. This is followed by a powerful quintet from the principals merging into another sonorous chorus (God Help Us).*

The fight itself is musically disappointing, sounding something like the hurry music for a D. W. Griffiths silent film. The post-fight rejoicings are noisy and lengthy and greatly enhanced by a notable moving bass figure in the orchestra. So Act I reaches a satisfactory conclusion.

Act II Sc 1

All three Lohengrin preludes are something on their own, and this one could be seen as a mini tone poem. It begins with a drum roll out of which emerges the motto Evil Ortrud in the lower strings. This is answered by a few bars of funeral march in the woodwind. Evil Ortrud returns, is passed to the bassoons and, with interjections, works itself up into a frenzy of gloom, then fades until interrupted gloriously by a bevy of trumpets from within the castle. After a quick reference to Elsa's Dream, back to the Ortrud tune which rolls on until the unhappy Friederich breaks in and Act II is under way.

6: *Du furlichter weib*

Friederich's outburst. This shout of rage and grief is sung in something nearer to aria than the sort of ongoing recitatif we have heard in Act I. It is a fine piece, ending in a rousing climax of despair.* The following duet with Ortrud in which she lays the grand plan for undermining Elsa's trust (Evil Ortrud) has some of the best music in the opera.**   6

21: *Euch lüften*

Elsa's sweet little hymn to happiness (introduced by a brief woodwind symphony) provides a pool of calm and serenity amongst the turmoil of ranting and plotting. It is in what we have now come to recognize as the Elsa childlike style – a crystal clear vocal line, slow dignified pace with light support from the woodwind and little or no bass beneath.* The long (12 minutes) duet between Ortrud and Elsa which follows is again one of the opera's chart-toppers. To begin with their exchanges are, perhaps, a little ornery, the chief interest lying in the vivid and adventurous orchestral accompaniment, but as Elsa's compassion is aroused the phrases become more rounded and Elsa's last piece before she leaves   21

29: *Wie schlect*

the balcony is deeply touching.** As Elsa negotiates the staircase Ortrud makes her appeal to her heathen gods – a splendid solo piece.*   29

33: *Wie kann ich solche*

Now, both grounded, Elsa becomes truly moved by Ortrud's alleged plight and abandons   33 her clear childlike tones, to sing like a grown-up woman. But when Ortrud starts her evil game of undermining Elsa's faith in her Swan Knight (Evil Ortrud and Forbidden Question) Elsa reverts to her childish innocent style as she protests her absolute trust in him and gives another heartfelt number (and note the gem of a phrase heard first in the woodwind, one of Wagner's most haunting obiter dicta). This long two-handed scene closes with the two sopranos singing together in a 'thinks' duet of dreamy beauty.**

After they leave Friederich gives vent to a final burst of declamatory hatred, this time directed against his wife. The scene ends with the orchestra reminding us of the Forbidden Question.

Act II Sc 2

In the interlude we have trumpet calls echoing round the turrets of the castle, followed by horns and imitation horns over a pedal bass, then a growing orchestral bustle until the military men join in with yet another manly chorus. More fanfares, more heralds, more choruses, all invigorating.

The quibbling of the four disloyal nobles and the unexpected appearance of Friederich pass off dramatically enough in a fairly conventional fashion. Then a little miracle takes place. The pages helpfully inform us that Elsa is on her way and as she moves downstairs we have, with a sudden modulation, a brief woodwind symphony playing Elsa's music in hushed tones.

13: *Gesegnet soll* This leads to the great God Bless Elsa chorus* at 13 first gentle, becoming magnificent and reaching a climax of almost religious intensity – until it is rudely interrupted by the evil Ortrud. In the tempestuous duet that follows Ortrud is on the attack, launching her accusations in almost hysterical style: Elsa's replies (she still trusts her knight absolutely) are dignified and serene. The chorus is definitely and vociferously on Elsa's side.

With the entry of Lohengrin and the King things steady up. Elsa, passionately contrite, begs Lohengrin to forgive her for taking pity on Ortrud, and now she is once again more the woman than the child. Lohengrin majestically bids Ortrud to lay off and, in a passage of great nobility, tenderly asks Elsa if Ortrud has managed to poison her mind against him. But before she can reply we have a couple of crashing chords from the orchestra. It's Friederich again. This stirs up general turmoil, but Friederich manages to get the ear of the company in his swingeing attack on Lohengrin's credentials (Forbidden Question) in a highly effective solo number (with something in common with Alberich's ill-tempered outbursts in *The Ring*). The tension rises between Friederich and Lohengrin with panting brass and sweeping strings which die away as he appeals to Elsa for her verdict. Then another wondering ensemble with solo 'thinks' parts interjected by the principals.* (Elsa in doubt). So swinging on to firmer ground we build to the climax as Lohengrin pops the question: Elsa gives the right answer (with organ accompaniment). The crowd and Lohengrin receive this with a kind of holy hush. But their enthusiasm (and volume) grow into a final great shout of joy, followed by a brief organ voluntary and brassy final chords.

30: *Den dort im glanz* 33

Act III Sc 1

This famous piece with its opening whoops and noisy bass tune provides a field-day for the whole brass section, and especially the trombones. It is meant to reflect the spirit of the wedding celebrations but we might just as well be in the middle of a thunderstorm or witnessing a foray by the Valkyries. An agreeable little woodwind intermezzo gives a little respite but soon the trombones are at it again and the prelude ends in a pretty well unsurpassable welter of brass sound. Absolutely ripping.**

5: *Treulich bewacht* Next comes Wagner's only number to get into 5 the all-time charts, a piece that is played a myriad times more than anything else he wrote and known all over the world as The Wedding March. It is not, of course, a march but a chorus and with its antique sound and carefully wrought stanzas has something in common with the wonderful pastiche chorale that opens *Meistersinger*. In the second stanza the music of the first is repeated but between the two we have a telling intermezzo – first some quiet rumination in the woodwind, then a brief octet for eight female voices and finally a sweeping romantic burst from the strings. All in all a smash hit.**

9: *Das stube lied*   The duet that follows (20 minutes) is one of   9
Wagner's great *tours de force*.** It begins with pure, passionate love music, Lohengrin singing to Elsa, then she to him, then both together. Everything in the world is lovely. The voices are given absolute priority with only the lightest orchestral accompaniment. But then the sky begins to cloud over. Elsa is worrying again. Lohengrin tries to soothe her, singing sweetly and strongly, but there are anxious little repeated chords in the woodwind which signify trouble. He changes the subject by directing her attention to the flowers outside the window [visible at 3 a.m.? Ed.] in a fine lyrical passage. But Elsa, still protesting one hundred percent love, worries on (the Forbidden Question) becoming more and more agitated and getting closer and closer to putting the dreaded question. Lohengrin makes his last appeal in something verging on an aria, and very fine too. But it is no go. Elsa becomes more and more frenzied, finally going a little potty, thinking she sees the Swan coming to take him away. In a mad climax of doubt she puts the Forbidden Question and it's all over. Amidst all this high drama Lohengrin kills Friederich. (His appearance and death seem musically incidental to such a scene of emotion). This scene is played out by the orchestra, sombre, and full of menace.

Act III Sc 2

After a good deal of dawn trumpeting and orchestral bustle – with one big Land of Hope and Glory tune – we are back again with King and chorus with hushed amazement as Friederich's men appear, then a sad mute Elsa, followed by Lohengrin, now declamatory. The drama progresses with a recitatif and chorus until, with a touch of Grail Lohengrin tells all. (Lohengrin's narration). Now he is in his Parsifal mode the music at first quasi-holy and not at all catchy but he gains power as his story unwinds and he finishes well.

50: *In fernem land*   50

After the standard hushed response from the crowd Lohengrin's farewell and Elsa's anguished appeals pass off well enough, but it is only in the great concerted piece that follows that the temperature rises. So the swan comes in again (Grail, piano) greeted warmly by Lohengrin who then delivers his farewell speech, a fine free-ranging piece, his best in the scene, with a ringing final flourish. Ortrud's moment of short-lived glory manages to avoid musical anti-climax by virtue of its high melodrama and the chorus, with telling orchestral interjections, see us through effectively to the final curtain.

63: *Mein lieber schwan*   63

NOTES

Lohengrin Wagner's sixth opera
First night Weimar, Grossherzogliches Hoftheater August 1850
Reception Divided, but the ayes had it
Libretto Wagner
Source *Parzival and Titurel*, poems by Wolfram von Eschenbach, also an anonymous epic poem featuring the story of *Lohengrin*

NEWS AND GOSSIP

Wagner first came across the legend of *Lohengrin* in 1841 when he was digging deep into legend-land to uncover the story of

Tannhäuser. He discovered more about *Lohengrin* (and *Parsifal* too) in poems by one Wolfram von Eschenbach and also in an epic version of the legend by Johann Joseph von Gorres. The story – with all its overtones of Holy Grailism, evil supernatural powers and a forbidden question – caught his fancy and he reports that as soon as he had read it he saw a vision of *Lohengrin* as a completed opera. This was in the summer of 1845 and he set to work at once, finishing a prose version of the libretto by November. This he read to a group of his friends, including Robert Schumann. Schumann was worried because the work was not divided into the conventional 'numbers' of a traditional opera. Wagner then applied numbers to the several sections of each act (goodness knows how) and so made Schumann happy.

He had the first draft of the score by July 1846 and completed it in full in just over two years. In his early life his speed of composition when he had a straight run at an opera was phenomenal: the *Dutchman* in a year and a half, *Tannhäuser* in less than three, *Lohengrin* in two and a half and this compares with twenty-two years for *Meistersinger* and for *Parsifal* twenty-five, both being subject to delays and distractions caused mainly by *The Ring*. Of the first three performed operas *Lohengrin* has by far the most elaborate and complex score and the speed at which Wagner wrote it is proof of his manic energy in tackling the huge operatic tasks he set himself. Gone were the days when Donizetti could boast that he could knock off an opera in a matter of weeks, but that, of course, is to compare the relative creative effort demanded by Milton's *Paradise Lost* and a Wordsworth sonnet.

The first performance of *Lohengrin* took place at Weimar in 1850. But Wagner was not amongst those present. Instead he was languishing in Switzerland, a political exile. Luckily he had Liszt as the musical director, an admirer and fan, who, when he studied the score in detail, found wonderful things there and this inspired him to write a eulogy on Wagner's work in general and on *Lohengrin* in particular.

Lohengrin is generally reported to have been 'well received' although there were, of course, some dissident voices which were to swell in the years to come into a mighty chorus. During the next five years and only within Germany *Lohengrin* was performed in provincial houses but Wagner did not see it until it was staged in Vienna in 1861. It was not performed in Italy until 1871 (twenty-three years after its premiere), and four years later it was given in London – in Italian! Its first performance in Bayreuth was in 1894.

In the opera houses of the world today *Lohengrin*, along with *Tannhäuser*, is the most frequently performed Wagner opera. This is not because audiences like these best but because they are the most manageable. Only major companies can easily tackle *The Ring*; *Meistersinger* is very long and heavy on sets; *Parsifal* and *Tristan* set artistic standards both for orchestra and singers that must be met if the show is to come off. But *Lohengrin*, although greatly enhanced by an orchestra of ninety and a chorus of a hundred and five star voices can be mounted with modest resources and still survive, which it does frequently all over the world. But most producers have now pretty well given up over the swan.

COMMENT

Lohengrin stands on the brink of fully fledged music drama. the *Dutchman* and *Tannhäuser* were early milestones on the road from Weber to *Parsifal*, but now Wagner passes into the promised land where poem and music are welded into a continuous whole. Despite what he said to Schumann there are only a few set piece numbers: the Bridal Chorus, Elsa's Dream, and Lohengrin's Narration. The great choruses have become part of the warp and woof.

The opera is slow to start. After a prelude (all three preludes *are* set pieces) we have some twenty minutes of good but conventional choruses, fanfares, musical flummery and the story told in somewhat humdrum Wagner recitatif. But once Elsa takes the stage the opera takes wing. Her music is Wagner at his lyrical best and has a quality of tenderness which is not found elsewhere in the operas, except perhaps for Eva's music in *Meistersinger*. At this point the story begins to grip and the music to cast its spell and from now on every scene is wonderfully well-judged, each one with a climax rising above the last. Although there are main and subsidiary mottos we are spared the profusion of abstruse and obliquely meaningful mottos that can make parts of *The Ring* into something of a motto-maze. Throughout, the orchestral writing is amazingly rich and inventive and the chorus is a major player and deployed throughout in a masterly fashion.

Indeed Lohengrin is Wagner's choral opera. There are memorable occasional choruses both in the *Dutchman* and *Tannhäuser* but here the chorus, except in Act II and in the Lohengrin/Elsa scene in Act III, is on stage for more than half of the full run of the opera – in all over two hours. Not only do they do the job of the Greek chorus – commenting on the action – and give voice to all the required jingoistic stuff – Hail! Hurrah! etc. – but they also contribute five major musical events, some of them sing-along with the principals. There are choruses which advance the course of the drama – the Arrival of the Swan and God Help Us (Act I), God Bless Elsa and Elsa in Doubt (Act II) and the Bridal Chorus (Act III). Here is choral writing the like of which, except perhaps in Verdi, we have never heard before, and will never hear again from Wagner. The nearest approach will be the set-piece choruses in *Meistersinger* (the church scene that opens the opera, the street riot in Act II and the final scene of the opera); *The Ring*, except for *Götterdamerung* is without chorus, in *Parsifal* they play a minor role and in *Tristan* there is none.

As always in Wagner the principals have clear musical personalities and their own individual keys: Lohengrin A major, Elsa A flat. Lohengrin himself has three musical personae – noble, tender and holy – and of these the first two, as in his championing of Elsa in Act I and the love duet in Act III, are preferable to the third (the Grail explained in Act III). Elsa has two personae – the innocent child (all of Act I) and the compassionate and then tortured grown-up woman (duet with Ortrud in Act II and then her struggle with doubts in Acts II and III). Friederich has only one musical persona although his mood changes from that of the suave and confident pretender in Act I to the broken hopeless man in Act II and again when he rises to launch his last desperate challenge for Lohengrin in Act III. Ortrud is dark and broody throughout, except when she puts on her pitiful act in Act II. For the rest the King is kingly, the Herald heraldic, Friederich's nobles ignoble and the pages fluting.

For all its virtues Lohengrin is not a loveable opera like *Meistersinger* nor does it purge us with pity and terror as does *The Ring*. Perhaps it is at times a little ponderous. But provided it is decently produced and sung and the dreaded Swan is handled with a modicum of discretion, it will always come off, usually triumphantly.

Tristan and Isolde   Erotic music-drama

The one with two lovers, a love potion and a love death.

CAST

Tristan, a Knight, and nephew of Mark, king of Cornwall	Tenor
Kurwenal, Tristan's ADC	Baritone
King Mark	Bass
Melot, a courtier of the Cornish court	Baritone
Isolde, an Irish princess	Soprano
Brangane, Isolde's lady-in-waiting	Soprano
A sailor, a helmsman, a shepherd	

3 acts: running time 3 hrs 30 mins

STORY

Act I On the deck of a ship at sea
Sc 1 In which Isolde expresses her wish that the boat should sink with all hands and thereby bring her life to an end and Brangane is worried lest her mistress be unwell

We are in the Dark Ages on a small boat en route from Ireland to Cornwall and there is this sailor up in the rigging singing modern music. Who's that and where are we? says Isolde waking from a nap. That's Nutty George singing says Brangane and we are in sight of Cornwall. Everything has gone to pot says Isolde my life is in ruins. I'd like a storm to sink this ship and all who sail in her. You feeling all right m'lady? asks Brangane. A paracetamol? Or is it a mental problem? Air! More air! shouts Isolde. Brangane pulls open the curtains and we see the whole of the deck and it is Scene 2.

Sc 2 In which Isolde sends Brangane to ask Tristan to come to see her and receives a dusty answer

See that Tristan skulking up there in the bow? asks Isolde as Nutty George sings his number again. Yes sure says Brangane he is very well spoken of. The stinker says Isolde he daren't face up to me just you wait and see. Ask him to come here. Brangane goes. Kind sir, she says to Tristan, my lady awaits you. We're nearly there says Tristan I'll take Isolde ashore when we arrive. I rather think she'd like to see you now says Brangane. I can't leave the wheel just now says he. Quit fooling around says she it's an order.

Get back interjects Kurwenal and tell Isolde that Tristan takes orders from no one. He goes on to sing a nasty song recalling Tristan's brave but unhygienic behaviour in chopping off Morold's head (Isolde's one-time fiancé) and wrapping it in a parcel and posting it to her. Ho ho sing all the sailors this is the way Tristan pays his respects to ladies. Ho ho.

Sc 3 In which Isolde tells Brangane the previous history of her relationship with Tristan and decides to end it all for both of them

Well what did he say? asks Isolde. He says he can't leave the wheel says Brangane. I heard it all says Isolde including that vicious send-up song. Let me tell you that once a guy called Tantrum sailed into Cork sick as a pig and yours truly nursed him back to life.

I saw his sword had a suspicious nick in it plus hairs like Morold's. I went to the fridge and got out Morold's head and sent the head and the sword to forensic. Sure enough they found a fragment of sword above Morold's left ear that fitted also the hairs were identical. Tantrum was an alias for Tristan, see? I could have killed him then. Missed my chance. I forgave him instead. And he said he loved me and then he went off bragging that he'd carry me off to be the bride of his Uncle Mark. I'm sick, sick, sick. I hate him. I wish he were dead and that I was too.

Steady on m'lady says Brangane you are going over the top really you are. Tristan behaved within the Cornish code of Courtly Conduct Section Two in fetching you out for his uncle. He's done nothing wrong. Honest. He's just out there breathing 23 feet away says Isolde *and he doesn't love me.*

Oho! Aha! Now I get it thinks Brangane. But m'lady she says no man could not love you. You are such a peach. But if he needs a bit of a shove how about that stuff your old Mum brewed up and left in the medicine chest which I happen to have by me quite handy? You mean the love potion? Not on your life says Isolde but the instant poison – yes good idea. Get it out. At this point the crew whose discipline is poor start singing and shouting because the ship is entering harbour.

Sc 4 In which Isolde tells Kurwenal she must see Tristan for a special purpose before disembarkation and instructs Brangane to get a death draught ready for them both to drink

Enter Kurwenal. Get your bags together ladies he says we're nearly there. Take a message please my man to your master says Isolde: say I require him to come and solemnly beg my pardon before we land. Very good Ma'am says Kurwenal I'll do it but it is quite likely he will tell you to get lost. Right Brangane farewell for ever get the drink ready says Isolde. Which drink? says Brangane. The poison of course stupid says Isolde. So who's going to drink this? asks Brangane. Tristan and I says Isolde. O God no! says Brangane. But yes says Isolde this is just the sort of occasion for which my mother gave me the travelling medicine chest. Enter Tristan.

Sc 5 In which Isolde recounts to Tristan past events, suggests that he says Sorry and they drink to letting bygones be bygones which they do with momentous results just as King Mark comes aboard the ship

So why didn't you come when you were told? asks Isolde. It's laid down in the Manual of Court Procedure says Tristan that a knight escorting a royal bride should never be alone with her within fumbling distance. It's also in the Manual that before you accept an enemy as a friend he does the pardon ritual including the toast-drinking says she. Enemy? says he who is the enemy? You are my enemy says she: you killed my man and you done me wrong. When I nursed you under that silly name Tantrum I swore I'd get you in the end.

Be my guest says he take my sword and do it now. That wouldn't be a nice thing to do to kill one of your king's best knights says she. Now let us do the pardon drink. (The sailors start shouting and carrying on as the ship docks.) Tristan goes broody. Come on Tristan says Isolde drink it. The pardon procedure will put you straight with King Mark with yourself and with me.

Hey there, two points starboard shouts Tristan to the sailors his mind on the job. OK. Right. Last time you did a good job as a physio to get me well let's hope this time this drink will help my problem [he means his love for Isolde which is a great aggravation and which he has to hide because it is his duty to escort her to marry his Uncle Mark – too bad: Ed.] so here goes. He drinks. Steady on says Isolde leave some for me. She drinks. They both go funny. They gaze into each other's eyes. They call out each other's names. It's love! [Chemically induced: Brangane switched the bottles: Ed.] Meanwhile it's all go on the ship. Brangane tries to get a pretty limp Isolde into her ermines. Sailors shout and bustle, King Mark arrives amidst an outbreak of royalist fervour. Huzza!

Act II In the garden of King Mark's Cornish castle
Sc 1 In which Isolde is anxious to give the signal for Tristan to join her and Brangane is unable to prevent her

I can't hear that hunting mob now can you? Isolde asks Brangane. Yes I can says Brangane they're still quite close and it would be crazy to switch that light off and give the signal now. You want to keep Tristan away from me don't you? says Isolde. You must be careful says Brangane everyone noticed something funny when Tristan handed you over on the boat.

And watch that Melot he's up to no good. Melot? says Isolde he's Tristan's best friend. Melot is a treacherous toad and Mark's informer and this hunting lark is no more than a trap to catch you two together says Brangane. Not true says Isolde Melot organized the hunt to give us a chance to have a good time together. Put out the light! No leave it alone says Brangane I should never have given you that love shot. You didn't know the power of Mrs Minne the goddess of love did you? says Isolde she's telling me now to give the signal. No for Chrissakes no! shouts Brangane. But it's no good. Isolde puts out the light [which is the signal of course: Ed.]

Sc 2 In which Tristan arrives and after a great deal of loverly talk we are meant to think they are lovers in the carnal sense although we don't actually see them do it

Tristan appears. Isolde he says. Tristan she replies. So we are off into unimagined rapture sublime bliss overwhelming joy and similar. Day is our enemy night is our friend says Tristan. Yes the day is really a drag says Isolde. Yes isn't it? says Tristan and the

night is tremendously friendly? Yes tremendously says Isolde.
Let's personify them and for a little while sing about them plotting
for and against us says Tristan. Good idea says Isolde let's. They
do.

For quite a long while they recap the past (remember the night
you put antiphlogistine on my wound instead of Friars' Balsam?)
But suddenly Tristan gets an unusual idea: wouldn't it be nice to
die together? But how do we know we'd be allowed to stick
together in the great unknown? asks Isolde. (Hey look out you two
it's nearly dawn, shouts Brangane.) Couldn't split us says Tristan
not enough power. OK let's do it then says Isolde what a terrific
idea. Tremendous says he. Terminal says she. Everlasting love
says he. Eternal bliss says she. Die in your arms says he. Never to
wake says she. Let's go on like this for about five minutes says he.
(They go on for six minutes thirty seconds.) But then –

Sc 3 In which Tristan and Isolde are discovered in a highly compromising situation by King Mark and his court

A scream from Brangane. A shout from Kurwenal. No good. The
hunters with King Mark at their head have arrived (without
making a sound): Tristan and Isolde exposed! There you are Your
Royal Highness says Melot what did I say? I've saved you from a
disgraceful marriage and should get an earldom or at least the
OBE. Saved me from what? says Mark. This is the most terrible
thing. Tristan is my best friend and he done me wrong. My belief
in human nature is seriously at risk. (It's all just a bad dream says
Tristan hopefully.) I have something to say to you Tristan says
Mark and he certainly has for he goes into a full appraisal of
Tristan's army record his career as a courtier his behaviour as a
friend (and all of this with poor Tristan lying amongst the gladioli
with his trousers down). You are a great disappointment Tristan
he says what made you do this to me? I can't answer that Uncle
says Tristan. I'd best be off to my old home in Brittany. Will you
follow me there Isolde? I will come says she.

Melot draws his sword. Traitorous rat he cries. Melot I thought
you were my true mate says Tristan but you sneaked on me to
Uncle Mark because you lusted after Isolde yourself. Take that!
But he drops his sword God knows why and Melot gets in with a
fairly good thrust and inflicts not a mortal but a stretcher-case

wound. Tristan flops back onto Kurwenal Isolde onto Tristan and King Mark gives Melot a sharp slap on the wrist. Curtain.

Act III Outside Tristan's castle in Brittany. A huge lime tree centre stage
Sc 1 In which we find Tristan at home and not at all well and anxiously awaiting the arrival of Isolde which eventually takes place

Tristan is asleep beneath the lime tree. A shepherd pipes as best he can whilst trying to keep control of his sheep. How's the patient, Kurwenal? he asks as he reaches the double bar. Poorly says Kurwenal I wish Isolde were here. I'll play my Mazurka in E flat as soon as I see her ship says the shepherd. Make it the one in G sharp minor says Kurwenal the fast one. OK says the shepherd. He plays on.

Tristan stirs. That sounds like my Dad's old bass clarinet says he. Where am I? Here says Kurwenal. Brittany. Kareol Castle. Your old home. Tristan surfaces. Kurwenal tells him what's happened since he flaked out in Cornwall. I can't remember a thing says Tristan except for Isolde. I keep thinking I see her but it's only a dream. I wish she was here. She'll be here today says Kurwenal. It struck me that she did a good job on you after you had tangled with Morold and she might do it again so I arranged for your UK solicitor to bring her over.

Isolde coming! Great! Terrific! Good man Kurwenal you done well you are this man's best friend get up that lighthouse, look out for the ship. . . ! There it is! [No it isn't he's just hallucinating: Ed.] No boss says Kurwenal no ship. So meanwhile I'll tell you of my extremely unhappy boyhood says Tristan (he does so) so you see he says I was brought up to yearn and I've yearned a lot since then and I am particularly good at yearning to die. (He now hallucinates again about Isolde, the wound, death and mixing a poison from lover's tears. He's really pretty well gone.) He passes out and Kurwenal thinks he has expired. But no. I see the ship! he cries. Isolde's on it!

Oh no not that again thinks Kurwenal but suddenly he hears the G sharp minor mazurka. It's a real ship. Told you so! shouts Tristan. She's coming in fast cries Kurwenal and she's flying the Cornish duster. Oops! she's gone behind some rocks. Not aground I trust? asks Tristan. No I don't think so says Kurwenal look there she is again I can see Isolde. They're landing. She's coming. I'll go and fetch her says Kurwenal.

Sc 2 In which Tristan tears the dressings off his wound and expires from loss of blood just as Isolde arrives

Oh what a beautiful morning sings Tristan Oh what a beautiful day I've got a beautiful feeling Isolde is coming my way. I feel great I'm going to take up my bed and walk. I won over Morold with a wound so I'll win over Isolde with a wound too [Not quite right in the head: Ed.]. He tears his wound open. Look at all the lovely blood he says streaming out all over. He gets up and staggers around. Tristan! cries Isolde offstage. Sounds like her says Tristan. Isolde rushes on stage: Tristan! she says. Isolde! he replies (expires). Wake up Tristan says Isolde I've come to die with you. Let's look at your wound. My God – no breathing – no pulse – you're dead! It really is too bad of you Tristan to die on me like this. She passes out.

Sc 3 In which Melot and Kurwenal are killed, King Mark says he now knows the whole story and Isolde joins Tristan in death

A second ship is sighted. Kurwenal and the shepherd plus local unemployed agricultural workers barricade the gates against King Mark and his men. No good. You are heavily outnumbered says a spokesman give yourselves up now and you will be well treated. Not bloody likely says Kurwenal brandishing his sword. Get back cries Melot (for it is he). Kurwenal kills him. You madman says King Mark. Hold back. But no there is a general mêlée. Kurwenal is wounded and lies down to die next to Tristan. My God! Everyone's dead round here says King Mark: Tristan Kurwenal Melot Iso . . . Isolde's come to! cries Brangane. Thank God there's someone still breathing says King Mark. Isolde I have to tell you I now know the whole story. I came to arrange for you and Tristan to be happily married but now everyone's dead and it's quite spoiled my plan. You all right Isolde? asks Brangane. Isolde clearly in a trance gazes at Tristan. Look at him she says he's coming alive again! He's opening his eyes! He's breathing! He's incandescent! He's levitating! Listen – do you hear that heavenly choir? They are singing for him! And that wonderful smell of sal volatile! There are clouds of it all around me . . . all around me . . . I think I'm going ... going ... going ... (She goes. Sinks onto Tristan's body. Dead.)

Tristan Mottos

Number	Name	Description
1	Tristan	A leap and a slow descent to the 'Tristan chord'
2	Isolde	Four notes going up and leaving you hanging in the air
3	Stab	A variant of Isolde, a stab of emotion: a long note followed by a short note over a notable chord
4	Gaze	A five-note motto (Tum-ta-ti-TA-ta) with a sizeable drop in the closing TA-ta
5	Sea	A downward waver followed by a triplet run up
6	Death	Long loud first note dropping a long way (an octave) to a muttered ending
7	Wound	A downward sliding phrase – semitones
8	Doom	Two strident opening notes and a third that fades away
9	Tragic	First a brassy fanfare, later strong and simple, a musical clove hitch
10	Day	A boom then a drop followed by an upward jerky phrase
11	Frustration	A snaky upward scale with semitones
12	Ecstasy	Sweet high smooth phrases – really nice
13	Minne	A slow downward sweep, twice, the same pattern
14	Night	Slow, dreamy, long first note, down and a tum-tum-ti-ta
15	Love at Peace	Sweet lyrical melody, longer than a motto, unmistakable
16	Love in Death	Hymn tune, notes of equal values, deliberate
17	Mark Disappointed	Very deep in the bass clarinet: long opener slipping down in semitones
18	Angst	A hitch upwards, down again to the starting note and a two-note tack

LOOK OUT FOR
Act I Prelude

0

The Prelude** opens with two mottos that are   0
Siamese twins. In a hushed voice and in four
bars this twin motto sets the mood of the love
story we are going to hear. Its first phrase
descends (from an initial leap) to a chord that
grabs you by the throat (the 'Tristan chord') and
the second rather plaintive phrase goes up and
leaves you hanging in the air. We can call the
first Tristan (his love for Isolde) [1] and the
second Isolde (her love for him) [2]. They are
followed at once by a variant of the end of the
Isolde motto, the Stab (of emotion), centring on
a long note resolving on to a shorter note and
here ending over a notable chord [3]. We shall
hear a lot of these three, the first two are so
much part of the work as to be mentioned only
when they stand out, but the Stab is hardly
mentioned at all because it is used as a sort of
emotional punctuation mark. (It comes into its
own at the very end of the opera.)

These mottos don't hold the stage long for
next on the scene is a five-note motto (Tum-ta-
ti-TA-ta, with a sizeable drop on the closing
TA-ta, the Gaze [4]). This, as we are to hear
later on, catches the moment when Tristan and
Isolde first looked into each other's eyes and
knew it was true love between them. The Gaze
is worked over intensively by the orchestra,
mainly the strings, for nearly ten minutes and it
is amazing that this modest little thing can offer
enough stuffing to carry this rather wonderful
piece almost to its close. After the climax we
close with Tristan [1] – Isolde [2].

Act I Sc 1

A young sailor sings a song about the girl he left
behind him – unaccompanied and unmemorable
but for a phrase (a downwards waver followed
by a triplet run up), the Sea [5].

11: *Wer wagt mich zu höhnen?*

Isolde wakes up* (a reminder of [4], she was dreaming of that magic moment). She is pretty cross owing to frustrated love and hopes the ship will run on the rocks and everyone will drown. Brangane tries to soothe her. This passage runs out in a sort of ongoing arioso at an easy speed somewhere between the pace of the 2,000 and the 10,000 metres, occasionally breaking into a sprint. There will be a lot of this in *Tristan* carrying the calmer part of the plot with the orchestra doing most of the work and having all the tunes. Lots of Sea [5] churning about. 11

Act I Sc 2

Brangane throws open the curtains and we see nautical life on the deck beyond. The young sailor repeats his number, this time with some rubbing strings beneath, and Isolde, still in a black mood, sees Tristan at the helm. She wishes him dead. Here we have the motto of Death for the first time, sung by Isolde (long loud first note dropping a long way – an octave – to a muttered ending [6]). Isolde asks Brangane what she thinks of Tristan (Brangane thinks he is lovely) and sends her to fetch him.* There are nice exchanges. But Isolde gives away her true feelings when we hear Isolde [2] – love for Tristan – in the middle of some loud anti-Tristan stuff. 17

17: *Was hältst du von dem Knechte?*

Brangane's errand. Some swirling horns (Sea [5]) tell us of the manliness of the crew as they fiddle with lanyards, mainstays, etc. Brangane's first exchanges with Tristan are in a polite quasi-recitatif and his replies are full and melodious* but as she gets stroppy the tempo changes and we move into a brisk set-piece ballad from Kurwenal.* As so often in a Wagner set piece, the voice takes a clear lead over the orchestra which drops back to become no more than an accompaniment for a while. The nasty mocking tone of this piece carries through to the short chorus that closes the scene. At the end of 21 24

21: *Grämt sie die lange Fahrt*
24: *Das sage sie*

Kurwenal's song and in the sailors' chorus we hear the Fighting Knight motto, Tristan the feisty warrior, a military flourish, up down up (Knight [unlisted], and if you happen to know Tchaikovsky's *1812 Overture*, you will be greatly helped by recalling the brassy tune in that).

Act I Sc 3

Isolde tells her story:

She is miffed by Tristan's snub. So she will tell all to Brangane and starts by recounting
27: *Wie lachend sie* Tristan's first Irish trip* including the disgust- 27
ing stuff about Morold's head being sent through the post and the good job that forensic did in fitting the splinter to the hole in Tristan's sword. She was going to kill him but their eyes met and the Gaze took place. Wagner's free-style writing at its best with a lot of Tristan [1] and Isolde [2] around and in various forms. Tristan was wounded (Wound motto, a sliding downward phrase, semitones [7]). She gazed at him and, of course, Gaze [4] comes in strong on cue.

She healed the wound and he swore to be her true love, now he has the brass neck to come to fetch her to marry his uncle for political
31: *Sein Lob* reasons.* This section goes marching on, Is- 31
hörtest du eben olde's fury is rising all the time with the earlier mottos, especially derivatives of Wound [7], and Knight (unlisted) also in evidence.

So now she really thinks very little of Tristan
34: *O blinde* and we have a cataract of abuse** in descending 34
Augen! octaves leading to a great musical and dramatic climax – Traitor – Revenge – Death – Death for us both. (More free singing but Death [6] still prevalent.) Here Wagner really piles it on and holds us spellbound as the distressed lady pretty well bombs out before our very ears.

It is a wonderful fifteen minutes, but tough going for the Isolde – as taxing a bout of soprano singing as you will find anywhere.

39: *Was meinst du Arge?*

Brangane tries to calm Isolde** and is doing a good job until she says How about your old mum's aphrodisiac? (a variant of Gaze [4] followed by Isolde [2]). What about the other bottle, the poison? says Isolde. (Death [6] and a new motto deepish in the bass, too noble to be called a squirm, two strident opening notes and a third that fades away, Doom [8].) These are dreamy exchanges as if the two ladies were already into some magic trance, out of which they are rudely brought to earth by the O-Ho-Hoing of the crew. They have sighted land.   39

Act I Sc 4

44: *Auf! Auf! Ihr Frauen!*

Kurwenal brings in a breath of sea air with some cheery stuff about going ashore.* A change of tempo, a break in the intensity, the orchestra cheerful too (an upbeat version of Sea [5]), only a little galumphing.   44

47: *Nun leb wohl, Brangane!*

The potions – which one? Highly charged exchange between Isolde and Brangane:* sometimes excitable with strings rushing all over the place, but later sotto voce and doomy. Quite a gripper. Lots of Death [6] and Doom [8] and Isolde [2].   47

Act I Sc 5

51

The first Tristan/Isolde duet:

1. Tristan presents himself with a new motto, Tristan Tragic [9] – a tremendously important four-note brassy fanfare here but after this much diminished to something strong but simple, like a musical clove hitch. Opening exchanges never descend to ornery but no star.   51

55: *Nicht da war's*

2. Isolde's indictment.** In two long solo pieces she tells Tristan about Morold, Tantrum's wounds, oaths, etc. and makes him feel pretty awful. He offers her his sword to let her kill him. Here one marvels at Wagner's resourcefulness: the music unwinds sticking close to the sense of the text all the time but spinning along with fresh delights and surprises at every turn. Few mottos – Wound [7], Tragic [9] and Doom [8].   55

59: *Wie sorgt' ich schlecht*

3. Isolde says it would be bad form to slay one of her future husband's best knights* (also his nephew). Let's make friends and have a drink on it – Gaze [4]. (From now on the duet is subject to interruption from the manic crew who seem to be unable to go about their business without yelling Ho! He! Mizzen! Bowsprit! etc.) She then goes skittish and does a send-up of the coming meeting with Uncle Mark,* not without a little Doom [8], but mainly jolly with a tripping, mocking accompaniment. Tristan is momentarily distracted by navigational matters but returns to the duet with a not-too-impressive oath of atonement – he drinks, she drinks, and as the liquor is doing its work the orchestra builds up expectations as to the effect. Is it a poison? An aperient? An aphrodisiac? A hurricane of strings susurrating up and down and all over is followed by breathless tension in the woodwind, [1] and [2].

59

64: *Du hörst den Ruf?*

64

An aphrodisiac! POW! And does it work fast! Tristan! she cries. Isolde! he moans, and they gaze [4] into each other's eyes, then embrace, and the orchestra billows up to embrace them too.**

70: *Tristan!*

70

72: *Wehe! Weh!*

Now several rather important things happen at once.*** The lovers go into a feverish love trauma, King Mark arrives, Brangane tries to get Isolde into her ermines, the manic crew go mad with excitement (Sea [5]), Kurwenal tries to get Tristan to attend to his duties, Brangane admits she swapped the bottles, Isolde faints. Musically this builds into a bustlingly effective finale, with the sailors doing their nut and the orchestra making huge *Meistersinger*-like noises and the dopey lovers still crying out feebly to each other, unable to relate to real life. Very satisfactory.

72

Act II Prelude

The prelude is a beauty** and with no effort at all gives birth to three entirely new mottos, first the opening motto Day [10], which keeps breaking in on the lovers' dream world, a boom then a drop followed by an upward jerky phrase – immediately followed by Frustration [11], a snaky upward scale, semitones and here followed by a hiccup and, again overlapping with Frustration, something really nice – Ecstasy [12], sweet high smooth phrases (here on the flute) swimming around in a state of great pleasure. The prelude is a midsummer night's dream and a winner.

Act II Sc 1

So to the unmistakable sounds of an operatic hunt (horns in their hunting mode)* and although they are mainly open notes, it must be hard to play them out there stumbling about in the brushwood in the dark. And what, for Chrissake, are they hunting *for*? Foxes, out of season and at midnight? Meanwhile, Brangane and Isolde have a great duet:

5: *Der deiner harrt*   1. Brangane tells Isolde Melot's a wrong 'un.* Watch him. This is free-flowing with references to Ecstasy [12] and distant cousins of [1] and [2] are never far away. The whole of this section holds the ear pretty well enthralled.

2. Isolde tells Brangane that the aphrodisiac was only a little help to her love for Tristan, which was always there. Late in her call to the

10: *Dein Werk? O tör'ge Magd!*   Love Goddess,** delightfully named Mrs Minne, we have a persistent new motto – a slow downward sweep, two legs the same pattern, one after the other, the second lower (Minne [13]). Now she works up to the great climax of giving Tristan the signal. This is swashbuckling loverly stuff, emphatic, committed and tuneful, with some of Ecstasy [12] and Minne [13].

Act II Sc 2

15: *Isolde! Geliebte!*   The first love duet*** – twenty minutes of Wagner at the top of his bent. As the lovers see each other we have a case of extreme orchestral excitement. The word climax has been used from time to time on these pages for quite minor storms. This one is a hurricane. The lovers ride into it with an exchange of rapturous one-liners

(Bliss! Mine for ever! Sublime joy! etc., etc.) and then launch into loverly outpourings in which the music and the emotion take a strong lead over the text. Such content as there is covers:

1. Night is our friend, day our enemy (O bliss!)

2. A recap of past events. Do you remember? (O joy!)

3. Hooray for the aphrodisiac (my beloved)

4. More night-versus-day stuff (my treasure)

The music in the early part of the scene gusts along in a mood of high passion (Ecstasy [12], Minne [13]) but when we move into the night and day, the storm blows itself out and from here on the exchanges, although still rapturous and high voltage, become more orderly. From time to time the lovers sing together, a rare event in Wagner and a signal of something special. The Day motto [10] is worked pretty heavily here and later a new motto, Night (slow, dreamy, a long first, down and a tum–tum–ti–ta [14]). The duet ends with a coda, a sort of grace before meat, or rather in this case, before love (introduced by a variant of Stab [3]). After the tearing passion of the love-in this quiet hymn-like piece comes in with good effect. This duet, together with part two that follows, is the centrepiece of the opera, it is wonderfully vivid, powerful and will sweep all but the Wagner-proof off their feet. A stunner.

29

Brangäne's warning.** Useless of course. A lovely slow-moving piece with words and phrases stretched out over a ravishing orchestral accompaniment.

35: *Einsam wachend*

So to part two of the duet,*** which starts in a very different manner, indeed one would say in a relaxed post-coital mood but for the fact that the poor things being continuously on stage have had no coital opportunity as yet (and never get one). But the climax in the first duet was pretty well as good as an orgasm. The lovers lie calmly developing the rather sick idea of dying

38: *Lausch, Geliebter!*

29

35

38

together to music about as far away from the smell of death as can be imagined. (A sweet lyrical melody much longer than most mottos and unmistakable, Love at Peace [15].) As they begin to get keen on the idea, another motto, destined to become the theme that opens the Liebestod, is sung by Tristan (starts rather like a hymn tune, notes of equal length, deliberate and strong, Love in Death [16]).

Brangane gives another warning (no good). Now things work up into a second mighty climax, not the great flurry that opened the first part of the duet, but a slow build-up, a lesser climax followed by a greater climax (Ecstasy [12], Love in Death [16] the chief themes) until the great joy in the idea of death together reaches a point of no return. Here we have a foretaste of the climax of the Liebestod.

This second half of the duet is every bit as good as the first. Although the emotions range only from A to B (Death to Love), their intensity is considerable and the music is quite beautiful.

Act II Sc 3

51

Suddenly the lovers are exposed. Not in fla- 51 grante delicto, for there has been no delictus, but things look pretty bad to King Mark. There is no saying what any one of us would do if we were a king who on returning from a night's hunting discovered his best knight having it off in the gladioli bed with his bride-to-be. A muffled oath perhaps or a quick swipe with a sword. But no: King Mark tells us at great length how very disappointed he is to find Tristan with his trousers down and what bad luck it is for a king to have so treacherous a best friend. He does a lot of this to a new motto (long opener slipping down in semitones – played very deep on a solo bass clarinet – Mark Disappointed [17]). The temperature drops. This is a little boring.

Nothing to say Your Honour, Tristan replies

(Tristan [1], Isolde [2], Love at Peace [15]). Then he asks Isolde if she will follow him to his home country.* This trance-like appeal works around with the original Tristan [1] and Isolde [2] to good effect. Isolde says yes she will (Isolde [2] and Love at Peace [15]). The world of the King and court are suspended motionless while these tender exchanges take place. But not for long. Tristan tells Melot what he thinks of him. Tristan attacks Melot. Melot wounds Tristan with noisy support from the orchestra ending with the Mark motto [17] punched out by the brass section. Musically this is a scrappy act end and indeed during the concluding twenty minutes the spell falters and we begin to consider the matter of a large scotch in the interval.

66: *Wohin nun Tristan scheidet*   66

Act III Prelude

The prelude** opens gloomily, as indeed it should, for things are looking pretty bad. We hear a variant of the Isolde motto [2] (over minor-key harmony) and this is ridden hard by the strings in a desperate fashion until we hear the shepherd's pipe. This shepherd is no country-and-western fan and his piece sounds something like a pibroch arranged for the cor anglais by Debussy. Followed by some desultory dialogue between Kurwenal and the shepherd. Tristan surfaces. By careful questioning of Kurwenal* he finds out who he is, where he is, etc. There is general rejoicing in the orchestra and Kurwenal too, greatly cheered by signs of life in his master, gives his answers accompanied by a cheerful little polonaise (Tum-ti-tum-tum like any polonaise), followed by bustle and fuss.

Sc 1

11: *Wo bin ich?*   11

Tristan delirious.* Tristan's sick-bed thoughts start grottily (Isolde [2]) but once he gets into his stride with the night-versus-day bit (again), the wild raving nature of the music carries us along with it (Night [14], Day [10]). He then works himself up into a mucksweat,

17: *Dunkt dich das?*   17

cries out for Isolde and sinks back exhausted. Kurwenal says she is coming. He has sent for her.

26: *Mein Kurwenal*

So Tristan launches into Round 2.* He tells   26 Kurwenal what a good chap he is and then spins into another whirl of anxiety. Where's that ship? Is it coming? There it is! I see it coming! (Mad of course: it isn't there at all.) Here we have a motto first heard at the start of the act – Angst; a hitch upwards, down to the starting note and a two-note tail [18]. This is repeated obsessively, faster and faster. The shepherd signals no boat gloomily on his cor anglais, this time more like a dispirited yodel. The yodel reminds Tristan of his father's death, the cor anglais melts into the orchestral texture and we move into Round 3

30: *Muss ich dich so verstehn*

with sad thoughts about childhood.* But he   30 soon gets back to yearning, yearning for death, yearning for Isolde, yearning for her healing touch (Wound [7]). He yearns on in similar vein with climaxes, calm patches, sometimes up but mainly down with remarkable stamina for a man so badly wounded. At last he sinks back unconscious (Tristan [1], developed and transformed).

Kurwenal thinks Tristan is dead. But he isn't. Up and out of his blackout and into Round 4.

41: *Das Schiff? Siehst du's noch nicht*

Here we have an oasis of calm.** Tristan   41 fantasizes; he thinks he can sense the ship coming towards him (and this time he's damn right: if Kurwenal was up that watch tower he'd see it too). He has a touching awakening (Isolde [2]) and then we hear again the sweet motto of the goddess of love Minne [13]. But what's that? The shepherd is piping like crazy and the message clearly is Ship Ahoy! Now it's all go, Kurwenal goes up the watch tower and gives a running commentary as she comes in safely. She's here! He runs off to fetch Isolde. Music apt to the scene and on the ball all the way.

Act III Sc 2

50: *O diese Sonne!*

Tristan bombs out.** In a fever of excitement   50

he goes over the edge and tears open his wound (a disgusting thing to do). Clearly he's a goner. Isolde rushes in as he flakes out. She calls out 'Tristan' (Ecstasy [12]) and once again 'Tristan' and almost with his last breath he whispers 'Isolde' (Isolde [2], Stab [3] and Gaze [4]). This is a special moment: all the world stops and in the sudden hush the music speaks to us person to person very quietly.

52: *Ha! Ich bin's, ich bin's*

Tristan is dead. Isolde discovers this with exclamations of shock as she examines his body and then with bewildered reproaches.* How 52 could he let her down like this? She has not yet taken aboard the fact of death. Grief (or perhaps joy?) is still to strike. The music tells us her emotions are still in suspense. Isolde moves from quasi-recitatif to broken phrases and then into a run of unanswered questions with the orchestra sounding uncertain and indecisive beneath (Angst [12], Love in Death [16]).

Act III Sc 3

Now the rough and tumble of the second lot arriving. Kurwenal kills Melot and is then killed himself. All supported by high-class theatre music or, as they used to say in the film studios, hurry music. King Mark steadies things up by addressing the dead Tristan and then Isolde,

63: *Warum, Isolde, warum mir das?*

explaining his good intentions.* This dignified 63 short aria is moving in its solemn way. It also prepares the ground for Isolde's big piece.

65: *Mild und leise*

The Liebestod,*** death for love or love in 65 death. Isolde's finest hour and one of Wagner's greatest inspirations. The Love in Death motto [16] steals in quietly in the orchestra and Isolde, almost certainly, as one would think, in a trance, sees all manner of things happening to the dead Tristan – smiles, opens his eyes, gives off sparks. She hears a sweet melody, surely the one she is singing. So far the Liebestod has had only one theme, using only the wonderful Love in Death phrase [16], all the time building it higher, broader and stronger as Isolde's voice

climbs with it and (now together with a variant
of Stab [3]) then soars out on the topmost peak
of this great climax. Great waves of sound surge
out and break over the Stab [3] as Isolde sees
celestial waves in her trance. The music fades
into a peaceful coda as she expires (Isolde [2]).
Nothing like it in all music.

NOTES

Tristan and Isolde	Wagner's seventh opera (but see below)
First night	Königliches Hof- und Nationaltheater, Munich, 10 June 1865
Reception	Intense hostility by one faction, stunned admiration by the other
Libretto	Wagner
Source	Celtic legend, mainly as recounted by a twelfth-century German writer, Gottfried von Strassburg

NEWS AND GOSSIP

During the early 1850s when he was still struggling with *Siegfried*,
Wagner fell in love with Mathilde Wesendonck. She was the wife
of one of his patrons and the affair seems to have been purely
romantic, maybe because Wagner was wary of losing a really
useful sponsor through adultery. Because of this affair he stopped
work on *The Ring* and began to toy with the idea of an opera based
on the legend of Tristan and Isolde. He set five of Mathilde's
poems (she was quite a good poet) to music. That was to become
the essence of *Tristan* and it is clear that he began to identify his
feelings for her with Tristan's feelings for Isolde (but there is no
record of their planning a love death together). In 1857 he dived
into a bout of intensive composition. By the end of the year he had
finished Act I. Then there was a domestic row (over Mathilde?)
and he wrote Act II in Venice in 1858 and Act III in Lucerne,
completing the whole opera by August 1859. Two years for an
opera that had no model, no antecedents, was very complex, very
long and initiated what was pretty well an entirely new system of
harmony. Not bad.

The run-up to performance was not so quick nor was it trouble-
free. It took six years before his sponsor King Ludwig of Bavaria

could get *Tristan* put on in Munich. Even then it was postponed. On the day fixed for the premiere the bailiffs walked into the Wagner residence and took the furniture (he was always in debt), also the Isolde lost her voice. No wonder. Even today when it has been proved that Isolde is a singable role, if only by a handful of very strong women, it is still a terrifying prospect. To face up to it before anyone knew whether it was singable at all must have been enough to frighten the voice out of anyone.

The premiere caused a lively row. Those in favour were affected pretty well as Bernard Levin is today. Wagner was a crusader as well as a man who wrote operas. He stood for enlightenment – political, philosophical, aesthetic and musical. Of those against, some were anti-Ludwig, a king who squandered taxpayers' money on the arts, and modern art too which nobody wanted and nobody understood. Some found they couldn't stand up to the blitzkrieg that *Tristan* unleashes on the emotions. Some were anti-modernists, some pro-Jewish and some just thought his music a load of old (or rather new) rubbish. The argument filled the arts pages of the Sunday supplements for years to come and was good for a silly-season feature right up to the turn of the century.

But as the years rolled on, and excluding the monster *Ring*, *Tristan* came to hold second place to *Meistersinger* amongst the serious Wagner public. They began to rumble the overblown pretensions of *Lohengrin* and *Tannhäuser*, and the *Dutchman* was not real Wagner and *Parsifal* was too long and too holy. It also came to be No. 1 in the quality stakes – fully integrated musico-poetic synthesis and stuff like that. Today opera managements draw a deep breath before pencilling *Tristan* in on the schedule and this is for two reasons: it is almost impossible to cast and it takes an age to rehearse it properly. But it sits in the CD catalogue with several splendid versions and if the Liebestod were picked as the theme for the next Olympic games, it would, like 'Nessun dorma', undoubtedly get into the Top Ten. But preferably not sung by three sopranos.

COMMENT

Tristan was something of a musical time bomb. At first the musical world was stunned. Here was a way of writing music that was entirely new. The classical key structure and harmonic system had been chucked. Here there was a sort of stock pot full of motto-like fragments which were pulled out from time to time and slid about all over the place in a sea of chromaticism. A fellow could scarcely tell what key he was in, never mind get a grip on the shape. There were no arias, no recitatifs, only one set piece. Etc. It wasn't until the next century that the time bomb exploded. A little preliminary burst from Debussy and his fellows, but the big bang came with Schoenberg and the Second Viennese school who picked up the baton from *Tristan* and abandoned the whole diatonic system as well. A lot of people (misguided of course) will wish that Wagner had stuck to the style of *The Flying Dutchman*. In many ways *Tristan* is a bit of a wonder. For one thing it is all of a piece. In the much earlier trio *Tannhäuser*, *Lohengrin* and the *Dutchman*, Wagner was trying to shake off old operatic forms and force his way into his own very private world of Music Drama. In all three there are bits of old and bits of new. During the twenty years it took for Wagner to compose *The Ring* his style was growing up through adolescence to maturity. This means that *The Ring* is patchy, with items fit for the old grand opera in parts of *Götterdämmerung* (written first) and with *Rhinegold* (written last) the nearest to his new ideal of Music Drama. *Meistersinger*, thought his best by many, is all on its own. *Tristan* comes in the middle of all this and he struck a style that was quite distinct and had a perfect unity. It's a style that many find hard to take, especially when ladled out in such huge doses. But the sheer beauty of the music holds most people under its spell and the use of mottos is not nearly so distracting as in *The Ring*. Here the mottos are about ideas rather than things. There are no mottos about such things as anvils, dragons, fire. Indeed it is often hard to know what the mottos are about, if they are about anything definite at all. There is one that has been variously labelled by the Wagner scribes as 'Tristan's Honour', 'Morold' and 'Isolde's Anger'. A pretty wide choice. But the mottos work their way into the texture in a highly satisfactory manner. There is no need to be a motto spotter to enjoy *Tristan*. The mottos can become subliminal.

Tristan also scores on the matter of plot. It is simple, it moves at a steady pace. The central characters are all strongly drawn. Along with *Meistersinger*, it has the most convincing cast with not one dud, if one excludes the unimportant Melot. King Mark is a wimp, it is true, but he is an honourable if long-winded wimp. His headmasterly speech to Tristan when caught with his trousers down is the only real longueur in the piece. Otherwise it drives along with hardly a pause. Kurwenal's quasi-comic song in Act I is a welcome break and does its work well.

The high spots in *Tristan* are high indeed but they rise from an already high plateau and not from sea level. Thus they don't stand out as much as do the three-star items in the other operas. But the preludes to Acts I and II are both wonderfully compact, closely-knit orchestral pieces. The Tristan/Isolde duet in Act I is a bit of a marvel in its variation of pace and mood and the finale to Act I gives it a resounding finish. Act II holds the great love duet between Tristan and Isolde. It is the central item of the opera and in it Wagner reaches maximum thrust. Some would say it is the greatest love duet ever written. There is less high-voltage music in Act III, but we are of course moving steadily towards the great climacteric – the Liebestod. Even if you can't stand the sentiment, you have to admit that this number has a great tune. As a finale it lacks the earth-shaking size of the last ten minutes of *Götterdämmerung* but although smaller in scale, it has the same manic intensity of feeling and we leave the opera house suitably stunned.

And yet there are reasons why *Tristan* can't be counted amongst the select group of alpha-plus operas, and they are three. The first is that the world of knights, ladies, honour and romantic love à la Alfred Lord Tennyson doesn't grab us as it did our great-grandfathers. Their eyes would grow misty as they read aloud the tale of Lancelot and Guinevere. Today we find Norman Mailer a more convincing read. Jung, Freud and Germaine Greer have done terrible damage to the great lovers of history as recorded in saga and story book. *Tristan* is therefore only wholly acceptable to those persons who like their operas clothed in white samite, mystic, wonderful.

The second is about the vibes we find in the music. Whilst *Tristan* will bowl over most first-time listeners pretty soon, as they lie emotionally prone listening to the second, third and fourth hour of this music of power and beauty, there begins to lurk at the back of the mind – aside from more normal reactions such as The mixture is too rich, I can't stand it, I'm suffocating, bring me a brandy and ten minutes of Scarlatti quick, or What time is tea? – apart from these, the question that grows is one that challenges the foundations of belief in Wagner and it is this: isn't this all just a little Hollywood? Hollywood in the sky, of course, but still with the phoney sentimentality of Hollywood at its core.

The last bugaboo about *Tristan* relates to Wagner's close interest in sex and death. The two treated separately are of course the stuff of all drama, but it does seem that Wagner himself got a sexual kick out of putting them together and creating a musical orgasm out of a love-death. This is moving towards the territory of the snuff movie and whereas in *Tristan* there are only three deaths compared to *The Ring*'s fifteen, and two of them are military, there is a sort of sublime gloating over the central death that is disagreeable. It is no good the Wagner lobby making the case for Wagner as a genius who had the guts to attack our primitive instincts through dwarfs, incest and magic sex instead of making operas about polite society. It is not that at all: the death-love in Wagner is decadent, not primitive. This is the Wagner that liked to spend time stroking velvet, the Wagner that invented Venusberg and Kundry and amongst the clouds of scented emotion Isolde describes in the Liebestod we pick up a whiff of perfumed obscenity. So, at the end of the day, alpha, no plus.

Meistersinger
(Die Meistersinger von Nürnberg)

Human comedy

The one with a disagreeable town clerk, a noble cobbler, a street brawl and a prize song.

CAST

Veit Pogner, goldsmith and Mastersinger	Bass
Eva, his daughter	Soprano
Magdalene, her maid	Mezzo
Hans Sachs, cobbler and Mastersinger	Bass
David, his apprentice	Tenor
Sixtus Beckmesser, Town Clerk and Mastersinger	Bass
Walter von Stolzing, a knight	Tenor

Mastersingers (nine), a night watchman
Citizens of Nuremberg

3 acts: running time 4 hrs 30 mins

STORY

Act I Sc 1 Inside the church of St Katherine's Nuremberg
In which our hero declares his love for a lady but fails to sing his way into the club of Mastersingers whose members will be allowed to compete for the lady's hand

We are in Nuremberg mediaeval city of song and there is a church service in progress. Handsome knight Walter sidles up to pretty young woman Eva and says excuse me but are you spoken for? Eva recognizes Walter as overnight houseguest. Well no not exactly says her maid Magdalene not actually engaged but father Pogner has booked her as the prize for an upcoming song contest. Whoever wins gets her as wife. I see I see, says Walter to Eva. Let me escort you home. No stay here says Magdalene, here's Mastersingers apprentice David (sure enough David is fussing about resetting the back of the church as venue for the monthly meeting of the Mastersingers club) he'll teach you the tricks of the Mastersinging trade: you stay and get your Master's certificate and then you can compete for her. Eva I love you, says Walter [suddenly]: see you tonight. OK says Eva. Exits.

Act I Sc 2 A makeshift arena

So you think you can get your certificate at first try? says David. Ho ho. How much do you know about the Meister method? Zero says Walter. OK listen to this says David. He launches into a farrago of rules regulations admonitions prohibitions. Meanwhile the apprentices set up the singers' dais all wrong. David sorts them out: they take the micky out of him.

Pogner and Beckmesser enter. You are odds-on favourite to win my girl Eva says Pogner to Beckmesser: such a good singer you are. But if I win and she won't have me will you push it? asks Beckmesser. No I will not push it says Pogner. Excuse me says Walter would the Masters accept me as a late entry? I must propose you for the Masters' club first old friend says Pogner. The Masters assemble: roll call: Pogner makes the opening address. In my travels he says I found Nuremberg's image very poor. We are generally perceived as stuffy starchy stingy also philistine so I dreamed up this song contest to improve the image of this great city of ours and I offer my daughter as wife to the winner. Nice one Pog! shout the Masters. Viva Veit! cry the apprentices. But just one thing says Pogner if she doesn't like the winner she has power of refusal.

Why not allow the people to exercise their democratic right and judge the contest? asks Social Democrat Sachs. Subversive left-wing talk say the Masters. Order! back to the agenda says Pogner: we have this late entry my friend Sir Stolzing. I propose him as candidate for the Masters' Guild. Excellent C.V., noble parents, property owner, Name at Lloyds, member of the Athenaeum, banks at Coutts. Vocal education? asks the baker Kothner. I studied these classic LPs of Caruso Gigli Chaliapin says Walter (All dead says Beckmesser). But what actual educational establishment? asks Kothner. School of Nature says Walter (He learned from the birds says Beckmesser). Are you prepared to submit a trial song? asks Kothner. Yes, says Walter (poetically and at some length). Right! Into your marker's box Beckmesser, says Kothner and remember Sir Stolzing, seven faults and you're out. Take a look at the conditions of contest (apprentices show a video to Walter whilst Kothner sings the soundtrack).

Cue! shouts Beckmesser. Walter takes off into a romantic rhapsody. Beckmesser jumps out. Seven faults already he cries gleefully: do you want any more of this rubbish? It's funny sort of stuff say the Masters. Is this what they call minimalist? asks one. More atonal I would think says another. Perhaps it's tone rows says a third. Can't stand this modern stuff says a fourth. I liked it says Sachs: the marker is clearly biased, jealous and emotionally upset. His intervention is unfair. I say – go on Sir Stolzing and to hell with the marker. Walter sings. Sachs and Beckmesser slag each other off: the Masters argue. Pogner tries to cool it: the apprentices dance: chaos. Beckmesser yells let's take a vote. Big majority against Walter's admission. Curtain.

Act II A street in Nuremberg. Evening
In which an elopement is frustrated and a serenade leads to an altercation which becomes a riot

The apprentices shut up the shops for the night. Lena comes on asks David how did Sir do at the trial? Flunked it says David. Lena is quite thrown by this news and flounces out. Getting on OK with your bint eh David? shout the apprentices. David goes after them: he gets physical. Enter Sachs: stop that mauling you impudent dog he cries and set me up for the night shift. Pogner plus daughter Eva come on. Excited about tomorrow? he asks. Yes but must the winner be a Master? she says. Sure says he but remember you have power of veto. He retires indoors. Lena comes on. Any news? asks Eva. David says he was ploughed says Lena. O my God I must get the full story from Sachs later says Eva. Both exit.

Sachs comes out to cobble but monologues instead. That Sir Stolzing sang pretty good today he muses but the Masters hated it. Funny. Eva comes on. Come for your shoes my love? asks Sachs. Not for my shoes says she. To ask you who will win tomorrow. Search me says Sachs. Why don't you have a go yourself? asks Eva (a new idea to Sachs: for a moment he sees a glorious vision. But it fades). How did the trial go? asks Eva. Badly says Sachs, the knight didn't make it. He's out. No chance? asks Eva. No chance says Sachs. (He spots that Eva is unduly concerned.) Lena comes on. That Beckmesser's going on about serenading you she says. What a bore says Eva, why don't you sit in my window. I'm staying here. Lena exits.

Walter enters. Hi! says Eva: bad luck. Bad luck? says he: so I'm not good enough for that po-faced toffee-nosed poxy lot of Mastersingers. Bastards! The watchman's foghorn sounds. Let's fly together whispers Walter. All withdraw as watchman passes singing at his work. Once he is out Walter and Eva immediately clinch. Let's go let's go now they say but Sachs shines a preventive torch up the alley. They cower. Beckmesser slinks in tuning his banjo. I'll get that toad says Walter. Shurrup: wait till he goes says Eva.

Wise clever Sachs taking aboard all of Wagner's plot quite easily embarks on a very loud cobbler's song. Jerum! Jerum! etc. Bugger that noisy cobbler, thinks Beckmesser. In an intermission between verses he goes up to Sachs. Working late tonight eh Hans? he says. Working on your shoes for tomorrow says Sachs Jerum! Jerum! etc. Shall we make a run for it? says Walter. No keep still says Eva. (Halloolaloola yells Sachs.) Beckmesser sees a female at the window. Sachs gimme a chance for Chrissake he says, I wish to rehearse this song: a dry run for tomorrow: I would welcome your views. Strums on his banjo. OK OK says Sachs you sing away I'll mark your faults with my hammer. Beckmesser sings (a lot of banjo too) Sachs hammers. More and more. David spots Lena being serenaded. Neighbours open their windows. David sets on Beckmesser with a sand wedge. Neighbours in night clothes pour out and join in the fracas. Full-scale civil disorder ensues. Walter attempts to make a path for himself and Eva. Sachs rushes out seizes Eva and pushes her into her father's house. The riot continues until the watchman's foghorn sounds again. The street empties. Our friendly neighbourhood songster watchman holds the stage alone. Curtain.

Act III Sc 1 Sach's workshop
In which our hero rehearses his bid for winning a song contest, a journeyman is promoted and an unscrupulous town clerk makes off with someone else's poem

Sachs sits brooding during a broody prelude. David enters fearing a wigging for last night's fight. He messes around: Sachs is oblivious – still brooding. At last he wakes up and asks David to sing his trial verses. Bemused David starts off to Beckmesser's serenade tune: corrects himself: sings nicely: asks Sachs why he doesn't have a go in the contest? Stoopid says Sachs go and get dressed for the festival. David exits.

Sachs is broody again. He goes on for some time delivering irrelevant and opaque thoughts on the nature of madness. Walter enters saying so you see I had this dream-song but it's no good I can't compete. Those bastards won't let me in. They are not bastards says Sachs. They are decent conventional elderly gentlemen who dislike the passion of youth modern music whole-tone systems and the like. Sachs and Walter debate matters of musical taste etc. Sachs says sing me your dream-song I'll make notes. Walter sings his song: Sachs offers some advice: Walter sings again: Hey Walter Sachs says you have a good number there we might be able to do something with it meanwhile go and get changed. Both exit.

Enter the loathsome Beckmesser with a black eye limping etc. Prying around he spots Sachs's transcript of the words for the dream-song. He reads it and deduces Sachs is a competitor for Eva. Enter Sachs dressed to kill. Hey Sachs you deceitful skunk so now I know why you hounded me last night says Beckmesser. My rival eh? But I'll beat you you bastard. Mistake mistake says Sachs I'm not competing. Then what's this? says Beckmesser. Oh that old dream-song says Sachs if you want it my friend keep it, keep it. A poem by Sachs! Goody! thinks Beckmesser. Thanks Sachs very decent of you always knew you had a heart of gold he says: my number and your lyric will make me a certain winner. Exits.

Eva enters saying her shoes don't fit (a lie). After some persiflage Sachs cobbles. Walter enters in his Sunday best unseen by Sachs. Eva gives a great cry. Sachs cobbles on. Walter launches into the third chorus of the dream-song. Listen to this girl says Sachs, pretty good stuff eh? Sachs you are a sweetie says Eva, if you were twenty years younger I would really go for you. Enter David and Lena. Sachs gives David left uppercut the traditional way of signifying his promotion to junior manager. All quinque sing a glorious quintet about their hopes and fears for the coming day.

Act III Sc 2 A meadow outside Nuremberg set up for a fair
In which our hero triumphs, Sachs is acclaimed by all Nuremberg and we are given a lecture on the holy nature of German art

Craft guilds compete in song and friendly insults. Shoemakers first bakers next then tailors each with a buzzword – Streck, Me-e-eh and Beck respectively. The girls arrive: they dance with the apprentices including David (on the run from Lena). The Mastersingers are sighted and greeted with a welcoming chorus for all and especially for the song contest president Sachs. Much obliged says Sachs I'd like to thank Brother Pogner for putting up Eva as first prize and remember it's all about art.

Beckmesser is seen in a mucksweat trying to sort out Sachs's lyric to his tune. The crowd is amused. Beckmesser is called: begins: gets his knickers in a twist: the poem is totally confused and ludicrous: the crowd laugh: Beckmesser flounces off the podium. It's that bloody cobbler he shouts, he conned me. Believe me folks that poem was authored by Hans Sachs. Sachs? says the crowd: it's not possible: he writes good stuff. There's nothing wrong with the song says Sachs if it's sung right. Anyone here volunteer? Walter steps forward. This is the chap who was wrongly refused entry into the Masters' Guild says Sachs and actually it was him what wrote the song. Would you like to hear it sung proper? Yes yes cry one and all.

Walter steps up and starts. He sings his very beautiful very romantic number. The Masters and the general public are amazed. It's new! It's good! It's magic! It's a wow! they say. Give him the prize Sachs! OK says Sachs. He puts the crown on Walter's head. Walter rejects it. I don't want to be a stuffy old Mastersinger he says. Listen to my advice young man says Sachs, which incidentally will also serve as a brief Party Political Broadcast on behalf of German art. Listen folks: we must keep it pure. Don't let any foreign stuff foul it up. Keep out the Wops and the Frogs and above all the Yids. Do you get the message? Got it shout the crowd. Hurrah for German art! Best art in the world! Hooray! Hurry up Hitler!

Walter accepts the crown. Everybody happy except the miserable Beckmesser.

Meistersinger – the main mottos

Number	Name	Description
1	Masters	Taa-ta-ti-taa. Decent, worthy and important
2	Prize Song	Four golden notes vaulting downwards with the melody flowing on after them. Becomes the third verse or Aftersong of the final version
3	Pomp	A fanfare, tum-ti-ti-tum, then a sequence of pompous chords rising and rising
4	Apprentices	Jerky downwards steps in the woodwind, ti-ti-tum
5	Festival	A short sweet phrase, could be birdsong
6	Satisfaction	Dotted quavers going downwards: ti-tum/

		ti-tum/ti-tum
7	Cobbler	Je-rum Je-rum followed by a downward scale
8	Wahn	I've-lost-my-mar-bles. Two slow notes, a kick and two quicks
9	Sachs/Eva	An eight-note phrase, beginning with two clear high notes

LOOK OUT FOR

MINUTES FROM START

Act I Sc 1

0

The overture:*** one of the great milestones in music. It begins with a full statement of the Masters motto [1] reflecting the decency, the worthiness and the importance of the Masters guild in the life of the community. We will hear it again and again. Next is a yearning motto in the woodwind which has to do with the mutual attraction of Walter and Eva (Love, unlisted). This is followed by the fanfare of the great brassy Pomp and Circumstance tune which displays the Masters in all their pageantry and glory [3]. This reaches a climax: after some fairly drastic modulation we are into the theme of the last verse of the Prize Song [2] of which we are going to hear a lot too. Suddenly the thick welter of sound explodes into a cheeky and piquant variant of the Masters in the woodwind with a fragment of the Prize Song in counterpoint. Then back to the Prize Song main theme [2] with a swinging accompaniment and chattering woodwind above. But what is this we hear in the bass? It's the tune of the Masters [1], used as a foundation. Now Pomp [3] joins in and these three run as a troika until Pomp wins, takes over and dominates the final stretch up to curtain rise. Wonderful: if Wagner had written nothing else this piece would have put him up there with the greats.

0

9: *Da zu dir der Heiland kam*

The chorale** might well be an authentic period piece and not ersatz: it is really fine. Delicious instrumental solos are poked in

9

between the heavy choral phrases: and look out especially for a snaky solo cello, for once not reprehensible, also for the organ chord which sits below, a long long pedal point as the congregation file out.

Walter makes his enquiries. This really lovely three-handed scene,** Walter, Eva, Magdalene, flows along with lots of bubble and squeak: all three in lyrical mood with Love (unlisted) and a soufflé version of the Masters [1] and Pomp [3] fizzing away in the background from time to time. To mark David's presence (he is messing about with the furniture upstage), we have the first full statement of the Apprentices theme between these two – downward steps in the woodwind in threes, ti-ti-tum [4]. There is a short final trio in which Walter seems to have worked out pretty well what the Prize Song is going to be even before he knows he has dreamt it. (Coming in Act III.)

12: *Verweilt! Ein Wort!*   12

Act I Sc 2

After David's very thorough tutorial in which he gives poor Walter a rundown of the rules and regulations of a song contest (references to both Masters [1] and Pomp [3] throughout and an odd hint of the Prize Song [2] plus a forecast of the Cobbler's song to come) we have some jolly knockabout stuff between David and the apprentices* who have put up the platform all wrong. They wonder – will the stranger knight make it? (As well as the Apprentices we have a new theme here – Celebration: with a jerky rhythm, unlisted.)

34: *Was macht ihr denn da?*   34

After Pogner's entry and the roll call (Pogner's motto, a four-noter played over and over, unlisted), Pogner makes his address.** He opens with the lovely Festival motto [5], a short sweet phrase of four notes which could be birdsong. He sings it to the words 'Das schöne Fest'. He goes on with something more like recitatif as he turns to foreign affairs but gets poetical as he

45: *Nun hört, und versteht mich recht!*   45

approaches his climax 'Eva my only child' whom of course he is offering as the prize (Masters [1] lurking around in the background quite a lot, but mainly Festival [5]).

The act rolls on splendidly in a sort of free-fall rhapsody – arioso-recitatif (quite a lot of the Masters [1] and Festival [5]) with no great musical landmarks until Walter gives the Masters his account of how he learned to be a poet.**

60: *Am stillen Herd*

The Masters chatter a lot between the three stanzas of this number. It has a fine lyrical sweep and phrases that linger in the ear, but lacks the higher voltage of the Walter songs to come.

A minor event but worth a mention: Kothner reads the rules in a pedantic tongue-in-cheek set piece* which might almost persuade one that Wagner had a sense of humour. (Some Masters [1].)

68: *Ein jedes Meistergesanges Bar*

More impassioned than 'Am stillen Herd', not so disciplined as the Prize Song, this trial song** is written to give us an idea of Walter's natural talent (it has the fragment of the Prize Song mentioned in the overture accompanying it). It is a real set piece and although Beckmesser thought little of it, we relish this patch of uninhibited Wagner in an otherwise plotty first act.

72: *Fanget an!*

The finale is an ensemble** of confusion – not the confusion of Rossini's finales with each character wondering what the hell to make of things, for here everyone knows exactly what he wants – Sachs and Walter to finish the song, Beckmesser to sabotage it, the Masters to restore order, Pogner to see his man does not finally lose out and the apprentices jumping for joy at the general chaos. Act II ends with a better class of chaos than this one which is musically too thick a mass for everything to register. Although we desperately want to hear Walter struggling through his last verse and can't, the general effect of all the cross-currents of sound is very satisfactory.

80: *Singst dem Herrn Merher*

Act II

4: *Lass seh'n, ob Meister Sachs*

4

After the rowdy start to the act (nearly all new music), Pogner and daughter Eva stroll on for five minutes of enjoyable dialogue,* too one-sided to be called a duet, for Eva, like a good Nuremberg daughter, only speaks when spoken to. Pogner is really pleased with life except for that little matter of the knight at the singing contest which went wrong. He tells Eva tomorrow she is going to have a nice day. The scoring is light with the woodwind darting around in the most melodious fashion and there is one new short motto (dotted quavers going downwards – ti-tum ti-tum etc., a first cousin of the Love motto in the overture) which seems to describe his pride in Nuremberg – Civic Satisfaction [6].

11: *Was duftet doch der Flieder*

11

Sachs sits and thinks under his elder tree and we are into the Flieder monologue.** Why don't I give up all this poetic stuff and just stick to my last? he asks himself (a lot of bustle in the orchestra and quite a big dose of the Cobbler's song to come). Then he worries over the trial held earlier in the day: Walter's singing had natural beauty but was so strange as to make it hard to size up. Funny. He made the others mad but I loved it. So ruminates Sachs. (Some of the Trial Song around, with its accompanying fragment of the Prize Song.) This is a great piece: it seems to flow out effortlessly and from it we begin to learn what a generous big-hearted character Sachs is going to become.

17: *Gut'n Abend, Meister!*

17

Eva calls on Sachs for news of the song contest. This *is* a duet,** freely written, leaping from point to point. At first they fence with each other. She taunts him: why doesn't he have a go himself? But in the end his concern over the contest and hers for Walter break through and they become passionately involved. Eva is really disgusted that the petty-minded Masters have rejected her man and unfairly gets after Sachs as party to the crime (ending with bits of Cobbler's music).

27: *Da ist er!*

Eva sees Walter approaching and Wagner gives us one of those great surges of orchestral sound* that so wonderfully reflect the quickening of the pulse when lovers meet. But ecstasy does not last long. Walter breaks into a tirade against the frightful Masters: the whole thing was a nightmare, he says. Turbulent violin music with some satirical side swipes at the Masters [1] and Pomp [3]. As Walter and Eva plan to elope they are interrupted first by the night watchman with his splendid ditty and then by Beckmesser tuning his lute.

27

36: *Jerum! Jerum! Hallahallohe!*

The Schusterlied*** – Sachs's rollicking Cobbler's Song [7], in three stanzas and an outright winner. Walter, Eva and Beckmesser all chunter over it a bit and although helpful to the plot, this does become tiresome and one longs for the clear concert version which gives Sachs a chance to belt it out without let or hindrance. One of the several items in the opera that are complete set pieces.

36

50: *Den Tag seh' ich erscheinen*

Beckmesser's Serenade.* The tune is a parody, some say, of the style of a Jewish cantor. After the long argument with Sachs the first and second stanzas of Beckmesser's serenade seem even longer and the hammer blows from Sachs begin to lose their charm, when – hey presto! – they start singing at the same time and in double time, and as the neighbours pop their heads out of the windows, things cheer up amazingly.

50

55: *Zum Teufel mit dir*

Turmoil.** Everyone out and all singing very loud. If it turns into mashed potatoes (which it often does) it will seem to go on too long. But if it comes off (and Toscanini had it rescored to make this more likely) then it is one of the best welters of sound in the business. Whatever happens earlier on, the end piece always works like a dream. The busy street is hushed, Sachs pushes Eva back to safety, the night watchman's horn booms out as he sings his comforting night lines once again, this time conclusively.

55

Act III Sc 1

0

The prelude*** is a pensive piece with noble   0
thoughts delicately expressed. First a full-bodied
strong tune in the cellos – the Wahn motto [8] –
see next page for a definition of this crazy word
– which we have already heard in the Schusterlied bit of Act II but only in a fugitive form.
This theme swells upwards to be taken up by
the strings in counterpoint and leads to a sort of
brass choir chorale, which will return as the
chorus that greets the Masters in the last scene.
This solemn fanfare is followed by a sequence of
strong new tunes, then the brass choir again,
and so back to Wahn [8]. One must suppose that
it has something to do with the serious side of
Sachs, although he reads a book right through it
and pays not the blindest bit of attention to what
is going on in the pit.

Nowhere in Wagner is there more mickey-
mousing of the action to the music than in this
scene between the dreamy Sachs (Wahn [8]) and
the jumpy David (Apprentices [4]): it is lively
but can be embarrassing unless David is kept
firmly under control. There are nice moments,

11: *Am Jordan*   as when David after his false start sings his well-   11
Sankt Johannes   tailored verses** to the Master in the style of
stand   Bach or Telemann.

Slice it how you may, it is not easy to make
14: *Wahn! Wahn!*   much sense of the Wahn monologue* in which   14
Überall Wahn!   Sachs gives us the benefit of his thoughts on this
midsummer morning. The word Wahn itself is a
bit of a block since it does not mean simple
madness but some combination of divine dis-
content, illusion, inspiration and mania for
which naturally enough there is no one word in
English and indeed the whole notion is very
German, very philosophical and very Wagnerian. The monologue can be split into three parts:

1. There is Wahn all over the world causing
war and mayhem. Quite a lot of reference to
Wahn [8] but mainly free and running up to a
sharp climax over the worldwide effects of Wahn.

17: *Wie friedsam treuer Sitten*

19: *Ein Kobold half wohl da:*

22: *Gruss Gott, mein Junker!*

26: *Mein Freund, in holder Jugendzeit*

31: *Morgendlich leuchtend im rosigen Schein*

2. Smug reflections on wonderful wonderful Nuremberg* Civic Pride (unlisted) Festival [5] so comparatively Wahn-free – but – but last night there was a riot. A lot of riot stuff from Act II.

3. Some sentimental thoughts about how the riot was caused* and then some constructive thinking about how this quality Wahn can be harnessed to do good (as, one imagines, in inspiring song contests, but honestly by now one is beginning to give up). References to Festival [5] and to the Prize Song [2].

So there you have it: one of the most celebrated pieces in the opera, musically coherent, aspiring to philosophical profundity but in truth just a bundle of old Wahn, and cobbler's Wahn at that. (Especially the bit about hunting which is quite impenetrable.)

The duet Sachs/Walter which leads up to the rehearsal of the Prize Song is a phenomenon.*** It does not advance the plot one inch and for ten minutes the two men discuss the nature, quality and appeal of romantic music. Not, one would have thought, a particularly lively topic. But the whole duet is set to music that is quite ravishing, a flow of lyrical ideas, most of them free, although Festival [5] (one of the most heavily worked mottos in the piece) is there at the start. Rhapsody takes over altogether when the duet reaches the point where Sachs gives Walter advice about the need for stamina in a composer.** Clearly this was a subject close to Wagner's heart and he throws all his energy into the discussion of this matter.

Sachs coaches Walter in the art of winning a song contest.*** Actually his help does not go beyond a little strategic advice, for Walter seems to have got the first two verses of his dream song pretty well pat. Sachs is deeply moved, and so are we by the first full hearing of this glorious piece. Sachs responds to the song with his reflective Wahn theme [8].

Beckmesser picks around in Sachs's workshop and finds the Prize Song poem. Wagner goes over the top here with motto after motto from last night's brawl used to mickey-mouse Beckmesser's actions as in a Tom & Jerry cartoon. But the duet* with Sachs has an amazing flow of fresh and sprightly melodic invention. It is however much too long. Musical references all over the place, especially to Beckmesser's lute music from Act II and the beginning of the Prize Song.

46: *Ein Werbelied! Von Sachs!* 46

Now we move into the clear upper atmosphere. Eva comes in. Her shoes don't fit. This touching scene*** has a new motto – hinted at before – the Sachs/Eva motto, introduced by an oboe and developing into a ravishing eight-note phrase starting with two high clear notes [9]. The two duet together with quick give and take over an orchestral accompaniment of tenderness and simple clarity. Then as Eva sees Walter (Sachs doesn't) she gives a great cry. Sachs busies himself with the shoes until Walter begins to sing the third verse of the Prize Song (which this time he has apparently dreamt up whilst awake). Then a great emotional moment – Eva weeps on Sachs's shoulder, Walter seizes his hand and all three stand in a tableau before a mighty orchestral climax. Sachs defuses the tension with some jolly stuff about the shoemaker's life (Cobbler [7]) and this marvellous scene ends with a set-piece solo*** from Eva telling Sachs how much she loves him, but not as a prospective husband. Sachs replies briefly, and affectingly (textual and musical references to *Tristan* here), the spell is broken and we are into the hustle and bustle of Midsummer morning.

58: *Gruss Gott, mein Evchen* 58

66: *O Sachs! Mein Freund!* 66

After Sachs has celebrated (to the tune of the opening church chorale in Act I) the birth of a new master-song and the promotion of David from apprentice to journeyman (Masters [1] and the Prize Song fragment), we are into the most magical moment of the opera, the quintet.*** It

73: *Selig, wie die Sonne* 73

is a 'thinks' piece as follows: Eva (Such a good song it's bound to win), Sachs (So I really must give up any idea of marrying Eva), Walter (Here's hoping), David (That was sudden promotion for you!), Magdalene (A journeyman! We may be married soon!). All these disparate thoughts are expressed most harmoniously. The opening themes of the quintet are new, look out especially for a long smooth phrase first heard in the accompaniment and then passed from voice to voice. The music drifts into the Prize Song [2], and spreads into a chorus of happiness and hope. One of the great moments in opera.

Act III Sc 2

The transition from Sachs's workshop to the Festival meadow is managed orchestrally by a bustling build-up of excitement with fanfares and flourishes and references to Festival [5] and the Masters [1] and so we are into the sing-about* of the rival guilds, the Shoemakers to the tune of the Schusterlied (Cobbler [7]), the Tailors and Bakers each to something new. The repeated monosyllabic war-cries (Shoemakers 'Streck', Tailors 'Meck', Bakers 'Beck') become a little embarrassing.

80: *Sankt Krispin, lobet ihn!*   80

83   The Dance of the Apprentices* – a little mincing for such rough lads but tuneful. Some horseplay with David. Followed by more fanfares, the Masters [1] and Pomp [3] and the Masters arrive on stage.   83

90: *Wach auf*   A rousing chorus*** – first heard when played by the brass choir in the prelude to Act III. All Nuremberg rises to greet the Masters and especially Sachs. They give us the surprising news that dawn is near although they are standing in a brightly sunlit meadow. This is Wagner at his most civic, the sort of anthem that could have been made to order for the City of Birmingham at the height of its municipal glory.   90

After Sachs has said Thank You for this tribute (Wahn [8]) we have the painful farce of Beckmesser's attempt to sing Sachs's words to

109: *Morgendlich leuchtend im rosigen Schein*

the tune of his serenade in Act II with its ghastly lute accompaniment. And now the Prize Song proper.*** Walter has done a lot of work on it since morning for although the musical inspiration is the same, the poem is different and more relevant. Now we have it in all its glory and as it casts its dreamy spell over the assembled citizenry it makes us believe for a moment that we too are standing in a meadow in Nuremberg overwhelmed by the beauty of song. If on the other hand we remain aware that we are sitting in an opera house, there is something wrong with the production, for this is one of opera's most magical moments.

109

The crowd take up the reprise of the Prize Song and Walter is acclaimed the outright winner. He then rather rudely rejects membership of the Masters guild. This provokes an outburst of rather nasty chauvinism from Sachs,* much of which is sung (at the beginning and the end) to snatches of the Prize Song [2] above Masters [1], plus several other references including Pomp [3]. The opera ends with all stops out. Walter relents. Everyone sings the praises of Glorious German Art, coupled with the name of Hans Sachs, to positively the last and easily the noisiest rendering of the Masters [1].

117: *Verachtet mir die Meister nicht*

117

NOTES

Meistersinger	Wagner's seventh opera
First night	Königliches Hof- und Nationaltheater, Munich, 21 June 1868
Reception	A tremendous success
Libretto	Wagner
Source	Research into sixteenth- and seventeenth-century history of Nuremberg. But no previous version of the story itself

NEWS AND GOSSIP

Surprisingly, Wagner first thought of *Meistersinger* as a short comic item to be performed immediately after *Tannhäuser*. Admittedly, after four hours of *Tannhäuser* one is ready for some refreshment, but most people would feel more like a glass of the strong stuff than another Wagner opera. Also his idea of 'short' would probably mean starting *Tannhäuser* off at noon. Luckily he dropped this curious notion. In 1845 he started delving into the history of Nuremberg in the seventeenth century and discovered quite a lot about the singing guilds and the civic poet Hans Sachs who wrote plays (one of them about the death of Siegfried). He linked the historical story with his own pet propaganda lines, such as:

1. Art is the most important thing in life.
2. German art is in danger of being taken over by foreigners and Jews like that frightful Meyerbeer.
3. It's about time that the establishment gave a decent hearing to modern music. Music like mine, for instance.
4. Music critics who don't like my stuff are small-minded malicious bastards, especially that Hanslick who writes in the Vienna Sunday Times.

All of these thoughts went into the hopper and Wagner worked on the *Meistersinger* libretto for seventeen years, in clear spaces during the writing of *Lohengrin*, *Tristan* and *The Ring*, finishing it in 1862. He completed the score three years later.

The huge success of the premiere (under Hans von Bülow) set all the musicos in Europe a-talking but *Meistersinger* did not immediately sweep the opera stages of the world. Although it was mounted in the German number two provincial houses in the following year it did not make it to Vienna and Berlin until 1870. Then London in 1882, the Met in 1886, Bayreuth in 1888. It seems incredible today that this great masterpiece should have hung fire. *Meistersinger* is not 'difficult' Wagner. Certainly expensive and hard to mount, but so wonderful, such a crowd-puller, that one would have thought that urgent faxes would have been flying in all directions – 'Maestro, I've seen a show we just got to put on!' But no.

Today *Meistersinger* is the best-liked Wagner opera, not such a monster as *The Ring*, clearly better than the slightly ludicrous *Tannhäuser* and *Lohengrin*, less holy than *Parsifal*, not so taxing as

Tristan. So it is played a lot, and loved by not only Wagnerites, but a lot of the generality of mankind as well.

COMMENT

Meistersinger is the acceptable face of Wagner. There are no hang-ups with sex and sin, no power-mad dwarfs, no sprouting staves, no swans and not a holy grail in sight. Even the racial propaganda mentioned in the notes above can be played down to zero effect except for the unavoidable and disagreeable final outburst about the ethnic cleansing of the arts.

The story is simple, strong and rather slow. Its strength lies in Walter's struggle and success in pushing romantic or impressionist art in the face of the sort of hatred that always springs up amongst the arts establishment in the face of anything that is good or new. Although Walter is the front man in this contest, it is really Sachs's support for him that gives the opera its gravitas. Indeed the smart way in which Sachs outwits Beckmesser and makes Walter into No. 1 in the charts at a single blow is something that even Brian Epstein would have envied when he launched the Beatles. The sub-plot with Beckmesser is not so strong and there is too much of it. In particular the long dialogue with Sachs before his serenade in Act II and the encounter with Sachs in his workshop in Act III Sc 1 could be cut with advantage.

David and his apprentices pad out the work with their Rolf Harris-boy-scout antics, but the music is so good not a second of this could be cut and the producer has to do with it what he can (but not too much, please). Again, it is the music that saves the long discussion between Sachs and Walter in Act III Sc 1 about the nature of poetic inspiration and Nuremberg's musical politics, for it does nothing to advance the plot. The street riot and the blaze of choral singing in the last scene both come off very well, but it is of course the Prize Song itself which is the high peak of the show and it is brilliantly managed.

Unlike *Lohengrin*, *Tannhäuser* and co., the characters in *Meistersinger* are recognizably human. Sachs, of course, sensible, wise, a little radical and clever with it, wins you over pretty soon, although after listening to the Wahn monologue we can see a club bore in the making and in his final utterances about German art a potential fascist. His sudden fantasy of winning the contest himself and taking Eva to be his wife gives him an extra dimension (and her too, for why does she suggest it?). This is not the sort of stuff you find in Verdi or Puccini with their raging black and white passions. It shows both characters with a genuine tenderness for each other and so when Walter enters in the shoe-fitting scene and we rejoice with Eva in her cry of ecstasy, we also feel a stab of pain for Sachs. Walter is a good standard romantic knight and a top-class artist to boot, but he does not win our hearts as does Eva. Beckmesser is less successful, partly perhaps because Wagner was keen to use him as an agent to vent his spite. He is too near a caricature to be taken seriously and too essential to the plot to be just a witless clown. It is an uneasy role which seldom comes off in performance. Pogner, on the other hand, is in kilter with real life: one meets at least one Pogner on every respectable borough council, and long may they pontificate – civic do-gooders, decent through and through.

But the great glory of *Meistersinger* is its music. The rich sonorities of the Masters' two themes full of pomp and circumstance fill the ear in a highly satisfactory way, the Prize Song beguiles as do few other songs, prize or otherwise. There are some great set pieces – Walter's account of his learning processes ('Am stillen Herd'), the Schusterlied, the last act choruses, the Prize Song itself and above all the Act III quintet which for sheer lyrical invention stands alone in Wagner's huge operatic output in the same way as does Beethoven's Act I quartet in his single opera *Fidelio*. The pastiche pieces are immaculate – the opening church scene, David's verses and Pogner's address. With such variety and apparently endless flow of melody, it comes as a bit of a surprise to discover that the use of thematic material in *Meistersinger* is very economical. The two Masters themes do a tremendous amount of work, as does the Prize Song. These three plus another six or seven much shorter mottos generate the music over most pages of the score, set pieces excepted. The music of *Meistersinger* is closely knit, there is nothing flabby about it and although perhaps twenty minutes too long, it is never really boring, as are patches in *The Ring*. It has no vulgarities, as has *Tannhäuser*, is not pretentious like *Parsifal*, and what pomposity it has is delivered with more than a whiff of send-up.

It is also nearly producer-proof. It cannot be set in a used-car lot nor in Hiroshima after the bomb. It demands a church, a street, a meadow and although these can be reduced to black drapes (when the opera can still survive), they cannot be transmogrified into symbolism without destroying the piece entirely.

So it's three hearty cheers for *Meistersinger*, a noble life-enhancing work which, although a long sit-down, can give you one of the happiest and most rewarding of evenings in the opera house. Alpha-plus.

THE RING

Contents

A General Hello

There is no need to be frightened of *The Ring*. Gone are the days when a pilgrimage to Bayreuth ranked equal in holiness with a visit to the Passion Play at Oberammergau. Today there is no need to spend a preparatory week hammering out leitmotifs from a piano score, for *The Ring* is now accessible on CD, which is the perfect medium for getting acquainted with it. Most people will want to job about amongst the tracks for a while before tackling the old thing in its enormity in the opera house. But if you are one of those who are content to let the music wash over them with only the vaguest idea of what the words are saying, and find it enough to know that Siegfried is good, the dwarfs are bad and there is something about the ring having a curse on it – don't bother to read on. If, on the other hand, you are an eager beaver who wants to hunt each motto to its lair and feel it imperative to find out the whole truth about the Norns, then you will have to buy some proper opera books. But if, like most of us, you feel a spot of homework is required in order to get reasonable customer satisfaction, then do read on.

The Ring is of course the biggest aspidistra in the world of opera and for a newcomer the voyage of discovery can be tough. But if you are *Ring*-prone or even just *Ring*-tolerant, it is quite a thing to hear this mighty work of genius unrolling before your very ears. But don't expect a lot of laughs.

It is of course the power of the music that makes the *Ring* experience different from just going to the opera. With the Italians, including Verdi at his greatest and even with Mozart, we are looking at and listening to the opera from outside. Brilliant, wonderful, marvellous they may be, but it's a performance. The music of *The Ring* engulfs us. We get right in there – into the saddle in the Ride of the Valkyries, we march in step amongst Siegfried's funeral cortège. We are in the middle of that ring of fire with Brünnhilde. It is possible to get too far in and get singed, like Bernard Levin. But *Ring* mania is only a mild inconvenience and it really does no harm. Nevertheless, it is a medically certifiable mental state and whereas there is no danger of anyone suffering from the bends after coming up from *Figaro* or *Aida*, *The Ring* can have you wandering around in a daze for a week.

It is not possible to explain why some music is great and some isn't. You can point out technical things as you can with a great painting. But what you can't do is to put your finger on why Rembrandt pulls it off and John Smith who rents your attic doesn't. In *The Ring* Wagner pulls it off. He commands mighty forces. To compare his orchestra with Haydn's is like comparing the Albert Hall organ with a harmonium in a Friends' meeting house. In particular he unleashed the power of the brass section and packed it with sonorous instruments, some of which he invented himself. He could write a good tune. He pushed the language of music (which had stood still for nearly two hundred years) into new territory. Like Debussy after him, he could make pictures with music, in particular fire, water, various states of the weather and the sort of scenery you get in national parks. He could write music of great intensity about love, hate, horror, happiness and bravery. He could construct a climax that climbed from peak to peak: and each time you thought you had got to the top he surprised you with something higher. He could build a scene with perfect judgement of tempo and contrast. But although he was a superman in all other departments and the great panjandrum of orchestration, this still does not explain the chemistry that makes him the great musical magician he was. You can only learn by listening. But you have to listen for a long time for, alas, he had no wit, nor any part of the soul of wit, brevity.

When it comes to the words, he was not so great. The best you can say about the story of *The Ring* is that its setting of myth and mystery and its huge imaginative scope doesn't let the music down. It is the sort of work where the tone is lofty, where nobility is truly noble and where evil is unspeakably bad, where a giant can turn into a dragon at the drop of a magicap and a dwarf into a toad. Wagner's judgement was spot-on in using a phantasmagoria of myth as a basis for *The Ring* for it is much easier to make heroes out of gods and villains out of dwarfs than to cope with human nature. Also any awkward plot points can be magicked out of the way in a trice.

The story itself is not all that hot. The three-tier system, as we would now call it, that Wagner built up out of those depressing old sagas – gods, humans, dwarfs – isn't complete and isn't rational. Although parts are worked out in great detail – far beyond their importance to the plot – there are great holes in the middle. And the detail is often otiose. We hear a lot, for instance, about the Valkyries who were bred by Wotan out of Erda to carry the corpses of dead heroes to Valhalla where they would be re-vived and retrained as stormtroopers. This is picturesque but unnecessary. Wotan surely had enough magic to call the corpses up to Valhalla without the need for a platoon of Valks. Indeed, why not recruit them whilst still alive and avoid the bother of resurrection.

At the centre, the motivation for the collapse of the system is unclear. Why does Wotan wander? Why does he lose his bottle? Is it the effects of the curse? If so, it has taken a long time to act. If it's not the curse, what is it? There are now plenty of the medicinal apples around in Valhalla. Maybe he had Alzheimer's and we weren't told. And why do the gods Downfall? Once the Rhinegirls get the ring back all should be gas and gaiters up there. But no, even when she knows she is going to give up the ring, Brünnhilde sends Loge off to arsonize Valhalla. Why?

But faults in the system – which is a pretty crazy one anyway – don't matter so much as the faults in telling the story. Here by far the biggest bugaboo is Wagner's habit of constantly regurgitating the *Rhinegold* story. Somebody tells us a bit of the story and half an hour later someone else tells us the same bit again, only for a third telling to surface in Part III. Even when a part of the story takes place before our very eyes – e.g. Alberich's theft of the gold – we are told about it again on four separate occasions. Meanwhile, all action stops. The narrative drive goes into neutral. Sometimes it seems like reverse. If it weren't for the soothing effect of the music it would drive us all potty. You could say that retelling No. 2 or No. 3 usually gives more detail and you could also say that the telling opens a door for some wonderful music (and some pretty ornery music too) but the balance of advantage must be against so much retelling.

The handling of the main characters is the second great weakness. Wotan, who we thought was going to be the king pin of the whole piece, fades out completely after Part III and is not up to much in Part II. We don't know why he fades out. He has no payoff except having his spear broken by Siegfried. So why doesn't he go back to base and have it repaired? Siegfried did it to Nothung. If it is a symbol that his magic power is running out of gas, again why? Siegmund passes over in Part II and Siegfried doesn't arrive on the scene until Part III. Only Brünnhilde is central to the story after *Rhinegold*. The story also suffers from the characters being such an unattractive lot. With Wotan one loses patience very early on. Ill-tempered, indecisive, cowardly and much too talkative, he is not a person one would want to invite into the home. The truth is that Wagner packed into Wotan so many different roles (chief god, hen-pecked husband, loving father, orbital strategist, power-mad plotter, Don Juan, dwarf-oppressor) that the result is an unfocused character who never really comes off. And why is he wandering? We don't know, and apparently he doesn't either. Maybe Fricka just wanted him out of the house.

The two heroes of the Strength Through Joy movement, Siegmund and Siegfried, are a couple of boneheads who in the real world would be best employed in the boxing ring ('My boy don't know what fear is'), the Gibichungs are brutish, the dwarfs abhorrent, and thus we have only one major character – Brünnhilde – with whom we can have some fellow-feeling. She is quite splendid and gives us hope that there is some spark of decent feeling in Wagner after all. But with all of these faults, the story and the characters have power and the sort of power that Wagner in his slightly obscene way was aiming for. By dealing in blood, death, incest, necrophilia, deformity, etc., he can touch those deeper and darker instincts that we have within us and wish we hadn't got. Occasionally he can make the music help him enormously in this rather disagreeable task. One feels he gloats over the dirty bits and particularly incidental items such as Alberich raping a human female in order to produce the ghastly Hagen. Not the sort of thing Barbara Cartland would put in her books. But for perverts who incline towards snuff movies, *The*

Ring can offer a worthwhile beginners' course. (See **Death Toll** page 139.)

Amidst all this death and doom Brünnhilde pretty well saves the day. She is brave, she is good, she is true, she is lovely, and – although in her desperation she helps to plot Siegfried's death – the only thoroughly respectable person in sight. We rejoice with her in her love for Siegfried and we share her grief at his death. She also gets the best music, and deserves it.

The story of *The Ring* is told not only in words but in mottos (see page 133). Wagner made a big thing of the motto system in composing *The Ring*. It doesn't always work. For instance, in *Valkyrie* Act II Sc 2 when Wotan does one of his tedious recaps to Brünnhilde the mottos respond to the text like a pack of Pavlov's dogs. Each one sits in its kennel and only pops its head out when it hears His Master's Voice. You mention the ring, you hear the Ring; you think of Valhalla, you hear Valhalla. It gets close to parody. At the other end of the scale the mottos can work splendidly in the orchestral pieces where they are turned over and developed, and in the great duets too. Here they become part of the fabric and not just descriptive labels. It is best, however, not to get too deep into mottology because it is easy to get lost in the mist. Everything can be related to everything and everything can have a deep and sometimes elaborate message. Some quotes from a musico:

Loge as the ambivalence of primal energy (Loge [8])
First stirring under the Rhine as a premonition of consciousness (Rhine [1])
The Valkyrie as the masculine element in women (Valkyrie [16])

Beware of writing too much on the labels.

There is a general belief that in the motto idea Wagner invented a wonderful new system for composing operas. Certainly all the Wagner scribendos, and they are legion, tend to give him good marks when he is laying on the mottos thick and fast and poor marks when he forgets about mottos and just writes a good tune. I quote from a scribendo who is worried about the master's performance in *Götterdämmerung*: '. . . retrogressive elements of grand opera exist side by side with mature passages of motivic integration'.

It is the word 'retrogressive' that tells the tale. This scribendo does not take account of the fact that a lot of the best music occurs when Wagner uses very few mottos or chucks them altogether (retrogressive) and some of the most boring music when it is tremendously well motivically integrated and bouncing along from one old motto to the next. No one can tell how Wagner's work would have developed if someone had persuaded him to junk this whole paraphernalia of mottos as a load of theoretical rubbish, or at least to have kept it within the sort of bounds set by *Meistersinger*. For the trouble with the motto game is that when you get really deep into it it is great fun for the composer and for the musicologist but not for the client. Like Bach's mirror fugue, which can be played backwards, forwards, upside down, in a mirror and in braille, it is not such a satisfactory piece for the listener as, for instance, that old warhorse the Toccata and Fugue in D minor, which can only be played one way – forwards and the right way up. One of the problems for the aficionado of *The Ring* is that you keep thinking you hear a relationship between one motto and another and the other problem is that you are usually right. So whilst you are occupied with this mental/aural struggle the dragon is killed and you miss it. However that may be, the composition of the motto itself is often a small-scale work of genius (as for example Fate [19], Anvils [9], Ecstasy [21]).

There is another part of the Wagner product that is beyond the reach of most clients and certainly all non-German-speaking clients, and that is the relationship between words and notes. When Wagner worked on the script he started with a prose draft. This he converted into a poem. There aren't any rhymes, but the lines scan and there is a lot of alliteration. Even without knowing the German, one can guess pretty safely that Wagner was no Keats, for some of the words that filter through in translation such as Wishmaidens, Battlefather and the constantly recurring Wondrous send a shiver down the spine. But in fitting music to the words he went to extraordinary lengths. Let me just quote a short passage about this from one of the best Wagner scribendos, Brian Magee:

> If, says Wagner, he writes a line like 'Liebe giebt Lust zum Leben' (Love gives delight to living) the concepts involved are obviously consonant and therefore no change of key is called for. But suppose the line is 'Liebe bringt Lust und Leid' (Love brings delight and sorrow) then delight and sorrow are opposites and the music should modulate between them. What should happen is that the key in which the phrase begins on the word 'love' should remain the same through 'delight' and then

change on the word 'sorrow'. But the modulation must express the interrelationship of delight and sorrow in the state of love, at the same time as their difference; it must articulate their conditioning of each other. . . . Now supposing the next line is 'Doch in ihr Weh webt sie auch Wonnen' (which might be very freely translated: 'Yet even its pain gives us joy'). Then the key of 'sorrow' from the end of the previous line should be carried through as far as 'pain', because the emotional mood remains the same. But then the verb in this second line starts a shift of the mood back towards that of the first half of the previous line; therefore the music should begin to change key on 'gives', and on the word 'joy' should arrive back at the key of 'Love gives delight'.

Or:

Sieglinde enters. She tells how an old man dressed in grey had thrust the sword into the tree at the wedding ceremony of herself and Hunding. This narration, 'Der Männer Sippe sass hier im Saal', is a choice example of the musico-poetic synthesis – the practical application of Wagner's principles of word-setting – that finds its most consistent expression in *Die Walküre*. Particularly noteworthy are the low-lying vocal line depicting the old man's low-brimmed hat, the shape of the melodic line portraying the flash of his eye and then its 'threatening glance', the falling chromatic intervals for his lingering look of yearning, the expressive appoggiatura on 'Tränen' ('tears') and the final rise to a top G for the physical act of implanting the sword in the tree. The sounding of the Valhalla motif by horns and bassoons announcing the real identity of the stranger, is one of the classic uses of leitmotif to comment on the action.

Amazing, isn't it? But no good unless you understand the German. And so all this intensive labour really goes for nothing unless you are an insider in the Wagner club.

In moderating this and other of his excesses, what Wagner badly needed was an editor. Until our Richard came on the scene the opera composer was a pretty workmanlike fellow. Verdi, for instance, and especially Mozart, would adapt and adjust to suit the needs of the house, of the sponsor and of the singers. They also had a librettist who was always a talking block and sometimes a critic, occasionally a partner. Wagner was his own librettist, his own manager, his own editor and his own hero. He thought he was

pretty good in all of these capacities. In the writing and putting on
of a show no other opinion mattered. The composer was always
right, which we now see he very often wasn't. Just as it was a
happy accident that Mozart had da Ponte, Strauss had Hofmann-
stahl and Hart had Rodgers, so it was a bit of a disaster that
Richard had no one to work with but Wagner, for he was not only
self-indulgent but also a megalomaniac. It is of course quite
possible that a sensible partner would have persuaded him not to
touch anything so outlandish as *The Ring* at all, and where would
we be then?

Even today *The Ring* could be much improved if the longueurs
were cut out, some of the sillier script points straightened out and
the whole thing reduced to more manageable proportions. This
would allow the big houses to put it on without the total
disruption it now causes, or at the very least give them more time
for rehearsal, the evening could be organized more sensibly for the
clients who would not have to suffer from an undigested chicken
salad bolted down at half-past five and timed precisely to ruin the
love duet. Alas, this will never happen because a cult of religious
veneration for the wishes of the composer now rules the musical
roost. Wagner himself played a big part in promoting this by
putting out a lot of self-serving propaganda about art being pretty
well the sole purpose of life and the wickedness of tampering with
the work of an artist, especially a great artist such as himself. To
be authentic, to do exactly what the scholars say Scarlatti,
Schubert or Monteverdi would want you to do, if necessary going
to the length of building a sixteenth-century ophicleide – this
today is pretty well the holy grail. Never mind that the piece
would sound much better played another way or that modern
acoustics are different, that pitch has gone up, musical taste
changed, musical marathons don't fit into our culture – never
mind anything at all, just stick a harpsichord into the Albert Hall
and not on any account a Steinway. If you can't hear it at least you
know what you're not hearing is authentic. The real obstacle to
producing a sensibly revised version of *The Ring* is not the chorus
of outrage that would go up, but the difficulty of finding a
musician of genius to do it.

But the thought of what we might have had can't dim the glory
of what we have got. There was a time when Wagner and
especially *The Ring* divided mankind into the Wagnerites and the
rest. Today the war is won. There are a few I-can't-stand-
Wagners still around and these are usually people who confuse

Wagner the nasty little man – and he certainly was racist, chauvinistic, a liar and a megalomaniac with fascist tendencies – with Wagner the composer of genius. They may also be people whose defences are too weak to withstand the sort of visceral attack Wagner makes upon them. But most of us can now be cool about Wagner and even the coolest must stand back and regard *The Ring* with wonder. It has been called the greatest feat of human imagination in the nineteenth century, and this is a statement that it is hard to deny. You can find in it what you like. Bernard Shaw found a socialist tract, others have called it fascist propaganda. Robert Donington saw it as an early statement of Jungian philosophy. The ecologists find in it a parable about polluting the world. No doubt equestrians, metallurgists, pyromaniacs and undertakers recognize some special message in it too. There had been nothing like it before and there has been nothing like it since. It is large, it is complex, it rides through the opera house like a juggernaut. Not much of it is lovable, some of it is repugnant. But when it makes its way through the ear and spreads across our sensibilities we know that we are listening to something that is a considerable event in the affairs of mankind and one that will stay with us to marvel at and to puzzle over for the rest of our lives.

After a performance of the last act of *Götterdämmerung* at a Prom in the mid-sixties the promenaders cheered for half an hour, then when the artists went home and the lights went out they stayed on and cheered in the dark. This could happen for no other piece of music.

Leitmotifs, Mottos and All That

In planning their history of England, *1066 And All That*, Messrs Sellar and Yeatman decided to include only those dates that were memorable. As a result of careful research they finally included only one – 1066. Deryck Cooke in his Companion to Decca's *Ring* quotes 191 leitmotifs. He is careful to say that deep down there are many more than this and he has just picked up a few of the more showy ones lying about on the surface. Robert Donington in his book on *The Ring and its Symbols*, by heavy pruning, gets the number of motifs down to 93. In the following section 29 main mottos are listed, all of them memorable, plus roughly an equal number of others which are mentioned but not thought to be memorable.

There are three ways of listening to *The Ring*:

1. Lie back and let it sweep over you. Don't bother about the plot too much, just . . . Ahhh . . . the Rhine . . . lovely music . . . Don't bother about the mottos at all. A lot of clients get their buzz out of *The Ring* in this way. Perhaps most.

2. Hunt every motto to its lair, if necessary reading books, even getting the piano score. Seek out family relationships. Set up your own theory of motto evolution. In fact, go motto mad. The trouble is that in the advanced stages of motto mania the patient ceases to hear the music as music. *The Ring* becomes a gigantic crossword puzzle – a quarry for new clues.

3. Take a middle course. There is no need to go poking about in the viscera of *The Ring* to get the maximum mileage from it. But you can't listen to it without noticing the mottos and you can't get a handle on the old thing unless you have some idea what the main mottos mean. So each individual in this third class, according to the sharpness of their ear, the efficiency of their musical storage capacity and their determination, will sort out for himself the level of motto-recognition that he must reach to give himself satisfaction. The number of mottos selected in this guide is calculated to suit an intensely musical child of ten or an intelligent but unmusical retired airline pilot of sixty.

So what is a motto anyway? Some carry messages like Love is the Sweetest Thing or Every Silver Lining Has a Cloud. Others are personalized. Walk-on parts have no mottos. Supporting roles may have only one motto (the Giants, when both are still in human, or gigantic, form). Erda, Gutrune and the stars get several. Siegfried has half a dozen and more. Each motto is telling you something, though sometimes it is pretty hard to make out just exactly what Wagner had in mind. In some cases one suspects he didn't really know himself, but just liked the sound. Valkyrie [16], Anvils [9] and Valhalla [5] are easy and indeed not far from the system of *Peter and the Wolf*. A tune for everyone: the jolly hunter, the evil wolf, etc. More mysterious are ideas like Fate [19] or Ecstasy [21], which probably mean something different to each listener.

A motto can be as short as two notes or can be stretched out like chewing gum to cover half-a-dozen pages of the score. In their virgin form mottos are seldom more than two or three bars. A motto can change into another motto. A motto can split in two like an amoeba and then the split bits can split again: and it is also like a chameleon for it can change its colour in a trice. All mottos are related to other mottos, say the Mottologists, indeed all mottos can trace their family tree back to the great Mother Motto, the chord of E flat with which the piece begins. Here a sceptic will suggest that with enough changes of gear, as in those funny fade-throughs of the early cinema, you can transform Winston Churchill's face into that of Madonna, but that when it's all over they still look different people. Pop Goes the Weasel can be turned into the Grand March in *Aida* in ten easy stages but that doesn't mean the tunes have any real relationship.

Many people find the mottos a bit of a nuisance. Conscious or subconscious groping for mottos can take your attention away from the game that's going on before your very ears and Wagner may be scoring a series of goals whilst you are grubbing about motto-hunting.

The matter of mottos is treated in the following pages as follows:

1. Longlife mottos. Can be recognized without difficulty. Are important. Crop up off and on throughout the show. These have a number.

2. Short Stay mottos. Can be recognized. Can be important in a single scene or within an act. May be referred to in other parts of *The Ring*, but seldom, and when they are they don't matter that much. These have a letter.

3. Momentary mottos. Can be recognized, but more difficult because they don't happen so often. They seldom crop up outside their own patch; some of them, although very insistent when doing their stuff, fade away completely. These are unlisted.

It is probably unwise for the lay listener to burden his memory with the unlisted lot or for that matter any of the 130 further mottos indexed by the scholarly Deryck Cooke but not mentioned in these pages at all.

The Mottos

Longlife	Short stay	Motto	Sounds Like

Rhinegold

| [1] | | Rhine | A smooth flow of water with eddies going up and down jerkily |

[2]		Gold	A bugle call that flies upwards and stops (played on a trumpet)
[3]		Rhinegold	One long note – Rhine – down to the adjacent note – Gold – shorter
[4]		Ring	Woozy chords rotating around in a vague way
	[a]	Rejection	A slow yearning sort of thing hanging on to an early high note
[5]		Valhalla	Pompous brass going down then up: very civic (related to [4] above)
	[b]	Stress	Jerky downward steps
[6]		Giants	BRRM-TI-TA (TA). A scoop up and the following notes hammered out in unison
	[c]	Apples	Slow horns with triplets towards the end. Rather nice
[7]		Spear	Downward scale that could go on for ever, often punched out by trombones
[8]		Loge	Flickering semitones and more. A sort of motto grouping which hangs together. No sweat
	[d]	Bad News	A two-note cry of grief, WOE-WA, twice
[9]		Anvils	Clinketty Clinketty Clinketty Clinketty
[10]		Tarnhelm	Or magicap. Horns moving about (but not that much) rather close to each other
[11]		Curse	The rhythm of DAMMIT-ALL rising to a high note – with a nasty low afterthought
[12]		Earth or Erda	An upward sweep in chords moving unevenly. Sometimes settling on the top note
[13]		Destruct	Earth [12] upside down

Valkyrie

	[e]	Sieglinde	A bass line going down followed by chords going up
	[f]	Lovers	A long, smooth, sweet, string melody
	[g]	Self-Pity	A slow item climbing upwards and ending with an unusual harmony

	[h]	Volsung	A majestic melody with dotted rhythms
[14]		Sword	Trumpet octave and arpeggio. Shining bright
[15]		Nothung	A downward octave twice, with a tail-piece
[16]		Valkyrie	Rocking-horse rhythm punched out by trombones. Unmistakable
[17]		War-Cry	A ferocious inverted yodel. Can be followed by a trill and peals of laughter
[18]		Frustration	Starts with a buzz like an angry bee, then fades away
[19]		Fate	A doomy three-noter. Long – short (down) – long (up). Often followed by ominous drumbeats
[20]		Siegfried Heroic	A call (often horn) with three upward steps and a tail. Can be confused with Curse [11]
[21]		Ecstasy	The sheer beauty of this phrase makes it impossible to miss
	[i]	Sleep	Semitones poncing around usually downwards (the first time they squirm)
[22]		Trance	A smooth downward phrase of five notes. Repeated over and over

Siegfried

[23]		Fafner	Grunting, sometimes squirming, tubas
[24]		Horn I	The daddy of them all. A horn call that winds about and can go on almost for ever
	[j]	Longing	Strings – sweet and slow
	[k]	Wanderer	Even-paced chords: semitones
	[l]	Blacksmith	Downward runs in the bass
	[m]	Muscle	Five-finger exercises taken from the schoolroom piano to the orchestra pit
[25]		Forest Murmurs	Shimmer shimmer
[26]		Birdie	Birdlike piping
	[n]	Heroic Love	A tender hiccup, soon smoothed out

| | [o] | Sigh | A downward sigh, then pretty |

Götterdämmerung

[27]		Horn II	Son of Horn I but regal
[28]		Brünnhilde	A sweet phrase – low note, twiddle, high note then three more
[29]		Gutrune	A gentle sighing woodwind phrase, soft and sweet
	[p]	Gibichun- gies	Brassy chords in a swoop up and down. Start and finish on the same note

Who's Who (and What's What)

GODS

Wotan Chief god, sometimes wanders on earth where he is known, unsurprisingly, as The Wanderer. Sponsor of Valhalla and has a finger in most pies but fades out in the last act of *Siegfried*.

Fricka His wife, goddess of marriage. Role model for Mary Whitehouse.

Freia Fricka's sister, goddess of youth and beauty, she guards the apples that give the gods everlasting life. Important only in *Rhinegold*.

Donner Son of Wotan and Fricka, god of thunder. Not important.

Froh Son of Wotan and Fricka, god on general duties. Even less important.

Erda Goddess of the Earth. An important god. Related to no one. Has had frequent sex with Wotan.

Brünnhilde Daughter of Wotan and Erda. Leads a flying squad of light cavalry under the command of Wotan.

Waltraute Brünnhilde's no. 2. Same parentage.

Seven Valkyries Rank and file illegits of Wotan and Erda.

MORE THAN HUMANS LESS THAN GODS

Siegmund Son of Wotan and a human unidentified female of the family Volsung.

Sieglinde Twin sister of Siegmund. Married to a human, a nasty piece of work named Hunding.

The Gods – A Family Tree

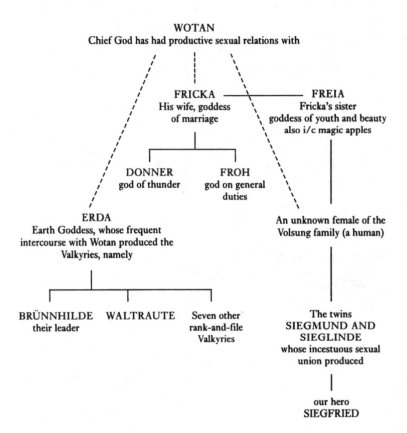

WOTAN
Chief God has had productive sexual relations with

FRICKA ———————— **FREIA**
His wife, goddess
of marriage

Fricka's sister
goddess of youth and beauty
also i/c magic apples

DONNER
god of thunder

FROH
god on general
duties

ERDA
Earth Goddess, whose frequent
intercourse with Wotan produced the
Valkyries, namely

An unknown female of the
Volsung family (a human)

BRÜNNHILDE
their leader

WALTRAUTE

Seven other
rank-and-file
Valkyries

The twins
**SIEGMUND AND
SIEGLINDE**
whose incestuous sexual
union produced

our hero
SIEGFRIED

Siegfried The son of the incestuous union between Siegmund
and Sieglinde. The hero of *The Ring*. Brünnhilde, whom he
loves, is his aunt.

Alberich Revolting headman of the Nibelungs, a race of dwarfs
who do appear to have some superhuman powers, though God
knows who gave it to them. A fascist. On one occasion turns
into a toad.

Mime Alberich's wimpish brother who fosters the young Siegfried. Not such strong supernatural powers here.

Loge The god of fire, but he's not accepted as a proper god.
Parentage uncertain.

Fasolt A giant with animal instincts who is killed while he is still a giant.

Fafner A giant who kills his brother Fasolt and turns into a dragon.

The three Rhinemaidens Mermaids with legs who live under the Rhine.

The three Norns Elderly females who spin the thread of time using very primitive technology.

A bird A creature with whom Siegfried can communicate after a dose of dragon's blood and who is helpful in that it has a good knowledge of the local topography.

Hagen Son of Grimhilde (see below) and the awful Alberich, therefore only just superhuman, indeed his behaviour marks him out to be subhuman rather than super.

HUMANS

Hunding Husband of Sieglinde. An ape.

Grimhilde (Grim Hilde) Wife of a senior Gibichung. Seduced by the dreaded Alberich resulting in Hagen (see above).

Gunther Legitimate Gibichung.

Gutrune Gunther's sister.

GROUPS

Nibelungs The race of dwarfs who live mainly below ground. Main occupations mining, smelting, being bullied by the ghastly Alberich.

Gibichungs Members of the disagreeable Gibich family. Land-owners on a big scale. Country seat on the banks of the Rhine which sometimes overflows.

Valkyries Wotan's flying squad of female equestrians. Main duty to carry corpses up to Wotan's HQ for heart transplants and subsequent resurrection into warriors.

THINGS

The Ring Whoever possesses it has the power to rule the world but it carries with it a curse put on it (unaccountably) by Alberich.

The Tarnhelm or **magicap** Headgear made by Mime to a formula known only to Alberich. Whoever wears it becomes invisible or can change his form (toad, snake, etc.)

Nothung Wotan's sword which was pulled out of an ash tree by Siegmund, shattered on Wotan's spear, put together again by Siegfried and used to kill the dragon and finally to shatter Wotan's spear. [Though why the shatter-power of the two weapons should have switched so decisively it is hard to know: Ed.]

The Ring: Death Toll

(Characters in order of disappearance)

Victim	Cause of Death	Person or Persons Responsible
Fasolt	Battered by a blunt instrument, perhaps his brother's fist	Fafner
Siegmund	Sword wound	Hunding
Hunding	Unknown	Wotan
Sieglinde	Died in childbirth	Natural causes, but surely the appropriate god could have saved her?
Fafner	Sword wound	Siegfried
Mime	Unprovoked attack: sword wound	Siegfried
Siegfried	Spear wound in the lumbar region	Hagen
Gunther	Sword wound	Hagen
Hagen	Death by drowning	Rhinemaidens
Brünnhilde	Burnt alive	Suicide while the balance of her mind was disturbed
Wotan Fricka Freia Donner Froh	Immolation	Loge

TOTAL 15

Rhinegold
(Das Rheingold)

Part I of *The Ring*

The one where we start under water, where a goddess is walled up in gold blocks, one giant kills another and a dwarf turns into a toad.

CAST

(see **Who's Who** page 136)

Wotan, chief of the gods	Bass–baritone
Fricka, his wife (goddess of family affairs)	Mezzo
Freia, her sister (goddess of youth and beauty)	Soprano
Donner, her brother (god of thunder and meteorology)	Bass–baritone
Froh, another brother (god on general duties)	Tenor
Loge, a demi-god appointed by the gods as their official diplomat, wheeler-dealer and agent on all matters concerning fire	Tenor
Woglinde ⎫	Soprano
Wellgunde ⎬ Rhinemaidens	Soprano
Flosshilde ⎭	Mezzo
Fasolt ⎫ giants	Bass–baritone
Fafner ⎭	Bass
Alberich, head Nibelung	Bass–baritone
Mime, his brother	Tenor
Erda, earth-mother, a goddess	Mezzo

1 act: running time 2 hrs 40 mins

STORY

Sc 1 Under the waters of the Rhine
In which the sun rises on the gold beneath the waters of the Rhine, Alberich renounces sex, nicks the gold and leaves the three Rhinemaidens in deep distress

We are submerged in mythical time and in the mystical waters of the Rhine and these three Rhinemaidens are swimming around like fishes wearing no diving gear whatever. Waga Woge? says Woglinde to Wellgunde. Yes, I'm coming replies Wellgunde. Sisters says Flosshilde watch over that thar gold girls: watch over it zealously.

A revolting dwarf Alberich appears through a crack in the Rhine: Hi sexy! he shouts. Who's that? ask the girls. From Greater Nibelheim says Alberich. Any chance of having sex with you girls? Dirty beast says Wellgunde. Let's teach him a lesson says Woglinde. Alberich slips over rocks scutters sneezes trying to get after the girls. The girls make provocative passes: dwarf-teasing. Alberich spurned.

The sun rises and lights up the Rhinegold. What's that stuff? asks Alberich. Ignorant pig say the girls it's the Rhinegold of course. It gives absolute power to anyone who swears to give up all forms of sexual satisfaction forever. Works best when formed into a ring. Great Scott I see I see says Alberich. OK I swear to give up all forms of sex forever. He seizes the gold. He runs/swims off with hollow laugh. The Rhinemaidens yell help! Stop thief! etc. No good.

Sc 2 A mountain top. The newly-built city of Valhalla visible in the clouds
In which Fricka gives Wotan a hard time for doing a foolish deal, the giants come to take away Freia and Loge suggests a way of saving the situation

Wakey wakey Wotan cries Fricka. Get off says Wotan I'm having a lovely dream [and why two gods should be sleeping rough on this mountain top I do not know: Ed.]. Wotan – says Fricka – it's about that Valhalla. Oh yes? says Wotan. Mad extravagance says she and Wotan what possessed you to offer my sister in payment to those building contractors? Crazy coot. I had to offer the giants something says he. If only you'd mentioned it I would soon have stopped you says she. Hell, woman, says he, it was you that egged me on. Only to get some fixed abode to make it more difficult for you to sleep around says she and anyway you stink. Hey – didn't I lose an eye for you when courting? says he. Anyway I'm not going to give Freia up to those giants. We depend on her for those magic apples that keep us young.

Enter Freia in panic. They're coming to take me away she cries those bleeding giants. Relax says Wotan relax. Seen Loge around? That tricky Dick? says Fricka. He's no good. When he did the deal with the giants says Wotan he promised me to get Freia out of it. I don't trust you Wotan I'm sending for my brothers says Freia: Heyup Donner: Heyup Froh.

Enter giants. Job completed boss they say. We want our pay.

What did you have in mind? asks Wotan. Don't come funny
Wotan they say: Freia of course that was the deal. Not Freia says
Wotan you clots that was just a joke. Joke was it? say the giants.
OK if you won't deliver we'll just take her now. Enter Froh and
Donner. Hands off our sister you big bullies they cry. Take it easy
boys no physical stuff says Wotan.

Enter Loge. Where have you bin? says Wotan kindly sort out this
mess right now. You got us into it. Now now now says Loge steady
on I negotiated this contract very very carefully. Clause 17B says
best endeavours will be used to find a substitute for Freia no more
no less. So what? says Wotan. We're taking Freia say the giants.
Loge you're a double-crossing bastard say Froh and Donner.

Wait wait wait says Loge I travelled the world to find a sex
substitute for these giants better than Freia and I found these
Rhinegirls who had lost their Rhinegold. This stuff gives absolute
power to any chappie who forswears sex and makes a ring out of
the gold. Nasty Albert Alberich the circus dwarf from down
under, swore the sex oath, nicked the gold, made a ring out of it
and now queens it over everyone down there. He might take over
up here soon too. By the way Wotan, I told the girls I'd ask you to
get it back for them.

I want that ring says Wotan. How can I get it? Nick it from
Albert says Loge. We like the sound of that gold say the giants:
Wotan – get us the gold and we'll give you back Freia meanwhile
she comes with us as a hostage. They trundle off. A fog falls. The
gods go grey. What's the matter? cries Loge. Radioactive fallout?
Ah no of course it's apple deficiency caused by carting off Freia
who made those magic medicated apples with monkey gland
effects. Oh Gawd Wotan look what you done to us now says
Fricka.

Hey Loge says Wotan on yer bike we'll go get that thar gold
from the horrible Alberich now. Which route down? says Loge the
water route or the sulphurous cleft? Sulphurous cleft says Wotan.
They go down a hole and it's intermezzo time.

Sc 3 The underground workshops of the Nibelungs
**In which we learn of the powers of the magicap and the
ring and Alberich is persuaded to turn himself into a
toad in which form he is apprehended**

Alberich drags on Mime by the ear. Has he met production
targets? Did the night shift meet its quota? He pulls his hair and

pinches him in little boy bully fashion. He grabs the tarncap from Mime. Says Abracadalberich: disappears. Where did you go? asks Mime. I'm still here says invisible Alberich whipping biting and kicking the poor sod. Ho ho. So you made the magicap so good now I can spy on you idle bastards at work. Exits.

Loge and Wotan creep out. What is this whimpering mess? asks Wotan finding Mime. Who done this to you? My brother done it says Mime he bosses everyone around something terrible since he got this ring. Before that we were just one big happy family of admittedly revolting dwarfs making toys for the Japanese market. Now it's bang bang bang all the time. Why did your brother beat the hell out of you? asks Loge. Well you see I make this invisibility headgear to his formula and when it's done I put it on to get invisible and escape him. So? says Loge. No good says Mime I forget the codeword. So he snatched it and disappeared on me. Who are you folks anyway? We have come to help you says Loge.

Alberich comes on shouting and screaming at the workforce something horrible. Whaddya want you two? he asks. We heard you are now the big man dictator of Nibelung County. We wished to pay our respects says Wotan. Cut all that crap says Alberich you two are up to no good. Steady on Alberich says Loge: who devised that new carbon ignition system for you? Also I am your second cousin once removed. You're just a tricky dicky says Alberich. Look at that pile of loot. Ever see anything like it? Never says Loge. Nothing to what it's going to be when my chaps really get extracting from them thar gold seams says Alberich, and once I reach fifty billion I will conquer the world I'll come up into your territory and I'll take over you lot. Having rejected sex I am all-powerful so look out you posh godly lot I'm on my way to conquer pillage and rape. [Rape? Howzat? Ed.]

Keep cool Wotan says Loge: now Alberich you've really done frightfully well starting with practically no capital and an unmotivated workforce but suppose some villain were to nick that ring? What then? Aha I've thought of that says Alberich I have this magic tarncap: when in danger I disappear. My my says Loge just think of that what an amazing thing I can't believe it. I'll show you says Alberich: turns into a cobra. Squirms. God you terrified me says Loge. Very clever Alberich says Wotan. I don't suppose you can do small ones as well as big ones says Loge. Sure thing says Alberich how small? Let's say a toad says Loge. Alberich becomes a toad. Wotan puts his foot on it. Alberich is captured and trussed up by Wotan and Loge.

Sc 4 The mountain top again
In which the ring and the magicap are traded for Freia, the giants fall out with fatal consequences and the gods move into new premises

Wotan and Loge come on with Alberich (no longer a toad) in chains. So we got you Alberich say Loge and Wotan now we want a pretty good ransom to let you go. What you got in mind? says Alberich. All that gold says Wotan. Gawd! says Alberich well I suppose even if you get the gold I can make a fresh lot by keeping the ring [a most injudicious speech: Ed.] OK you can have it. I will issue instructions to my chaps. Could you get me a portaloo. I'm embarrassed to be seen all chained up or maybe set me free now? Not until every penny is paid says Wotan. The nasty dwarfs bring on many tons of gold. OK now? says Alberich. Gimme the magicap says Loge. All right I suppose they can make me a duplicate says Alberich. OK now? Gimme the ring says Wotan. O Lord help us Mary Mother of God expletive deleted says Alberich not that. The ring says Wotan. No no no says Alberich you bastard you I do all the dirty work you pick up the ring no bother. No no no. The ring! says Wotan. He seizes it. Now I am the Lord of Creation says Wotan I gloat – hear me. Let the dwarf go. All right but before I go I will put the curse of death on any owner of the ring present or future says Alberich. [So who gave little Albert Alberich the power to curse? Ed.] He lays the curse. Goes.

Froh, Donner and Fricka are amongst us once again. Fafner and Fasolt are on their way says Loge. How did you get on? says Fricka. Mission accomplished says Loge. Hooray I could do with a few of those apples says Froh. The giants and Freia enter. Money's ready says Wotan. Here it is. Look Wotan I really fancy this girl says Fasolt. I couldn't leave unless the gold blocks conceal her entirely one glimpse and I'm back like a yo-yo. The junior gods and Loge brick up Freia in gold blocks. I can still see her left tit says Fafner coarsely. (Oh dear says soppy Fasolt such a sweet girl so sorry to lose her.) All the gods are upset.

What a disgraceful scene says Wotan why did I ever get those crazy giants on the job? Donner thunders. Shut up says Fafner. More gold! cry the giants I can still see it. There is no more gold says Loge. OK let's chuck on this here item says Fafner. My God that's the magicap gone says Loge. She's still visible! says Fafner: get that crack blocked or else. Stick that ring into it pronto. What!

says Wotan this ring!!! No. Negative. Not never. It's mine. It belongs to the Rhinemaidens anyway says Loge. Finders keepers says Wotan. Stuff it in that crack or we carry off Freia says Fasolt. Help! Help! cries Freia. Give it up Wotan says Fricka. Give it up says Froh give it up says Donner. Shan't says Wotan.

The earth opens and an elderly lady namely Erda the Earth Mother is elevated to a prime position centre stage. As you know Wotan she says, my family send you a fax every night with advice about future strategy but today this is a matter of such importance I bust out of the earth in person to tell you: *Leave that ring alone.* Most impressive says Wotan. Anything else? No says Erda: *Now mind what I say Wotan* (she sinks without trace).

OK giants says Wotan. Here's the ring. Take it. Fafner starts shovelling gold into a burlap bag. Hey steady says Fasolt leave some for me. Push off says Fafner if we'd kept Freia you would have been humping day and night so it's only fair that since it's gold not Freia I get more than you. Not fair says Fasolt. Is fair says Fafner leggo that ring. Shan't says Fasolt. OK then take that says Fafner: kills him. My God that curse is really hot stuff says Wotan. You did well Wotan says Loge. Let's get up to your Valhalla then says Fricka. Oh Lord I feel guilty says Wotan. Maybe I should have a Fernet branca or a session with my shrink.

Meanwhile Donner gets to work on the weather to produce:

1. a sultry haze
2. pale clouds
3. lightning
4. mist and drizzle
5. thunder

all pretty simple so far but now wait for it:

6. a rainbow pedestrian bridge to Valhalla.

The gods tramp up the bridge to Valhalla. Whassit mean 'Valhalla'? asks Fricka. Riddle-me-ree says Wotan. An odd bunch these gods says Loge; think they know everything. In fact they are doomed. I might burn them up myself one day if I have time.

Rhinemaidens strike up from the valley below. We want our gold back they sing we want our gold. Tell those Rhinemaidens to belt up says Wotan to Loge. Pack it in girls shouts Loge. You're not getting your gold. But they don't pack it in and go whingeing on until the curtain comes down.

LOOK OUT FOR

Sc 1

(For motto numbers see the Table on page 133.)

0   The prelude** takes us back to the beginning of   0
time even before the Rhine began to flow. But at
last above the famous long-held chord of E flat
we hear something stirring: soon the Rhine is on
the move and amongst its waters we hear the
Rhine motto (a smooth flow of water with eddies
going down and up jerkily [1]): now we are
engulfed and out of the watery arpeggios

4: *Weia! Waga!*   Woglinde's morning song floats up.* The girls   4
on sentry duty exchange tribal cries like sea-
lions. Rather nice.

Alberich and the girls. Although it goes on a bit,
this scene is full of watery magic. After the girls
have identified Alberich he scrambles over the
rocks slipping and sneezing (you hear this
mickey-moused in the score). He slavers with
lust: each of the girls in turn teases him by
singing sexily as they swim towards him and
then dart away at the last moment. Perhaps

7: *Heia Du holder!*   Wellgunde's love music is the nicest.** Then all   7
three together mock him in close harmony with
a good deal of ringing laughter – really rather an
unpleasant way to treat a person of restricted
growth and not at all politically correct.

The sun rises on the Rhinegold. This is a big
event and perhaps the finest moment in the
opera. First we hear lazy horn arpeggios floating
around with water susurrating above. This is the
Gold motto and as the first rays of the sun strike
the gold we hear it more powerfully (a bugle call
that flies upwards and stops, here played on a
trumpet [2]). The girls sing a hymn to this

15: *Heiajaheia!*   morning miracle*** with a lot of Heijaho Heia   15
stuff in it, then the Rhinegold motto [3]: one
long note – Rhine – down to the adjacent note –
gold! – shorter. (There has been quite a lot of it
around already but not so you would notice
much.)

17: *Des Goldes Schmuck*

Now the girls tell Alberich the tale:** 17

1. The gold is all-powerful if forged into a ring (the Ring motto [4] – woozy chords rotating around in a vague way – hard to pick up here but no sweat, there will be lots of it shortly).

2. But to make it work you've got to give up sex (Rejection motto [a] – a slow yearning sort of thing hanging on to an early high note – Easy).

20: *Der Welt Erbe*

Alberich does it.* No more sex he swears. High 20 drama. To a great scoop on the horns he seizes the gold and exits with hollow laughter (much hollower in the recording studio than on stage). The girls go frantic. And so they should for they have really messed it up.

24

The linking intermezzo** between deepest 24 Rhine and highest mountain top plays over two pretty important mottos: firstly the Ring [4] (already heard) – here it's clearest on the horns that move about in thirds – and Valhalla [5], pompous brass going down then up (over a harp): very civic. (It's related to the Ring motto.)

Sc 2

After some early morning bickering between Wotan and Fricka (Wotan in trouble for the mad extravagance of Valhalla and the idiocy of promising Freia in payment), Freia herself

33: *Hilf mir, Schwester!*

comes on the scene in panic.* The giants are 33 coming to get her! Quite a lot of the Stress motto [b] – jerky downward steps. Wotan tries to calm her: but what is this we hear? The coarse, brutal motto of the giants [6] – BRRM-TI-TA-TA (sometimes without the last TA), a scoop up and the following notes hammered out in unison – unmistakable. This booms out as Fasolt and Fafner come on. Now there is a

35: *Sanft schloss Schlaf dein Augen*

parley,* musically rewarding but not much cop 35 for Wotan. Although the giants' utterances – really quite melodious – are quite at odds with their motto, they are tough guys. We done a good job for you boss, says Fasolt, now we want Freia. Without those apples she manufactures

you will all die Ho Ho says Fafner. Apple motto
[c] – rather nice, slow horns with triplets
towards the end.

42: *Zu mir, Freia*   But the marines, in the shape of Froh and
Donner, are coming.* Wotan tells the boys not   42
to get rough – Spear motto [7] – downward
scale that could go on for ever, we've had it
before as punctuation but now it's punched out
boldly by the trombones and incidentally
Wotan's spear symbolizes about a dozen things
including power, authority, doing deals, his
problems, his inhibitions (and probably his
thoughts on Islamic Fundamentalism too). Just
behind Froh and Donner, Loge – motto [8] –
flickering semitones in the strings, and more. A
sort of motto grouping which hangs together.
Always easy to spot. So now we are into a
dramatic patch, Wagner in his forceful driving
mood: no longueurs.

After Loge, in true shyster fashion, has
disclaimed liability for the Freia/Valhalla deal
the giants begin to come the heavy and demand
their rights. This leads to a lengthy debate:

48: *Umsonst sucht'*   1. Loge tells the tale.** He looked all over   48
ich   the world for something the giants would like
better than sex and by chance lighted on the
story of the ring. A piece that begins as
recitatif, is then interrupted by the orchestra
and continues in something more like an aria,
ending with lots of Gold [2] and Rhinegold [3].
Everyone muses rather quietly for some time.

56: *Den Ring muss*   2. I must have that ring says Wotan.* How to   56
ich haben!   get it? Steal it says Loge in a shout. We would
consider a barter deal say the giants – the ring in
exchange for Freia. Not likely says Wotan. Very
good say the giants and trundle off dragging
Freia with them. Lots of Giants [6] around.
Vigorous and tuneful stuff but the confrontation
not so gigantic as one might have hoped.

61: *Was sinnt nun*   3. You gods don't look so well says Loge.*   61
Wotan so wild?   Oh my Lord, it must be for lack of Freia's
apples. Here the stage goes into a sort of grey

mist and so does the music. The Apple stuff at the start [c] is brisk enough but the gunpowder runs out of Loge's boots as he watches the gods wilt. Lots of Loge [8] about.

4. Let's get that thar gold cries Wotan who has more stamina in the face of apple deficiency than the others. Loge come with me.** They set off to one of Wagner's quite magical transformations (the intermezzo between Scene 2 and Scene 3). First we have lots of Loge [8] then a motto indicating Bad News (d) – a two-note cry of grief WOE-WA, twice – (we heard it first but only incidentally when Alberich failed to catch the Rhinemaidens); next a heavy dose of Gold [2] and then, with a carefully calculated shock, into Anvils in Action motto [9]*** – clinketty clinketty clinketty clinketty. For a little while, as the Nibelungs' production line becomes visible, we have nothing but clinking (from a battery of eighteen backstage anvils, if Wagner's wishes are respected) and no orchestra at all. By now we are well below the Rhine and the disgusting Nibelungs are all around us.

Alberich bullies Mime and extracts the Tarnhelm from him – Tarnhelm motto [10] – horns moving about stealthily, but not that much, rather close to each other. Loge and Wotan arrive and listen first to Mime being bullied by Alberich and then to Mime's sob story. All of this is pretty low voltage and too long, but there is one lively reminder of the Anvils* as Mime recalls the good old days before Alberich started his productivity campaign. Alas this scene is not a gripper. There is no way in which we can get emotionally involved in the spectacle of two singularly unpleasant dwarfs having a family quarrel. The music is as clever as ever but for a while we seem to be watching a puppet show. No star.

Alberich becomes power-mad, cracking his whip and screaming at his revolting gang of gold

66: Auf, Loge, hinab mit mir!

66

69

69

Sc 3

74: Sorglose Schmiede, schufen wir sonst woh!

74

78: *Hieher!*
Dorthin!

workers. He tells them to get moving again fast,* orders Mime back to his bench. He flaunts the ring – Ring motto [4]. Musically this scene is compulsive but nasty.

78

83: *Die in linder Lüfte*

Alberich boasts he will take over upstairs,* kick out the gods and rape their women. Recitatif-ish at first but he works himself up into a pretty fair frenzy. Lots of Valhalla [5] about.

83

89: *Riesen-Wurme winde sich ringelnd!*

Alberich's party piece:* first the transmogrification (Tarnhelm motto [10]) into the serpent (unison squirming in the tubas) and then the toad (toadish leaps in the woodwind). We have another crafty transformation intermezzo which plays around with a parade of mottos, including Anvils [9], Giants [6], Valhalla [5] and Loge [8]. Fascinating, but not as good as the earlier intermezzos.

89

Sc 4

99: *Wohlan, die Niblungen*

After an opening exchange to strangely ill-fitting light-hearted music the trussed Alberich agrees to trade in the gold so long as he keeps the ring [4] and summons his frightful horde to drag in the loot. This is an effective little episode* to a rumbling background of Anvils [9] and a good deal of Bad News [d] too.

99

106: *Bin ich nun frei?*

The business of getting the ring off Alberich is played in hushed tones, almost sotto voce. This is really effective, for when he lets loose his storm of hatred it has all the more power**. It culminates in the curse [11] sung twice at the beginning and end of this piece; the rhythm of DAMMIT-ALL rising to a high note – with a nasty low afterthought. It is Alberich's swansong: frightening in its animal-like ferocity.

106

112: *Wie liebliche Luft wieder uns weht*

On Freia's return we have a welcome patch of blue sky. Froh, a god of little consequence, gives vent to the first decent sentiments we have heard this last hour.* A sweet burst of melody based on Apples [c] – Nice to have you back, he says to Freia. And Fricka greets her politely too. This oasis of lyrical music disappears slowly as the vocally gentle giants

112

parley about screening Freia with gold blocks. This to a walking bass and a good deal of Giants [6] and Anvils [9].

Fasolt, the more decent giant, is going to miss
118: *Freia, die* Freia. He sings to her rather fetchingly.** Then   118
Schöne we have the debate about the next destination for the ring with music that is – considering the raging passions all around – surprisingly light and airy: Rhinegold [3], a little Anvils [9] and Ring [4]. This ends in the impasse between Wotan and the giants.

Erda's solemn warning. First we have the primaeval Earth motto [12] – an upward sweep in chords moving unevenly and here settling on the top note – all deep down on Wagner tubas
122: *Wie alles war* and then Erda's sombre and beautiful aria.**   122
The Earth motto [12] is around pretty well throughout as is a new motto, Destruct [13], forecasting the final downfall, or twilight of the gods, or Götterdämmerung, or whatever. It's the Earth motto [12] turned upside down. Dust to dust, earth to earth. (Nice one, Richard.)
128: *Zu mir,* Now things happen rather more quickly.**   128
Freia! Wotan gives up the ring: Spear [7]. The giants, no longer gentle, quarrel. One kills the other noisily with a lot of banging on the timps. Wotan marvels at the power of the curse (very loud rendering of Curse [11], twice on the trombones).

The biggest and best of all the transformation
134: *Schwüles* scenes.** Donner, who has not yet had much to   134
Gedünst schwebt do, swings his hammer and the violins shoot up like rockets to create a shimmering upper-air world – not unlike the opening water music. In the midst of this Rhine in the Sky a fanfare breaks in (which clever musicos have related to half a dozen of the earlier mottos, but let's just take it as a fanfare). Bang! Thunderclap! The Rainbow Bridge has sprung up. Well done Donner we say, and the orchestra shimmers and purrs in recognition of his good work. Now there is a sort of brief symphony – Valhalla [5] –

followed by Wotan taking possession of the premises. Another resounding trumpet fanfare which again we would be wise to take on its merits here because it really belongs to *Valkyrie*. And now it must be confessed that things hang about a bit. Why is it called Valhalla? asks Fricka. Dunno says Wotan. Tell you later. These gods, says Loge, think they've got it made. Poor silly things. I might burn them up sometime if the fancy takes me.

142: *Rheingold!*
Rheingold!

In the final scene** we hear the Rhinemaidens whingeing away in the valley, asking for their stolen gold back – Rhinegold [3] and Gold [2]. Wotan tells Loge to shush them. But they carry on and sing us out of the opera, moaning on about their terrible loss. Though less than climactic, this makes a satisfactory end to the great prologue and the orchestra winds things up by playing on magnificently beneath the Rhine.

142

NOTES and NEWS AND GOSSIP See **The Birth of** *The Ring* page 215

COMMENT See also **The Ring – A General Hello** page 123

The general effect of *Rhinegold* is far finer and bigger than would seem to be the case just by looking at the number of stars. Apart from the transformation scenes there aren't many big set pieces like the Ride of the Valkyries, Siegfried's Journey down the Rhine, or the anvil-splitting bit, and again, except for the intermezzos, there are not many big climactic moments. The prelude is stunning and after that the watery scenes swim along very nicely so long as they remain innocent and jolly, although they tend to wear out their welcome as each of the sportif ladies makes much the same pass at Alberich. But the sun striking the gold is a stupendous event and the Rhinemaidens' hymn that follows lifts our spirits to rejoice with them in this great hullabaloo over sunrise. Freia's music is a joy, the giants are melodious. But in Scene 2 there is nothing to make us sit up much until Loge appears. His report bringing us up to date with the Rhinegold situation, although too long, is a musical journey of some interest, as is the following parley with the giants. But perhaps the greatest moment of the opera comes when we are shot into the Nibelung workshops and are half deafened by the eighteen anvils, each of a size carefully specified by Wagner. This liveliest scene is followed by the most tedious, the power-mad Alberich bullying his brother. Even when Wotan and Loge arrive, the opening exchanges are less than thrilling and here in particular you feel you are looking at the rough cut of a film before it has been brought down to anything near its right length. Wagner is of course up against a problem that bugs all dramatists – a wily person must be given enough time to show that he is wily and persuasive (although we don't seem to mind too much when Don Giovanni talks Zerlina round in two minutes flat).

The sound pictures that Wagner conjures up in *Rhinegold* are vivid. To start from the beginning of time is a really good idea. We are in an empty world, static, asleep, waiting for something to happen. Then when the flow of the Rhine starts it is truly majestic, and the underwater music is as underwatery as music can be. When we recollect the taste of the spume and spray of the *Dutchman* we must see in Wagner a water composer extraordinary. Sunrises are pretty easy, but the early sun lighting up the gold makes this one special. The mountain-top music has no picture power whatever but the Valhalla references do. We can see the towers and turrets floating about up there amidst the high cirrus. The greatest sound-blow is of course the Nibelung workshop. The snake, toad and gold building-blocks don't come through visually despite Wagner's Disneyland attempts, but Donner's great trick of throwing the rainbow with the appropriate props of thunder, lightning and a crash in the wings works a treat. Strangely enough it is perhaps the dying fall of the opera that has strongest visual magic: the petulant Wotan striding up to his new home, the disaffected Loge lurking, the three Rhinemaidens singing plaintively in the valley below.

Rhinegold gains its power from its size, its length, its intensity and its sustained invention. When it flags it is not because the music is particularly weak but because that kind of music has gone on in the same mood for just a bit too long. But this is a small complaint in the face of this great feat of musical imagination, the curtain-raiser for the mighty saga that is now on the road and which casts its spell over everyone who isn't Wagner-immune. And bad luck on them we say because we are going to have a great time.

Valkyrie
(Die Walküre)

The one about a sword being pulled out of a tree, the ride of the Valkyries and a ring of fire being ignited around our heroine.

CAST (see **Who's Who** page 136)

Wotan, chief of the gods	Bass–baritone
Fricka, his wife (goddess of marriage)	Mezzo
Brünnhilde, Wotan's daughter, chief of the Valkyries	Soprano
Siegmund, Wotan's son	Tenor
Sieglinde, twin sister of Siegmund	Soprano
Hunding her husband	Bass
Eight **Valkyries**	Sopranos and contraltos

3 acts: running time 3 hrs 50 mins

STORY

Act I Interior of Hunding's house
Sc 1 In which Siegmund meets his twin sister to whom he is magnetically attracted

Time and place are both mythological but Siegmund's problems look real enough as he staggers in and slumps down in a heap by the fire. What's this then? says Sieglinde: it looks like a case for casualty. Water water cries Siegmund. You look scrumptious he says: who are you? This says Sieglinde is the Hunding residence and I am Mrs Hunding pray make yourself at home. Thanks says Siegmund by the way I am wounded. Had a bit of scrap. Here's a large scotch says she. Thanks says he that's better now I'd best be off. Why not stay on here? says she. OK thanks says he. Stays. By the way, he says, I call myself Dismal.

Sc 2 In which Siegmund meets his brother-in-law who says he will kill him

Enter Hunding. This guy Dismal dropped in in pretty poor nick says Sieglinde. Get him and me a meal right away woman says Hunding. You can stay here Dismal owing to the laws of holy hospitality. I lost myself getting here says Siegmund just where exactly am I? Is it somewhere near Basingstoke? This is the Hunding residence says Hunding and who pray are you?

Well I can't call myself Homebird nor Happy nor Smiler says Siegmund because I am prey to self-pity so Dismal is the name I go by. My father was a wolf and I had a twin sister. One day our home was vandalized my mother murdered and my sister abducted. After that my wolf father and I became free-range hunting wolves and I enrolled as a wolf cub. Then the same hooligans got my father. I found his wolfskin but his credit cards and watch had gone. After that I had a hard time wolfing on my own. It makes you very unpopular you know does wolfing. That's why I've called myself Dismal.

Who are you running away from now? asks Sieglinde. Another gang who tried to make a girl marry a bloke against her will. I went along and killed them all says Siegmund. Then their relatives arrived and quite unreasonably tried to kill me. That's why I'm not called Homebird Happy or Smiler. Great Scott! says Hunding I was one of that girl's clan. You killed two of my second cousins once removed: you can stay here tonight Dismal owing to the laws of holy hospitality but tomorrow I will kill you. Hey Sieglinde get my horlicks goodnight all. Exits. Also Sieglinde.

Sc 3 In which Siegmund gets his name, a sword and carries off his twin sister with conjugal intentions

Gosh thinks Siegmund that girl is a knockout. She gives me funny vibes. Apropos of nothing he says my dad promised me I would always find a sword somewhere around if I got into a fix. Like I am now. I see nothing. But yes – what's that shiny thing stuck in that there tree trunk?

Enter Sieglinde. I spiked his horlicks with soneryl so you can get away she says and there's an old sword you could use stuck in this tree if you can get it out. An old man stuck it in there years ago [Wotan of course: Ed.] and so far nobody's been able to shift it. Must be a knack. I'll take the sword and you too if I may says Siegmund you see I love you (sings loverly song about spring with heavy hints about brothers carrying off sisters). You look very like me says Sieglinde and you look very like me says Siegmund. You must be my sister. Golly! I don't like your name Dismal says Sieglinde nor is Smiler suitable nor any of that wolf stuff: I name you Winner which since this is a German opera will be translated as Siegmund.

OK says Siegmund and pulls the sword out. I will call this sword Nothung he cries [obsessed with names: Ed.] for nothing can be done without it and now nothing remains but to carry you off my twin sister and make you my bride. OK she says. Let's go.

Act II A wild rocky mountain ridge
Sc 1 In which Wotan is worsted by his wife in a marital disagreement

Wotan and Brünnhilde are on this mountain top together and he says to her get down there right away Brünnhilde and see that Siegmund wins against Hunding in this fight that's billed for 1600 hours. Oho says Brünnhilde better wait until you've had a word with the wife and she's on her way now.

Enter Fricka furious in a sheepcart. What's this Wotan are you on the side of adultery and incest? Steady on old girl says he love is love And as minister responsible for marriage I must insist that you stop favouring those bloody wolf cubs of yours says she and what about you anyway sleeping around in the most brazen fashion embarrassing the hell out of me. Listen woman says he in this crisis we have over the ring I need a hero to return the blasted thing to those Rhinemaidens. I need Siegmund. And trample underfoot the sacred laws of marriage? says she. I demand you withdraw magic from that Nothung sword and let Hunding kill the adulterous lecherous incestuous – OK OK OK says Wotan you win. No magic protection of any kind – you swear? says Fricka. I swear says Wotan. Good says Fricka.

Sc 2 In which Wotan unburdens himself of a great deal of the plot of *The Ring* to his daughter Brünnhilde

How'd it go? asks Brünnhilde. Badly says Wotan. It's the pits. I'm knackered. Fricka has done for me. How come? asks she. Well let me tell you all says he. He embarks on a lengthy narration from which the following are the main points:

1. I won the world by making some pretty dodgy deals with certain doubtful operators. Loge was of course a bad influence. And all the time I longed for love.

2. That Valhalla business stank a bit. I eventually paid off those

tiresome giants with the gold I nicked from Albert Alberich and he put this curse on the ring he had made from the gold.

3. Erda told me to get it back to the Rhinemaidens but didn't tell me how to do it.

4. This bothered me so I went down below the earth and had a good deal of sexual intercourse with Erda resulting in you and your eight Valkyrie sisters.

5. The purpose of all this begetting was to produce an elite corps of female cavalry to haul up the corpses of dead warriors to Valhalla where they would be revived and retrained as stormtroopers to defend my HQ.

6. All this went pretty well but now I'm in a panic lest Albert Alberich gets the ring back from Fafner [Fafner now a dragon: Ed.] and takes over all my corporate affairs.

7. I can't attack Fafner because the deal I did with him specifically excludes aggression.

8. So I need a hero who is a free agent not my son not a part of my establishment not created by me not in any way complicit to get the ring back. Bugger it! How do I do that?

OK I get your problem says Brünnhilde [more than most of us can manage: Ed.] how about that young wolfperson Siegmund? I wolfed along with him as a kid says Wotan and that Nothung sword has some of my stainless steel magic on it. But he's my son and not a free agent. Fricka rumbled that blast her.

Will you let Siegmund be killed then? asks Brünnhilde. It's all hopeless says Wotan. It's the curse of Alberich. Erda said a son of his would smash me up and now I hear a dwarf has made a woman pregnant. He's the one that will get me. It's all simply terrible (he bombs out). Pull yourself together Wotan says Brünnhilde *what do you want me to do*? Don't protect Siegmund says Wotan. Fricka has won. Shame on you cries Brünnhilde. I won't do it. You mutinous bitch you'll do what you're told says he. I've never seen you chicken out before says she. But OK I'll do what you say.

Sc 3 In which the runaways pause for a moment to allow Sieglinde to panic about pursuit by dogs

Hey! Steady! Not so fast stop! says Siegmund to Sieglinde we're both knackered. You must leave me my love says Sieglinde for I am guilty guilty guilty I made love to my brother whilst married to Hunding. Never mind I'll kill him shortly with this Nothung sword says Siegmund. No sweat. Listen! That's the baying of his hounds says Sieglinde (going a bit potty) they'll tear your flesh to ribbons. Faints.

Sc 4 In which Brünnhilde tries her best to obey her father's disgraceful instructions but is overcome by her noble nature

Look at me Siegmund says Brünnhilde I want you to follow me to Valhalla please. Will I meet my wolffather there? asks Siegmund. You will meet your wolffather says she. Who else? asks he. A lot of dead soldiers she says officers of course now revived and retrained as stormtroopers. Any girl guides? he asks. Several girlguide troops says she. Can I bring along my sister and wife same person? asks he. Negative she says. Then I won't go says he. If you don't go that Hunding will kill you says she. Faugh! says he – that ape? My magic Nothung sword will soon polish him off. I've got news for you says Brünnhilde Wotan has de-magicked that sword. The treacherous sod says Siegmund, OK I'll fight, die and go to hell rather than oblige him by trundling up to this Valhalla place. At least let me look after your wife says she. If I'm going to die I'll kill her first says he. Madman she says think of the babby. [Sieglinde now pregnant: Ed.] My mind is made up says he: we will both die. Siegmund she says you're wonderful! I can't resist your chutzpah. I will re-magic the sword and you will kill Hunding and to hell with Wotan.

Sc 5 In which Siegmund expects to kill Hunding with his magic sword but is killed himself owing to Wotan's intervention and Hunding also drops dead from shock

Siegmund watches over Sieglinde in a deep sleep. She is having a terrible dream. Save me Siegmund! she cries just as the dreaded Hunding appears. Hey Dismal come out and fight he shouts. You think I'm still unarmed or something? says Siegmund I got this sword from out your ash tree boy: watch out. Stop it you two, kill me first before you kill each other says Sieglinde. (They pay no attention.) Attaboy Siegmund says Brünnhilde. Kill! Kill! Kill! Wotan materializes and holds out his spear which shatters Nothung. Hunding attacks. Siegmund falls down dead. OK Hunding says Wotan run off to Fricka and tell her what a good boy am I. But Hunding also falls down dead. [Why? Ed.] Brünnhilde will pay for this says Wotan, snarling.

Act III A mountain top
Sc 1 In which Brünnhilde returns to barracks with Sieglinde across her saddle and a council of war discusses plans for her escape

The Valkyries are at their exercise: a vigorous form of airborne dressage combined with the transportation of dead bodies. Hoyoyoho! cries one. Heiaha! replies another. I gotta nice dead second lieutenant here cries a third. I got the tank captain that killed him cries a fourth. So it's all go with plenty of innocent girlish fun and laughter in Valkyriland plus a lot of horsey talk with sly jokes about mares and stallions. Hey shouts Helmetwig looking up from her pocket calculator, there's only eight of us. Should be nine. Brünnhilde's missing. Better wait for the captain says Walltrout.

But who is this they spy? Why it's Brünnhilde galloping split-arse with a female across her pommel. She arrives. Get up there and watch out for Wotan he's after me she yells. What's the matter? they all cry. I got in there to protect Siegmund in a fight, she gasps, against Wotan's instructions: he turned up and caught me at it. Siegmund was killed this here female is his wife. Wotan's not far behind.

My God! Defying the boss! You're in real trouble Brünnhilde! they all say. Don't worry about me please says Sieglinde just kill me quietly and I'd really much prefer that. But what about the babby? asks Brünnhilde have you the right to deprive a half-human embryo of life? O Lord I hadn't thought of that says Sieglinde please save me. Right you slip off on your own says Brünnhilde and mind the dragon on the left and the nasty thick forest on the right. And by the way I'd keep these broken bits of Siegmund's sword. Could be useful. Thanks a lot B you're really kind says Sieglinde. Exits. Wotan's coming yells a Valk. Hide me girls! shouts Brünnhilde.

Sc 2 In which the Valkyries fail to protect Brünnhilde from Wotan's wrath and he pronounces a terrible punishment

Where's Brünnhilde? asks Wotan. Stop messing about I know she's here. Cool it Wotan they cry. She's here sure enough but calm down a bit please before you see her. She's for it girls I tell you says Wotan she'll be chucked out of Valhalla without a penny to her name and without a roof to her mouth. D'ye hear me

Brünnhilde? Yes I do father says Brünnhilde appearing quietly. This hurts me more than it hurts you says Wotan: you're cashiered from the service. You're out. You're finished. You're done.

What exactly does that mean? asks Brünnhilde. Well banished from Valhalla for a start says Wotan, no more dragging up corpses no more serving the drinks no more family fun. How awful! cry the Valkyries poor Brünnhilde! And I will put you to sleep on this mountain top and – wait for it – whatever fellow finds you first and wakes you up will take you for wife and you will skivvy for him in some peasant's hut for the rest of your life. Got it? Hey Wotan! Steady on! Be reasonable! Please! say the Valkyries. Get off you lot says Wotan (they get off).

Sc 3 In which Brünnhilde makes a powerful case in defence of her conduct leading Wotan to decide to reduce her sentence in such a manner as to ensure that her future consort will at least be a hero

So was it so terrible what I did? asks Brünnhilde. I only did what you really wanted to do yourself. You wanted to stand by Siegmund. It was only after that terrible Fricka had argued you into a trance that you caved in. I did you a favour. And another thing when I saw Siegmund was such a dreamboat and so feisty a fighter I knew I couldn't let him down. So that's it says Wotan you see this guy about to be killed and you disobey me because he's cute. I had a hard time I will tell you in reaching that decision – I didn't like it at all – so what do you do? Jump in there with a light laugh and do it your way.

I couldn't believe my ears when you gave those orders says Brünnhilde. Not like my Dad. Not worthy of you. Nonsense says Wotan you just fell for that guy. Look father if this sleep business is on then OK but I don't like the waking up bit. Suppose some wimp like William Hague were to find me? I come of a good family I have the DBE the DSO and Bar you made me an OM I am in fact a gallant honourable and very distinguished person. Can't you arrange things so that only a good class of man preferably brave would find me? You're asking too much and anyway I must be going says Wotan.

Dad how can you do this to your little girl? says Brünnhilde. Please please Dad throw a ring of fire around me so that whoever it is that gets through must have nerve and may even be Mr Right. OK good point I'll do it says Wotan and I'm really sorry to have to say goodbye to you my darling girl. Loge! Come here. A ring of fire round this lady at once please. (A ring of fire springs up.) Curtain.

LOOK OUT FOR

MINUTES FROM START

Act I Sc 1

0

0

(For motto numbers see the Table on page 133)

The prelude* is stormy, indeed a storm, with the middle strings buzzing on one note whilst the lower strings range up and down restlessly. They repeat a figure based on Spear [7] over and over. This builds up until the brass give out the cue for thunder (the same as Donner used, to get thunder at the end of *Rhinegold*: unlisted) and the timps bang out the thunderclap. Now we have a bit of peace after the storm and the music softens and sweetens as the curtain goes up.

Love's Awakening. The hunted Siegmund staggers in and collapses to his motto – cellos moving purposefully in a firm short phrase (unlisted). Sieglinde fetches him water and as they make eye contact and get into each other's C.V.s we have some of the tenderest music imaginable.*** In particular there are short orchestral passages amidst the action which speak softly of their sudden strange mutual attraction using mainly two mottos, the first Sieglinde's very own – a bass line going down followed by chords going up [e] – and the motto for their mutual love, Lovers, a long romantic smooth sweet melody [f] heard first on a solo cello when Siegmund is brought the water (we will hear a lot of this one). Until Siegmund gets active about leaving, the whole of this scene is played in a dreamy cocoon of romantic music, much of which is woven by the woodwind.

4: *Ein fremder Mann?*

4

Act I Sc 2

But hark! What is that we hear? Hunding the hunter with his huntsman motto (a brassy hunting fanfare – unlisted). But, alas, when he enters the temperature drops and we are into a patch of quasi-recitatif as Hunding quizzes Siegmund – quite a lot of Hunding – and then we have Siegmund's dreary account of his early life – three long instalments, none of them by any means thrilling, but some lovely references to the Lovers motto [f] poked into the chinks in this sombre tale. The last bout of autobiography is the best,* when Siegmund describes a second massacre largely conducted by himself. He ends up with a rather ghastly burst of self-pity: now, he says to Sieglinde, you know why I'm not called Smiler. This to a Dismal Desmond of a motto – Self-Pity [g], a slow item climbing upwards ending in an unusual harmony. Almost immediately after this we first hear the noble Volsung theme – a majestic melody with dotted rhythms [h].

29: *Ein trauriges Kind*

29

Hunding's challenge to Siegfried is surprisingly gentlemanly. It is followed by a lot of business onstage as Sieglinde goes to prepare Hunding's spiked nightcap. This has a gentle but portentous orchestral accompaniment* (Sieglinde [e] but only the last part) ending in a prospective burst of the Sword motto (trumpet octave and arpeggio [14] – unmistakable, shining bright, first heard at the very end of *Rhinegold*).

35

35

Act I Sc 3

Now for something more considerable. A fine lyrical soliloquy** from Siegmund. He remembers his father promised him a sword (a lot of Sword [14]) and this is mingled with excitement about Sieglinde – Lovers [f].

39: *Ein Schwert verhiess mir der Vater*

39

An equally good reply from Sieglinde.* She tells the tale of how some mysterious old guy (Wotan of course, and we hear a bit of Valhalla [5]) stuck the sword into the tree. And towards the end we get a blessed break in the tempo,

45: *Der Männer Sippe*

45

which has been going at a slow canter for the last zillion bars. Suddenly it's fast. A lot of Sword [14] throughout, some of it pretty triumphant.

51: *Winterstürme wichen dem Wonnemond*

The Spring Song. Something that nearly amounts to a set-piece aria from Siegmund.** He sees a considerable affinity between love and springtime. This is a fresh lyrical inspiration (in triple time – what a nice change) and one feels it sprang from Wagner's pen with some relief after the workshop labours of the earlier pages. We are in the same territory as Walter's 'Am Stillen Herd' in *Meistersinger*. Virile, heroic, and very very romantic.

54: *Du bist der Lenz*

The last part of Act I consists of a rather wonderful duet,** though true to Wagnerian principles the two duettists do not sing together but turn and turn about. It is an impassioned and freely written piece gaining in intensity as it goes along and taking aboard the dislodgement of the sword Nothung in its stride. Siegmund and Sieglinde are brother and sister – so what? Love is stronger than the taboos of consanguinity, much much stronger, if this cataract of passion is admissible evidence. Valhalla [5] crops up when Wotan is mentioned and during the actual sword-pulling bit, as well as the Sword [14] and Rejection (a), we have a new motto, Nothung (it means the sword is needful or needed), consisting of a slow downward octave twice, sung by Siegmund to 'Nothung, Nothung!' plus a tailpiece [15].

Act II Sc 1

0

The prelude starts with the Sword [14] and Lovers (f) echoing around all over the place. Then what is this? Do we hear the sword beginning to turn into a Valkyrie? Perhaps a little but then Ta-tum-titi-ta-ra and the horses begin to run. This is the Valkyrie motto: rocking-horse rhythm rolled out by the trombones [16]; unmistakable. Hojotoho!* The great war-cry of Wotan's female warriors first sung by Brünnhilde herself (War-Cry, a ferocious inverted

4: *Hojotoho*

yodel [17] often followed by a trill and a peal of laughter). Brünnhilde warns Wotan that there will be trouble with the wife. There is trouble, sure enough. Wotan and Fricka embark on a twenty-minute argument, much of it dry and recitatif-ish but with some appealing passages. The course of events is roughly as follows:

1. After the opening formalities Fricka says it's quite disgraceful about these Volsungs (see **Who's Who** page 136): adultery and incest, what next? I don't consider marriage without love a binding contract says Wotan – some Spear [7]. Quite appalling says Fricka. All the above to pretty ornery run-along Wagner.

9: *Heut hast du's erlebt!*

2. Love will always find a way says Wotan. So let these two be. Rather nice references to Siegmund's Spring Song.*   9

3. Fricka gives him a real earful. You're going to pot, Wotan, she says. And just look at the record of your own adulteries. The second part

11: *O, was klag' ich um Ehe und Eid*

of this outburst* shakes off all mottos and takes wing into free writing. It runs along ferociously and grabs the attention.   11

4. The argument now becomes metaphysical (when is a hero not a hero) and the music less interesting. A good deal of the Sword [14].

5. Fricka is winning. Well what do you want? asks Wotan. No more protection of Siegmund says Fricka. OK says Wotan to a new and insistent motto – Frustration: starts with a buzz, like an angry bee, then fades away [18]. So Nothung will lose its power (lots of Sword [14]). Brünnhilde yodels offstage (War-Cry [17]). Collapse of Wotan, game set and match to Fricka, who celebrates her victory with a calm and

23: Deiner ew'gen Gattin

dignified request** that Wotan goes on oath to keep his word. He does so. We hear Spear [7], but it is broken up, also Curse [11]. A thoroughly eventful and musically satisfactory ending to the long, long debate.   23

Act II Sc 2

26: *O heilige Schmach!*

Wotan bombs out.* He explodes with anger, 26 shame, guilt, misery, etc. Lots of Frustration [18], and an upside-down Sword or two [14]. Lively and dramatic.

Wotan on the couch. An extended self-analysis taking in a lot of his life and history. This dismal monologue addressed to poor Brünnhilde runs for some fifteen minutes in a dry sort of quasi-recitatif, almost parlando, with little help from the music. This is nondescript stuff, except for a generous sprinkling of mottos which pop out like cuckoos from clocks, mickey-mousing punctually with Wotan's thought processes and including Frustration [18], the Ring [4], Valkyrie [16], Valhalla [5], Sword [14], Curse [11], Earth [12] and a new one, an amalgam of Earth [12] and Frustration [18] (unlisted). Things do perk up a bit when Wotan works himself into a fury over Alberich's role in the

44: *Und für das Ende*

ring saga,* and when, after that, Brünnhilde 44 brings him to the point, asking him Well, what now? The final exchanges have real feeling and we are left with something of the same sense of desolation as are Wotan and the mutinous Brünnhilde.

Act II Sc 3

50

There is a short orchestral prelude* before 50 Siegmund and Sieglinde arrive on this popular mountain top. It is based on Lovers [f] and you could be excused for not noticing this. But love in any form is a relief from a gloomy Wotan.

52: *Raste nun hier*

With the Siegmund/Sieglinde duet* we are 52 back in the land of the lyrical Wagner although all is by no means sunshine and sea air. Sieglinde is running away in panic. Siegmund tries to stop her – lots of Lovers [f]. I'm your brother, husband, companion, minder, etc., etc., he cries, with no sign of breathlessness. I'm guilty, guilty, she replies in sweeping rushing phrases. Don't worry, I'll deal with Hunding says he: Nothung will see him off nicely –

Sword [14] – and the whole musical texture stiffens. No! No! she screams, Hunding and his dogs are out after you now (loud hunting horns, real or imagined). She faints into an orchestral trance which dies away, but it takes an unconscionable time a-dying.

Act II Sc 4

The encounter between Brünnhilde and Siegmund – a really good scene.

1. The Wagner tubas speak out with a new motto – Fate [19], a doomy three-noter – long – short (down) – long (up). It is sombre and sonorous and very pregnant. Brünnhilde accosts Siegmund:** she tells him of her mission. Enormously impressively paced, with the deep, deep tubas sounding Fate [19] and the brass choir putting in quite a lot of Valhalla [5] with just a whiff of Valkyrie [16] from time to time, plus references to Lovers [f]. This sounds like a bran tub but it isn't. The mottos fall into place in the context of the music's flow. There is plenty of air, plenty of room. Everything works wonderfully well.

64: *Siegmund! Sieh auf mich*   64

2. Siegmund's negation.** I won't go. Lots of Fate [19] (and Fate extended to four bars). The pace quickens. Brünnhilde comes the heavy: You've got to go. Siegmund is stoical: I won't go. This piece is lyrical and uninhibited.

71: *Zu ihnen folg ich dir nicht*   71

3. The argument.** The tempo speeds up, the volume grows, the number of notes per minute increases – there is a splendidly controlled accelerando and crescendo – or speed up and sound up – as the two parties get really dogged with each other. Although there are a few references – Lovers [f], Fate [19], the inevitable Sword [14] – and the tubas are still there in full voice, we are now into really great lyrical writing and it is thrilling.

76: *Der dir es schuf*   76

4. Brünnhilde converted.*** In agony and at the same time in ecstasy, she defies Wotan and tells Siegmund it's OK she will be on his side:

80: *Halt ein, Wälsung*   80

he will win. This wonderful outburst from Brünnhilde raises the hairs on the nape of the neck, and not a motto in sight (or if there is it does not notice).

Act II Sc 5

83: *Zauberfest bezähmt ein Schlaf*

88: *Wehwalt! Wehwalt!*

Siegmund and Sieglinde alone.* After the storm of Brünnhilde's departure we have the soft sweet music of the orchestral prelude that began Scene 3 with some of Fate [19] but more of the love music, Lovers [f], which runs under Siegmund's address to the sleeping/fainting Sieglinde. But suddenly – bang crash – he hypes himself up for battle, Sword [14]. He makes such a racket as to wake Sieglinde who is having a bad dream. This leads to musical turmoil as Hunding turns up blaring his horn all ready for the fight. He bleats bloodthirstily.* Action! A lot happens very quickly. Hunding and Siegmund square up for battle in rather a muffled manner except for the Sword [14] shining out clearly. Kill me first! shrieks Sieglinde.* Get after him with Nothung! yells Brünnhilde – Sword [14] again and Valkyrie [16]. Watch me do the spear trick! says Wotan – Spear [7]. He does the spear trick: Siegmund falls dead (BONK!) – Bad News [d] followed by Volsung [h] and Fate [19]. Jump on my horse love, says Brünnhilde to Sieglinde – Valkyrie [16]. Now everything stops as slow trombones give the scene some gravitas. Then (CRASH! POW!) Hunding drops dead (cause of death unknown) and we are into a furious endpiece; Wotan very cross with Brünnhilde – Frustration [18] – and then a noisy orchestral finish. Rousing stuff, but this finale lacks the expert pacing of the great Siegmund/ Brünnhilde scene that has gone before.

83

88

Act III Sc 1

0

The Ride of the Valkyries.*** As famous as any musical ride in history. We start off orchestrally with only reasonably light forces engaged. After the opening trill (wonderfully exciting), we have both Valkyrie [16] and soon, as the girls join in,

0

War-Cry [17] as well. The Valkyrie tune drives along its course relentlessly until it lets up to allow the girls to have a little gossip about their horseys. But then BINGO and we're off again with greater force than ever and some nice girlish laughter (a pendant to War-Cry [17]) until we get to BANG! WHAM! the final rendering of the ride with all the massed fire-power of the brass section pounding out the tune in unison. A really big noise, and very satisfactory. Now we have some more stable-yard chatter and lots of laughter until we get to the count, when, after careful calculation, the girls find they are only eight, not nine. Brünn-hilde is missing.

7: *Nach dem Tann lenkt*

The Valkyries' meeting.** Brünnhilde rides in over some sweeping scales, deriving from Earth [12]; although they do a lot of work in this scene, they don't appear again. She explains herself and Sieglinde to the waiting Valks in breathless recitatif; all very fast. Oh Brünnhilde! say the Valks, disobey father Wotan? Yer on yer own lady. Good exciting stuff. In earlier days this section might have been called arioso, but it is arioso in fast forward, faster than any of the Italians – even Verdi – could have managed.

Brünnhilde plots Sieglinde's escape. After some discussion about escape routes and some plotty stuff updating us on Fafner's change of lifestyle (now a dragon), we reach one of the most lovely passages in the opera and one that decides the future course of the whole saga:

14: *Fort denn eile*

Brünnhilde tells Sieglinde to push off quick:** she is pregnant with Siegfried: she must take the fragments of Nothung for future reconstruction. This is Brünnhilde at her best – heroic, prophetic and at the same time a kind, decent woman. In this fine piece she sings an important new motto (doubled by horns), Siegfried Heroic: it starts with three upward steps, a

16: *O hehrstes Wunder!*

heroic call with a follow-through [20]. This leads to Sieglinde's reply,*** the most inspired

7

14

16

melody in the whole pantechnicon, Ecstasy [21]. Too long and too beautiful to be called a motto, it reappears again at the end of the whole *Ring* and its message in both places is to tell us what a glorious woman is Brünnhilde.

Act III Sc 2

Wotan's arrival, with his habit of never saying in ten bars what can be said in a hundred, heralds some boring stuff to come, and indeed his verdict on Brünnhilde paid out inch by inch in recitatif/arioso (Spear [7] prominent) is tedious, but the situation is saved by the Valks who panic on his arrival in the most pleasing fashion and who once again revive interest when they plead for mercy for Brünnhilde in eight-part counterpoint.** Their disappearance to strains of Valkyrie [16] and with the descending scales of laughter turned to tears, is also agreeable.

25: *Halt ein, o Vater!*

25

Act III Sc 3

So we enter the forty-minute marathon duet between Brünnhilde and Wotan that runs us through to the final curtain.

1. Brünnhilde pleads with Wotan: What I did was what you really wanted me to do. She starts with rather a lovely melody perhaps derived from Spear [7] – but then anything can be derived from anything else if put in enough gear-changes – which stays with her until the end of the round. Wotan's utterances tend to be pretty dry, but hers are sweet and persuasive and particularly when she tells Wotan that it was sympathy for Siegmund that compelled her to help him.* (Frustration [18], Valkyrie [16], Curse [11] and Spear [7] around early in this section.)

40: *Scheu und staunend stand ich in Scham*

40

2. The debate continues at much the same musical temperature, Wotan (dry recitatif-ish) saying he has renounced the Volsungs, Brünnhilde (more lyrical) saying they are great and that there is a new Volsung hero to be born (Siegfried Heroic [20]). No stars.

3. Now Wotan turns to the matter of Brünnhilde's punishment. He decrees sleep and whoever wakes her up – finders keepers. Reference to Fate [19]. A new motto, Sleep [i]: slow chords poncing around in semitones, usually downward, but on this first appearance they squirm. Brünnhilde wants her waker-up to show he's up to snuff and her passionate appeal** to Wotan pays off. Very fine, Wagner at his stormy imperious best – Siegfried Heroic [20], some Spear [7] and Valkyrie [16]. Brünnhilde is granted her ring of fire.

49: *Soll fesselnder Schlaf fest mich binden*   49

4. Wotan's farewell. At last he comes out of his corner singing like a loving father rather than a crusty Victorian paterfamilias. Goodbye my girl he says:** you shall have your fire. He warms to his work; only a warrior shall have you, he says (Siegfried Heroic [20]). Then as he puts his magic on Brünnhilde we move into a splendid orchestral intermezzo.*** A lovely motto here (we have had a hint of it before) – Trance [22]: soothing five-note downward phrase. It carries on under Wotan as he squares up for his last kiss. This is a different Wotan, quieter and quite touching (Rejection [a] and some of Sleep [i]). Now another intermezzo – mainly Trance [22].*** Peaceful, sleep-inducing and quite beautiful. Suddenly both Fate [19] and Spear [7] break in harshly and Loge music [8] starts spurting out all over the place as Wotan calls on him for fire. As the fire laps over the rock we have a last forecast of Siegfried's heroism [20] and as Loge [8] dissolves into Sleep [i] the opera glides away, trance-like [22], into the distance. But not without a reminder of Fate [19].

52: *Leb wohl, du kühnes, herrliches Kind*   52

55   55

66   66

NOTES and NEWS AND GOSSIP See **The Birth of *The Ring*** page 215

COMMENT See also **The Ring – A General Hello** page 123

The story of *Valkyrie*, if not exactly humdrum, is simple and straightforward. Man runs into hut, falls in love with long-lost twin sister. They elope. Gods disagree as to whether or not the man should be sponsored in duel with sister's husband, senior god withdraws sponsorship, man killed. Wife/sister, now pregnant, saved by junior god. Senior god punishes junior god by dumping her in a ring of fire to sleep until Mr Right comes along to wake her with a kiss. If the script had been kept down to the narrative and the digressions, in particular the metaphysical arguments, dropped, *Valkyrie* would have come out at something between two-and-a-half and three hours, instead of nearly four – about the same length as *Rhinegold*. The main hold-ups are Wotan's now-read-on stuff, which has an immense amount of retrospective detail explaining the whole saga of the ring, and also two lengthy debates, Wotan/Fricka on the nature, function and status of a hero and the Wotan/Brünnhilde debate about crime and punishment. We also have a shorter now-read-on from Siegmund himself in Act I. These digressions are a drag on the show because:

1. They hold up the forward thrust of the narrative.

2. No one can understand them without doing a lot of prep. Even German-speakers are unable to catch this sort of stuff when it's sung over an orchestra of a thousand, and surtitles can't properly cope with anything beyond fairly straightforward narrative and dialogue.

3. The actual subject matter is deeply boring. The ring saga told as a tale could be magic, but synopsized in a scrappy sort of flashback to justify Wotan's conduct, it is hardly a gripper. As for the arguments, they are legalistic if not donnish, a million miles away from the direct emotional clashes that were the stuff of Italian opera. We listen with impatience to clever points being made in slow time.

This is not to say that the music of the slow bits is boring too. It is true that Wotan's ramble through the past in Act II is musically tedious, but the two arguments are not. But even Wagner can't write consistently thrilling music for singers who are scoring debating points off each other and therefore in these sections the voltage drops and so does the listener's interest.

In the rest of the opera the music is always gripping and often quite wonderful. Wagner deploys his best romantic/mystical strain in the love music in the first scene (and in lots of later references), in the Spring Song and in the final duet. This is the music of sexual magnetism and also of the tearaway romantics, not unlike Walter's music in *Meistersinger*. The heroic music that is the most powerful in *The Ring* is the stuff written for the collective of the Valkyries which musters more force than ever Siegmund could drum up on his own. The Valkyries are quite wonderful in sound and concept, and their music has as much zing as any that has been written for the opera house. Pity the poor designer: how can he possibly match such majestic pictorial music?

On the softer side, the best scene in *Valkyrie*, both dramatically and musically, is Act II Scene 4, between Siegmund and Brünnhilde. The opening exchanges in this confrontation are marvellously impressive with Wagner's very own tubas doing exactly the work for which he had designed them, and then we have a slow build-up to the climax with mottos abounding yet adding to the rise and rise in the tension up to the final explosion. If only every page of the score had the forward drive and absolute command of pace as does this one, how happy we would be.

The other great scene in *Valkyrie* is the last. The forty-minute duet between Wotan and Brünnhilde is too slow and too long and does not really warm up until she makes her appeal for a more honourable sentence, but then it takes wing and carries us with it to the glorious end with fire lapping the stage and the five-note Trance motto repeated mesmerically over and over and over again, but not once too often.

There are two short items of pure joy in *Valkyrie*. The first is Sieglinde's farewell to Brünnhilde – 'O hehrstes Wunder!'. Suddenly Wagner pulls out of the bag a phrase more striking and more beautiful than anything else in the opera. It is one of those rare moments of musical elation that may occur only once in a month's listening (and Wagner uses this piece of magic only once again – at the very end of *Götterdämmerung*). The second is when the eight Valkyries beg Wotan not to be too rough with Brünnhilde. This is clever stuff – eight separate parts in counterpoint – and it sounds dense and tightly-knit, but it catches the ear and sticks in the mind, as great music should, whether it be clever or just good.

So there it is, *Valkyrie* sprawls, has its longueurs, its miracle patches, its scenes that are compulsive and scenes not so compulsive, also, of course, the Ride itself, but whatever your reservations and vexations with the opera may have been, if you are a fair listener you will acknowledge it as a work of genius, and you will leave the opera house or stow away your CDs marvelling that the human imagination could stretch to such a huge enterprise and should then, more or less, pull it off.

Siegfried

The one where Siegfried turns blacksmith and forges a sword with which he kills a dwarf and a dragon and then walks through fire to discover eternal love.

CAST (see **Who's Who** page 136)

The Wanderer, Wotan, chief of the gods, in disguise	Bass–baritone
Siegfried, a hero	Tenor
Mime, a dwarf	Tenor
Alberich, his brother, chief dwarf	Bass–baritone
Erda, Earth goddess	Contralto
Brünnhilde, chief Valkyrie, suspended from duty	Soprano
A bird	Soprano
Fafner, once a giant, now a dragon	Bass

3 acts: running time 4 hrs

STORY

Act 1 A cave in some rocks in a forest
Sc 1 In which Mime fails to piece together the magic sword Nothung and our hero learns the story of his early life

It seems I've been at this forging bit forever says Mime to himself and every time I produce a sword from these sodding fragments that bastard Siegfried smashes it up. In talkative mood Mime goes on to tell us:

   1. Siegfried is fearless

   2. Fafner is now a dragon and guards the Rhinegold in his cave (adjacent)

   3. Siegfried is very strong

   4. He plots to have Siegfried kill the dragon and get the gold for himself.

Enter Siegfried leading a bear. Why the hell do you keep bringing in bears? says Mime climbing up the scenery. I prefer their company to yours says Siegfried. Is the sword ready? Yip says Mime. Siegfried smashes it. Another dud he says. You're hopeless. Ungrateful boy says Mime: have some minestrone? Not your pigswill says Siegfried I ate an antelope in the forest. You are horrible to me Siegfried says Mime and yet I did all the work of

mother nurse tutor P.T. instructor skivvy chef barber religious
adviser and you hate me. Because you are a revolting deformed
dwarf says Siegfried also because you smell. I can't think why I
come back here. Parental affection says Mime.

Nuts says Siegfried and talking of parents who was my mum?
There wasn't one says Mime. Parthenogenesis. Did it all myself.
Liar says Siegfried a pretty person like me couldn't have a toad
like you for one parent never mind both. He beats Mime up. Stop
it you're killing me screams Mime. Who were my parents? asks
Siegfried screwing Mime's neck. OK OK I'll tell you says Mime:
you see I came on this woman giving birth. Name? asks Siegfried.
Sieglinde says Mime.

Where is she? asks Siegfried. Dead says Mime she said if it's a
girl call her Mary Lou if a boy Siegfried. Expired. Father? asks
Siegfried. Not known says Mime that's how I became your mother
nurse tutor. . . . Belt up says Siegfried any other material facts?
Your mum gave me these bits of your dad's sword says Mime. Get
moving you disgusting dwarf says Siegfried, make me a decent
sword and I'm off hunting and wish I could never see you again.
Exits. Dear dear says Mime. This is not how I had planned it at
all.

Sc 2 In which Wotan in disguise challenges Mime to a quiz game in which the stakes are high

How do? says Wotan strolling into Mime's cave. Get off says
Mime no travellers. But I am not a commercial says Wotan I am a
consultant. No consultants required says Mime: get out. Wotan
doesn't go. OK says Mime we'll play this game. Rules as follows: I
ask you three questions. You get 'em right you stay. You get 'em
wrong I kill you. OK? OK says Wotan.

Your starter for ten says Mime what kind of persons live under
the earth? Nibelungs says Wotan. Correct says Mime. No. 2: what
class of persons live on earth? The giants says Wotan. [No one
else? Ed.] OK No. 3 says Mime: who lives in heaven? The gods
says Wotan. OK you win says Mime. I won't kill you.

But now for the second leg says Wotan it's my turn. Go ahead
says Mime. Your starter says Wotan: what is the family Wotan
loves best and punishes most? The Volsungs says Mime. Good
enough says Wotan. What was the name of Siegmund's sword?
Nothung says Mime. OK says Wotan No. 3: who will weld
Nothung back into shape? Dunno says Mime. So I win the right to

kill you says Wotan. The correct answer is 'The man who never knew fear' and I hereby delegate to him whoever he may be the right to murder you in his own time. Cheerio. Exits (Mime wets his pants).

Sc 3 In which before our very eyes Siegfried forges an excellent sword and tests it upon a defective anvil

Mime is having a nightmare about the dragon. Siegfried wakes him. Is the sword ready? he asks. Napoo says Mime a man told me no one can do it except someone who never knew fear. Fear? says Siegfried whassat? Makes you wet your pants says Mime. I'll take you to visit the dragon. He should do the trick.

OK says Siegfried but let's make the sword first. You can't do it says Mime the instruction manual got burnt in the forge. Stuff that says Siegfried I'll do it somehow. He starts. Want some solder? asks Mime. No says Siegfried no patching up this time. A complete re-forge. By the way what's the sword called? Nothung says Mime. Nothing attempted nothing done says Siegfried. He forges on singing Ho Ho Ho quite a lot and hammering the sword on the anvil. Mime thinks (out loud) hey this guy doesn't know fear yet let's hope the dragon scares the hell out of him. If not he could be the one Wotan delegated to knock me off. He could pinch the treasure too. I'll poison him after he's killed the dragon, that's what.

Ho Ho Ho sings Siegfried forging on. He gives a running progress report. At last (Ho Ho Ho) the sword is finished and for some incomprehensible reason he strikes the anvil a mighty blow. The anvil splits in two (Ho Ho Ho).

Act II Deep in a forest
Sc 1 In which Wotan the Wanderer has a disagreeable encounter with Alberich outside the dragon's cave and nothing much happens

Alberich is watching over the dragon's cave to make sure no one else pinches the gold. Enter Wotan thinly disguised. Go away Wotan says Alberich you've already played one dirty trick on me: I don't want you stealing the gold a second time. Ho Ho wait till I get that ring Wotan and I'll fairly sort out you gods. I'll be the king of the castle I will. Anyway I know your tricks. All this stuff about an earth-born hero. Have you got one yet?

If you want to pick a fight says Wotan do it with Mime that nauseating brother of yours not with me. Did you know he was double-crossing you and will pinch the gold himself? And he was bringing a hero with him to do it? Why don't you tell the dragon he'll be killed unless he gives you the gold now? Fafner wakes up. Alberich puts the proposition. Be quiet *please* says Fafner lemme sleep. Well that was a no go says Wotan. Exits. I'll get you gods in the end says Alberich rather feebly.

Sc 2 In which Siegfried kills the dragon and gets good advice from a bird

Enter Mime and Siegfried. Is this where I learn about fear? asks Siegfried the simple soul. If you don't learn it here God knows where else says Mime. In there lives the most horrendous beast sabre-toothed lethal claws deadly tail saliva of vitriol urine of nitric acid breath of phosgene . . . . OK OK does it have a heart if so where? asks Siegfried. Usual place says Mime. Noted says Siegfried. I'll take a little nap by the stream says Mime you go ahead and kill that beast when you come out then wake me up. Exits.

Siegfried muses what a revolting little dwarf is Mime I'm so glad he was not my dad. Wonder what my mum was like (gets all soppy) I wonder if that bird could tell me (also crazy) maybe I could talk to it if I made similar sounds? (And ridiculous too.) He tries blowing on reeds and makes embarrassing noises. Tries his horn which he can play to about standard Grade IV. The bird is not impressed but the dragon wakes up. Stop making that bleeding noise he shouts can't a fellow sleep? I've come to learn fear also to kill you says Siegfried. Pshaw says the dragon I'll eat you for breakfast first. Will you indeed? says Siegfried and plunges sword into the dragon. Mother o'God says the dragon fancy being killed by a fresh-faced lad like you mark my words you'll suffer for this: what's your name? Volsung, Siegfried V. Volsung says Siegfried licking the dragon's blood off his fingers in a rather beastly fashion.

Hey Siegfried says the bird: a German composer called Wagner made that dragon's blood an enabler to the comprehension of ornithological linguistics – God knows why – so we can now talk to each other so long as you don't use long words and I'm telling you for starters that there's gold in that thar cave also the Tarnhelm magicap and the laser-ray ring that could make you

Superman Batman or whatever. Thanks says Siegfried be my Robin.

Sc 3 In which the two dwarfs quarrel, Siegfried avoids being poisoned, kills Mime and follows the bird in search of a lovely lady

Alberich slinks on also Mime. Keep your thieving fingers off my gold says Alberich. My gold says Mime. Mine says Alberich. Mine says Mime I made the tarncap and the ring you lost them. Anyway it belongs to the boy now says Alberich he won it. Let's split says Mime you take the ring I take the magicap. Not bloody likely says Alberich no deal. (Withdraws.)

Siegfried exits the cave carrying the ring and magicap. What the hell do I do with this stuff I don't know says Siegfried. Don't give it to those devious dwarfs says the bird. Did you learn fear? asks Mime. Don't think so says Siegfried. You need a drink says Mime: take this it will kill you. Whassat? says Siegfried. It's poisoned says Mime and for some reason which neither I nor anyone associated with this show can fathom I'm blurting out the truth all the time although I mean to conceal it. You think you're funny or something? says Siegfried. Cuts his head off. Pushes corpse into the cave. Drags the dead dragon across the mouth. Sits under tree. Pity poor lonely me he says no brothers no sisters mother dead father unknown – hey you bird could you please find me a mate?

I know just the girl says the bird but there's a slight disadvantage. What's that? asks Siegfried. She sleeps all the time says the bird also a permanent bushfire rages round her. Any hope for me? asks Siegfried. Only if you have never known fear says the bird. Snap! says Siegfried that's me never had a tremor. Would you kindly fly towards this lady at the pace of a rather slow marathon runner? Only too happy to oblige says the bird.

Act III The foot of a mountain
Sc 1 In which Wotan the Wanderer has a pretty unsuccessful interview with an old associate, namely Erda the earth mother

Wakey wakey Erda cries Wotan get your feet on the floor. Whosat? says Erda. It's me I'm an incognito VIP traveller says Wotan. Lemme be says Erda. If you want anything go to Norman's office it's full of Norms they're paid to give information. I'd rather have it from the boss if you don't mind says Wotan.

Go and ask my girl Brünnhilde says Erda: it may interest you to know that she's the result of my liaison with Wotan a distinguished god. She's in trouble says Wotan she went against her dad Wotan. He punished her by putting her to sleep in a bushfire. Who's that pig to punish anyone for being uppity? says Erda he's been getting above himself this last two million years. Excuse me I want to drop off again. Hey Erda wake up, your old lover Wotan's in trouble and he wants to know how to stop the end of the world. Whassat? says Erda kindly stop bothering me with foolish questions. She goes to sleep.

She's gone off says Wotan but I could tell her something namely that I'm not that much bothered about the end of the world any more for I'm going to duck out pretty soon and hand over to that young Volsung grandson of mine he's got his hands on the ring already. He's a good chap and will sort out that bastard Alberich good and proper. It would be nice too if he married his aunt Brünnhilde. Such a fine woman. Have a good sleep Erda.

Sc 2 In which Siegfried is extremely rude to his grandfather and breaks his spear

That bird goes too bloody fast I've lost it says Siegfried but here's an old man. Hey you have you seen a female asleep on a rock in a bushfire? he asks. What's all this? asks Wotan. Well you see there was this dwarf who got me to kill this dragon whose blood made it possible for me to understand birds so I asked one to bring me here which it did but I've lost it says Siegfried. How did you kill the dragon? asks Wotan. With a sword says Siegfried. Who made the sword? asks Wotan. I did says Siegfried. From what? asks Wotan. Splinters says Siegfried. What splinters? asks Wotan. Oh for Chrissake stop it you tiresome old bastard says Siegfried. Kindly show some respect for age says Wotan. The last guy who lectured me had his head cut off says Siegfried get out of my way. Shan't says Wotan. Lemme past says Siegfried. My spear will stop you says Wotan. Faugh! says Siegfried. He smashes Wotan's spear with Nothung. Walks by: arrives at a rockface which slowly starts to move downwards until we reach –

Sc 3 The mountain top
In which Siegfried walks through fire and learns about the female shape through waking up an extremely attractive female with whom he falls in love

What's that? says Siegfried passing through the fire unsinged, why it's a sleeping horse! And there's a sleeping fella. His armour looks a bit tight better cut it open. Somewhat riskily he uses Nothung as tin-opener and cuts a slit down the person's chest. Peers inside. Good Lord he says – Lord bless me – looking very carefully at the contours of the person's chest – well I'll be damned that ain't no fella. I've got a funny feeling all over and especially in my trousers – why I know what it must be – it's – it's a woman! How impressive! God I'm terrified! Scared rigid! I have learned fear at last! Doesn't she look just stunning?

Whassa time? What year is it? Who woke me? says Brünnhilde. I did. Me. I'm Siegfried says Siegfried. Thanks Siegfried says Brünnhilde I knew you before you were born when your mum was pregnant I was her best friend. Good to see you Siegfried I always thought my dad would make things work out right. You've got lovely lips says Siegfried. O Lord there's my old Sam Brown and my Smith & Wesson .310 says Brünnhilde now I no longer hold HM's commission I am no longer a royal I am just a mortal. Zut! How ornery!

This Siegfried looks a sexy fellow best not to get involved. I'm scared stiff of human sex having been for many centuries above that sort of thing. Brünnhilde I love you says Siegfried employing quite a lot of poetry. Actually I love you too says Brünnhilde weakening. They clinch. Rapture. Bliss. I'm on fire. I'm no longer afraid. Yours forever. Forever mine. You are sublime. You are lovely. You are just a pet they say to each other. They are in love. Curtain.

LOOK OUT FOR
MINUTES FROM START
Act I Sc 1

0

(For motto numbers see the Table on page 133)

The prelude* opens dark and very deep, first with a couple of bassoons soon joined by a double-bass tuba, a startling sound indeed. It moves upwards from the bowels of the earth, first giving some play to Frustration [18] and then, rather hesitantly, to Anvils [9], gaining

0

speed and strength all the time. So on to Bad News [d] on the cor anglais, Ring [4] and finally Sword [14] rings out loud and clear. Quite a story in sound and an effective curtain-raiser.

After a bit of solus forging and brooding by Mime – one new motto, Fafner (as dragon): four notes on grunting tubas [23] – we hear a hurried burst of Siegfried's Horn: a winding horn call, unmistakable [24] and he bounces in with a bear. The poor creature has no motto, something that must distress the Animal Rights fraternity. Siegfried tells Mime how he came by the bear in a fine lyrical burst,* Siegfried Heroic [20].

8: *Nach bessrem Gesellen*

Siegfried tells Mime he doesn't think much of him as a metal-worker and rejects Mime's offer of a nice roast beef breakfast. (A new version of the Anvil motto [9], Mime the tiresome, Mime the nanny: fidgety fiddles – unlisted.) Mime replies in a set-piece saga of pained self-pity* – I done everything for this lad and he spits in my eye. This is a particularly attention-catching patch in a scene that swims along at a good pace and melodiously.

12: *Als zullendes Kind*

Siegfried replies that he just can't stand Mime and then a tiny miracle. Wagner turns Mime's longing for affection into an orchestral phrase of melting beauty which for a moment stops the show in its tracks (Longing – strings sweet and slow [j]). Mime begs for love but Siegfried is more interested in the birds and the bees. He indulges in a brief wildlife rhapsody* (you can hear the birds fluting away) which has a fine careless rapture.

17: *Ei Mime, bist du so witzig*

When he asks about his parents (Siegfried Heroic [20]) Mime won't tell him until Siegfried gets physical (climax) and forces the story out of him (an unlisted motto of the Volsung family here in the woodwind, not to worry with it) and Longing [j] then in hushed tones Mime tells of his birth and Sieglinde's death – Siegfried Heroic [20] again. Persistent quizzing of Mime extracts from him the news of the fragments of

27: *Und diese Stücke*

Nothung and now we go into a fine flurry as the excited Siegfried tells Mime to get forging fast* (a lot of free writing). He goes and Mime sits dolefully at his anvil (sad version of Anvils motto [9]). 27

Act I Sc 2

31: *Heil dir, weiser Schmied!*

Wotan drops in to Mime's cave with a noble new motto – Wanderer (even-paced chords: semitones [k]). His stately greeting* is answered by Mime in a pert fashion and they parley on until the incomprehensible guessing game begins (Spear [7]). Wotan's answers are mickey-moused punctually by the motto for every item mentioned including Anvils [9], Giants [6], Fafner solus as dragon [23], Valhalla [5] and Spear [7] – this last very loud. Wotan keeps things on the boil all the way, but the one star at the head of the scene will have to do for all this riddle-me-ree stuff. 31

53: *Dreimal solltest du fragen*

Now it's Mime's turn and he runs through his catalogue of mottos until Wotan asks him the sixty-four thousand dollar question which he can't answer. Mime explodes into a frenzy and Wotan addresses him in a good final burst* of the sort of running arioso he has been dealing out for most of the scene. He tells Mime that: 53

　　1. Your head is in hock to the guy who does the remake of Nothung

　　2. And he will be a man who never knew fear. There is a good deal of Siegfried Heroic [20] around at this point.

Act I Sc 3

56: *Verfluchtes licht!*

Soon we have the rippling fire music of Loge [8] as Mime has some sort of brainstorm.* He also hallucinates that Fafner the dragon is breathing down his neck. Vivid. 56

60: *Sonderlich seltsam muss das sein!*

After Mime's rather feeble attempt to make Siegfried's flesh creep by goosing him with forest fears, Siegfried replies manfully* that he'd love to be scared but finds it frightfully difficult. This is a good burst of natural song which traffics mainly in three mottos – Trance 60

[22], quite a lot of this distorted at first but soon smoothed out, Siegfried Heroic [20], Loge [8] and then a lot more Trance [22].

Siegfried brushes Mime aside and in a scurry of excitement prepares the fragments of Nothung for the forge.* This is sung to, around and within a welter of sound in which the strings play around with Siegfried's Horn motto [24] in a dozen different ways.

65: *Her mit den Stücken*   65

Siegfried's forging song – a set piece.** Well, not all that set, for each strophe tends to drift off into highways and byways. But it is all one continuous piece of rolling anvil-hitting music fifteen minutes long with interjections by Mime and not a million miles away from Hans Sachs's Schusterlied in *Meistersinger*. But this is heavier metal with Nothung [15] and two new mottos: Siegfried Blacksmith [l]: rolling downward runs in the bass with some fancy trimming on top (octave leaps), this last so heavily used that it is almost hammered to pieces; and finally Siegfried's Muscle (m): a motto which comes in various forms, here a five-finger exercise played not on the piano but thumped out in the bass in octaves by all manner of instruments. This mighty outpouring ends noisily and in great triumph with Siegfried busting the anvil in half (Horn I [24]).

68: *Nothung! Nothung!*   68

Act II Sc 1

0

The prologue* growls and booms along its sluggish passage to curtain up. The bass tubas play basso profundo with that deep rasp that sends a frisson down the spine. We have the rhythm of Giants [6] (before Fafner's transformation) on the timps and besides Fafner's squirm [23], quite a lot of the Curse [11]. The long confrontation between Alberich and Wotan is not exactly musically dull, it just doesn't seem to be getting us anywhere. There are patches of quasi-recitatif but some arioso as well, some little climaxes and some big climaxes. They rake over old ground. They threaten. They finish up

0

7: *Zur Niedhöle fuhr ich bei Nacht*   7

exactly where they started. References to Wanderer [k], Curse [11], Spear [7] and for Wotan a little Frustration [18]. No stars.

13: *Mit mir nicht*

At last Wotan threatens Alberich with Siegfried's arrival and calls to Fafner in his cave.* 13 Now we have some mildly diverting pantomime stuff, timps still sticking to the old Giants [6], some squirming [23], Fafner singing out of an echo chamber. Alberich flings the Curse [11] after the retreating Wotan. But all a little below par, only just a star.

Act II Sc 2

22: *Wir sind zur Stelle!*

This scene opens with brisk exchanges between Siegfried and Mime in a sort of recitatif,* 22 heavily dotted with mottos – Blacksmith [l] on a solo horn, the old Giants [6] on the timps, Fafner [23], a reminder of Anvils [9]. Siegfried's interest in the dragon's anatomy is to discern the position of its heart which we hear beating rather revoltingly for a few bars.

28

At last the evil Mime goes and we are into Forest Murmurs:** shimmering strings [25]. 28 This has an outdoor sound like the music of the waters of the Rhine or the clouds around Valhalla and it comes as a wholesome change from loathsome dwarfs and dragon's heartbeats. The rest of the scene goes as follows:

30: *Aber, wie sah meiner Mutter*

1. Siegfried wonders about his parents. Who was his mum he asks himself in soft and melodious tones.** Lovely, and related to Long- 30 ing [j] and an unlisted Volsung motto.

2. More Murmurs [25], very agreeable. A bird springs out of a bush and sings (Birdie [26]: birdlike piping).

32: *Du holdes Vöglein*

3. Siegfried in a really nice lyrical free passage* debates whether birdtalk can be under- 32 stood by humans. Tries to ingratiate himself with the bird by blowing on reeds. Horrible results. Tries his horn instead. Lengthy and taxing solo* which has every First Horn in a state of panic until it is safely over – Horn I [24], Siegfried Heroic [20].

4. Fafner makes disgusting noises – growls and rumbles – from his cave. O Boy! shouts Siegfried, he's coming out. Now a dialogue between Fafner and Siegfried,* pretty witless but it helps to build up the tension. Shouts and growls – lots of Fafner [23] of course and the old Giants [6].

38: *Haha! Da hätte mein Lied*

38

5. The battle itself** – Fafner [23] played against Horn I [24], Giants [6] banging on in the timps and in victory a whiff of Nothung [15]. A rousing encounter.

42

42

6. The dragon's deathbed speech.* As well as the above mottos, the old Giants [6] played full and proper and the Curse [11].

44: *Wer bist du kühner Knabe*

44

7. Siegfried licks the dragon's blood off his fingers and can now understand the bird, who has a message for him. A novelty number* with quite a bit of charm.

47: *Hei Siegfried*

47

Act II Sc 3

And now for something entirely different – a change of mood, change of music, a queer scene. Alberich and Mime lurch on to a lumbering syncopated accompaniment arguing the toss about who gets the treasure. Few mottos – a little Anvils [9], Ring [4] and Rhinegold [3]. Then Siegfried comes out of the cave wondering what to do with the pretty stuff. A nice reflective piece* with a cushion of horns heaving about below Siegfried's voice and leading into Murmurs [25]. Out pops the bird again singing in perfect German [26] and gives its anti-dwarf warning. Then (surprise) Mime muses to some sweet and rather dreamy version of the motto for the Volsung race* [h] interrupted by Frustration [18]. Mime's version of this motto is shorter than Wotan's – of a size more suitable for a dwarf.

53: *Was ihr mir nützt*

53

55: *Er sinnt und er wägt*

55

Mime meets his end. The dialogue between Mime and Siegfried is strange indeed:* the music is halting and uncertain, making its own path as it goes along. And as for the words – one has the awful suspicion that Wagner thought he

57: *Willkommen Siegfried!*

57

was being comical in making Mime blurt out his true thoughts very much as did Basil Fawlty on the memorable night when the German guests dined at Fawlty Towers. Whatever the intention, the scene doesn't work. A star because it is such a curio. Mottos – Frustration [18], fleeting references to Birdie [26], Anvils [9]. Mime's subsequent death and Alberich's echoing laugh do, however, give a measure of satisfaction.

Siegfried triumphant. After he has pushed Mime's body into the cave, dragged the dragon's body across its mouth and said Thank You to Nothung – whew! – Anvils [9], Giants [6], Horn I [24] and the Curse [11] – whew! again – Siegfried settles down to a little quiet meditation.** This is Siegfried lyrical, and very nice too; he wonders did he have brothers? Sisters? Who was his mum? He asks the bird, how about a suitable wife? References to Mime's Frustration [18] and, of course, a lot of Birdie [26], who now has an additional motto as a bonus for having done so well – a two-bar musical rocket (unlisted). So now the bird steers him towards Brünnhilde and for a moment the downward scales in the orchestra seem to be going to break into the Trance [22]. Siegfried is told to be brave, the bird flies off and Siegfried brings down the curtain with a lyrical outburst that might almost be birdsong too.

66: *Da lieg auch du*

66

Act III Sc 1

0

A stormy prelude,* going at a fast canter and pretty loud. The main subject is the dotted downward bit of Spear [7], and two others that stick out are Earth [12] and Earth upside down, which is Destruct [13], also a hint of Frustration [18]. We are also treated to a welcome clap of thunder to allow the earth to open up and release Erda.

A duet for Wotan/Erda takes up the whole scene (seventeen minutes) which advances the

0

action not one whit and could be summarized as follows:

> *Wotan*: Erda, wake up, I need some advice.
> *Erda*: Don't bother me. Try the Norns. Try Brünnhilde.
> *Wotan*: OK, then let me tell you something: our number's up. We gods are doomed. Got it? (Erda sleeps on.)

But musically this long meander by the Wanderer is rich, sensuous and a little marvel in itself. It goes something as follows:

2: *Wache, Wala! Wala!*

1. Wake up.* Wanderer Wotan tries to rouse Erda: Spear [7], Erda [12], Destruct [13] and Sleep [i] before Erda says Whosat? Help me, says Wotan, I need advice – Erda [12], Wanderer [k] and Spear [7]. Erda: Get off; ask the Norns. Wotan: I'd rather ask their boss – a new motto for the Norns ending with two notes and a jump (unlisted, echoes of both Stress [b] and the Ring [4]). All of this nothing dialogue rests on a cushion of the most ravishing orchestral sound. One wishes one could listen to it without the singers. (Some enterprising recording manager might try this one day.)

9: *Männertaten umdämmern mir den Mut*

2. Down Memory Lane. Erda recalls she once had sex with a chap called Wotan* (although all-wise, she apparently fails to penetrate Wotan's somewhat flimsy disguise – that eye-patch wouldn't fool a child) and the result was Brünnhilde. Ask her, she says. Wotan goes into a now-read-on about Brünnhilde's unusual situation and pesters Erda again, as she tries to go to sleep (Trance [22] and Sleep [i]). Again the music rages and soars under this low-level, low-interest dialogue. Now there are fewer mottos, less mickey-mousing, although Erda [12] and Spear [7] are still around.

13: *Du bist nicht*

3. Wotan's final oration: a fine piece.** Don't be fooled by an important-sounding motto (two

long string notes and an upward run), it's a one-off and has no special meaning. Minor mentions of mottos about, but they don't impede Wotan's rapturous sweep as he sings Stuff it then! OK it's all going to fall apart. So what? (Big climax.) His elation dies away after easily the best session he has given us so far. A scene to relish – in the study.

Act III Sc 2

Now it's Wotan/Siegfried for fifteen minutes and quite a change in mood and sound. The early exchanges between the two are brisk, dry and tuneful, all now-read-on stuff (with appropriate mottos) until Siegfried begins to get rude and uncouth. In an opening passage of great musical sweetness** he asks the stranger why he   23
laughs at him? Words and music do not seem to fit at all, but they lead to an excited outburst from Siegfried* and the row between the two   24
warms up, the most prominent mottos being Spear [7] versus Sword [14]. The war of words and mottos ends in a clap of thunder and in the clatter of the shattered spear. (Last time remember it was the other way round: Spear 1 Nothung 0, so now it's 1–1. But the spear seems to be out of it for good.) Good action stuff.

23: *Was lachst du mich aus?*

24: *Das wär' nicht übel!*

So Wotan disappears and Siegfried looks hungrily towards the fire. He exclaims a bit and we are into a busy noisy intermezzo,** a real   30
buster in which every motto tells a story and there are a lot of them – Siegfried Heroic [20], Rhinegold [3] [Why is this here? Shome mishtake surely? Ed.], Horn I [24], Loge [8] and associated fire music, Sleep [i], Trance [22] and Siegfried Heroic again [20]. Got it? But this does not prevent the pieces being all of a piece and there is a magic moment that causes a frisson down the spine when the Trance floats in serene and calm as ever at the end.

30

Act III Sc 3

At the end of the intermezzo the first violins all alone climb up the rock to where Brünnhilde lies. They are slow climbers, and towards the end it sounds as if they could do with a whiff of oxygen. Siegfried pokes around singing a bemused sort of recitatif over a bed of rich orchestral sound* (some snatches of Valkyrie [16]). Here again is a section that would surely play better without the vocal lines. Siegfried opens Brünnhilde's breastplate with Nothung (tricky). But, goodness me, who and what is this man with bumps on his chest? The woodwind wanders around describing the contours of Brünnhilde's bust. Then POW! Musical Explosion!*** Sex in all its mighty power hits Siegfried full in the solar plexus. Really quite a knockout with Siegfried shouting excitedly amongst the whirling strings. He comes out of his delirium and things quieten down. Motto-spotters may have an anxious time because it seems there are a lot moving around, but most are freelances on short-term contracts and the only long-serving staff member is Trance [22] which steals in as beautifully and as quietly as ever. We are now into a magical orchestral poem:** awakening, sunrise, wonder and finally – love. Shimmering strings, melodious wood-wind, bold brassy chords held for a very long time.

Now things get ecstatic. Brünnhilde says who woke me? It was I says Siegfried. Siegfried she says. Oh goody, and for once in the height of their ecstasy Wagner breaks the ground rules and both sing at the same time.*** This duet is pretty overwhelming and with twenty-five minutes to go one wonders how he can top that. But without actually topping it he successfully pulls us off the climax with some full-blooded godlike love music** based on a new motto, a tender woodwind figure followed by a smooth ending (Mutual Heroic Love [n]). This, first heard on the woodwind and infinitely change-able, rolls on and out as the two gaze into each other's eyes, spellbound. Variously orchestrated.

35: *Selige Öde auf sonniger*

35

37: *Das ist kein Mann!*

37

48

48

52: *O Heil der Mutter*

52

54: *O Siegfried! Siegfried!*

54

Now for a bit of a rest. There's my old horse Grane grazing over there says Brünnhilde – snatches of Valkyrie [16]. My trappings of power have gone. She muses a bit sadly and Siegfried too, although he has his bursts of fire, decelerates gradually into recitatif until, great moment, he swings into his second love tune – Lover's Sigh (a downward sigh, then pretty [o]).** My eyes grow dim I cannot see I have not brought my specs with me sings Brünnhilde in a panic. [Why? Ed.] But Siegfried soothes her with Lover's Sigh.

67: *Sangst du mir nicht*

67

Now Brünnhilde sings an important number – better known as the Siegfried Idyll. An outpouring of young love to music that is older and wiser than young love.*** The combination of the two tells us what a glorious woman Brünnhilde is. Siegfried jumps in with all his boyish charm and we are into the final and miraculous stages of this marathon duet.*** Mottos can go by the board now (though there are several) as we are swept along by Wagner doing the thing he does best, piling on the agony and generating wave upon wave of passion each one higher than the last until we are overtaken by the surging climax of Siegfried's love for Brünnhilde and hers for him. Stunning.

70: *Ewig war ich*

70

73: *Dich lieb' ich*

73

NOTES and NEWS AND GOSSIP See **The Birth of *The Ring*** page 215

COMMENT See also **The Ring – A General Hello** page 123

The trouble with *Siegfried* is that when it is good it is very very good but when it is bad it is boring. The same can be said, of course, of *The Ring* as a whole, but in *Siegfried* we get the extreme case. The problem lies mainly in the script. There are at least two scenes which have no dramatic value whatsoever and one of these is just plain silly. Why should a host suddenly suggest to his guest that he should play a word game with him with death as the penalty for losing? And why should any guest accept such a ridiculous challenge unless he is a loony? The game itself is so poor that it would not have survived even on the tackiest local television channel in Nibelungenland for more than a second and turns out to be no more than a cover for yet another regurgitation of the Nibelungen saga. This is also true of the second scene – Wotan's unsuccessful try at interviewing Erda. Again there is nothing here but a churning-over of past history and we get no fresh news until the interviewee goes to sleep and the interviewer addresses her with a monologue which he might just as well have addressed to us in the first place and have saved poor Erda the annoyance of being woken out of her delicious eternal slumber. But this scene is musically rich and although the crassness of the libretto may be a pain, the music makes up for it.

Several of the other scenes wear out their welcome – the terribly slow speed at which Siegfried finds out about his parents, Wotan's predictable ding-dong with Alberich in the first scene of Act II, the two dwarfs quarrelling over the gold in Act III Scene 3, and the scene in the last act where Siegfried is so gratuitously rude to Wotan.

In the first half of the opera these dramatically damp patches seem more draggy because some of the music is fairly ornery, but in the second half where Wagner was a more advanced pupil (see **The Birth of *The Ring*** on page 215), the richness of the score beguiles us into feeling that things are going along pretty well. So we have an opera with a three-star final half-hour, two two-star episodes – forging the sword and the forest scenes – plus elsewhere a lot of gorgeous music, so let's just revel in that and for the rest be a little thankful.

For the good music in *Siegfried* is brilliant. It has no stirring set pieces for the concert hall, like the Ride of the Valks (although Forest Murmurs used to be played quite a lot in a mildly effective concert form), but Act III, especially, is full of great orchestral writing and the orchestration has its own special brand of sonority throughout the dragon-related parts.

The opera offers tuba-lovers a field day and whereas *Valkyrie* has the loudest music Wagner wrote, *Siegfried* has the deepest. The dragon's noises are really something to frighten the horses. The two set pieces – the forging song and the Siegfried Idyll – work well, but for those who know the Idyll in its orchestral form, it sticks out as a bit of an import, like the 'Stars & Stripes' in *Butterfly* (well, perhaps not quite like that). The musical character of the bird is as cute as the dragon is grotesque; Erda's music is even more beautiful than it was on her first appearance (but sleepier); Brünnhilde is as glorious as ever; the two dwarfs as tiresome, except for the moment in Act I Scene 1 when Mime (inexplicably) for a moment becomes a beautiful person. The Wanderer has a noble entry but after that his musical persona is even more unfocused than when he was himself. This may be because he doesn't seem to know why he is wandering or what he is supposed to be doing.

Siegfried himself has all the musical panache needed to make him the brave bonehead he has to be, although when first heard his absolutely memorable horn tune may be a little too close to operatic fox-hunting for comfort. But with his love music he becomes a grown-up human being – or almost, for his panic is still adolescent. He gives the impression of being a Wagnerian Cherubino who, if he had found Tosca, Desdemona, Carmen or even the Marschallin in the middle of the fire, would have fallen for any one of them just as madly. He was, after all, and a little late in life, discovering sex for the first time and this quite naturally made him very excitable.

But it is not the thing to question the bona fides of one of the parties in what is (possibly excluding the one in *Tristan*) the greatest love duet in Wagner. It is a *tour de force* and at the same time something more genuine than that. Wagner believed in this sort of passion as a central item in his scheme of things and with his genius for building a climax he raises this scene to an incredible pitch of emotion, emotion truly felt by him, by Siegfried, by Brünnhilde and so by us. Or rather most of us, for there will be those anti-Wagners, poor souls, plus that quite large section of mankind who have the misfortune to have tin ears who will fail to be moved by this great climacteric. But in the opera house where aficionados gather, as the curtain comes down you will hear the applause start hesitantly, in a whisper, as the clients slowly haul themselves back, as from an anaesthetic, into the land of the living. In the closing minutes of *Siegfried* Wagner deploys the full power of opera and if you are not overwhelmed, too bad – go and listen to Vivaldi – but if you are, it is the experience of a lifetime – and it will not do you the slightest harm.

Götterdämmerung
(The Twilight of the Gods)

The one where Siegfried makes new friends who stab him in the back, where Brünnhilde is very brave and Valhalla goes up in flames.

CAST (see **Who's Who** page 136)

Siegfried, a hero	Tenor
Brünnhilde, one-time chief of the Valkyries	Soprano
Waltraute, a Valkyrie	Mezzo
Alberich, chief of the Nibelungen	Bass–baritone
Hagen, son of Alberich and a human female	Bass
Gunther, his half-brother, King of the Gibichungs	Bass–baritone
Gutrune, Gunther's sister	Soprano
Three Rhinemaidens	One mezzo, two sopranos
Three Norns	Soprano, mezzo, contralto

Prologue and 3 acts: running time 4 hrs 15 mins

RELATIONSHIPS IN GÖTTERDÄMMERUNG

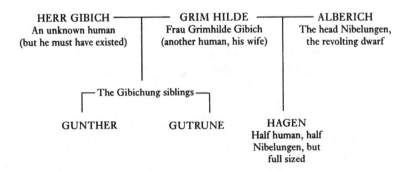

HERR GIBICH — An unknown human (but he must have existed) ——— **GRIM HILDE** Frau Grimhilde Gibich (another human, his wife) ——— **ALBERICH** The head Nibelungen, the revolting dwarf

— The Gibichung siblings —

GUNTHER   **GUTRUNE**   **HAGEN** Half human, half Nibelungen, but full sized

Subsequently: Siegfried when doped marries (or nearly) Gutrune
Gunther when pushed by Siegfried marries (or nearly) Brünnhilde

STORY

Prologue The Valkyries' rock: the same as the last scene in
Siegfried
**In which the Norns tell us rather more than we want to
know about the past, have some interesting information
about the future and meet with an industrial accident,
Siegfried and Brünnhilde swear eternal devotion, he gives
her the ring, she gives him a horse and he sets off for his
musical journey down the Rhine**

In the vague timescale of *The Ring* we move into timelessness.
Three Norns sit spinning the Rope of Destiny and recall amongst
many irrelevances that Wotan (having no filofax) cut his spear
from a very superior ash tree nearby in order to record on the
shaft in extremely small writing details of deals done. Siegfried
smashed the spear: Wotan's employees chopped up the ash tree
and piled the logs round Valhalla. Meanwhile Wotan has
preserved the bits of his shaft to use as firelighters to ignite the
logs round Valhalla in case he wants to arsonize it.

At this point the Rope of Destiny snaps which is lucky for us
since otherwise the opera would never have got started. The
Norns vanish: day breaks: it is some twenty-four hours after the
last scene in *Siegfried*. Siegfried and Brünnhilde come on
exchanging sweet somethings. OK I love you too much to stop you
going on this business trip says she and anyway I'm not really
good enough for you. Yes you are says he and sorry if I wasn't all
that hot in bed last night you see I'm a little inexperienced. Think
of me when you're away says she. Sure says he. Must be off thanks
for the sex lessons now here's a ring (*the* ring!) for you. Thanks
says she. Here's my horse as a present for you. Very nice of you
says he. Together we are one they sing and more fancy stuff in this
vein. Siegfried moves off.

**Act I Sc 1 The hall of the Gibichungs on the banks of
the Rhine. In which Gunther and Hagen plot and
scheme to get Brünnhilde as Gunther's wife and to get
Siegfried to assist them**

Hey Hagen says Gunther – how's my popularity rating this week?
Not good says Hagen, about the same as Hague's. How can I raise
my profile? asks Gunther. Royal wedding says Hagen nothing like
them I know just the girl – name of Brünnhilde – only one snag

she lies in the middle of a bushfire. Oh I see says Gunther am I
brave enough to get in there and fetch her? Frankly no says Hagen
you must get someone much braver than you to do it for you.
Who? asks Gunther. Young Siegfried Volsung is probably as good
as any. Comes of good stock and he killed a dragon [also Hagen's
uncle Mime: Ed.], says Hagen, and owns the ring which makes
him Lord of Creation.

Listen says Hagen: suppose Siegfried fetched in Brünnhilde to
be your wife and we got him to marry your sister Gutrune. Good
idea eh? How could we do that? say Gunther and Gutrune.
Remember that stuff in the magic medicine chest? asks Hagen:
forget-all pills and love philtres and stuff like that? Make a
magimix and dose Siegfried. Great idea say the other two – Hagen
you're a genius. I wish Siegfried was here says Gutrune. On this
cue Siegfried sounds his horn for he is drifting down the Rhine in
a punt with a horse.

Sc 2 In which Siegfried after drinking a magimix potion loses his memory and falls for another woman, namely Gutrune Gibichung

Hey Siegfried the Gibichungs shout. Hey to you he says can you
direct me to Gibichung Hall? I believe it is near Basingstoke. This
is it they cry. Siegfried gets out. Welcome welcome welcome says
Gunther: are you *the* Siegfried? That's me says Siegfried. Owner
of the Rhinegold? asks Gunther. Now you mention it yes says
Siegfried I only kept this yellow balaclava that's the magicap
Tarnhelm: I gave the ring to a nice girl called Brünnhilde.

Gutrune comes on with magimix medicine. Like a scotch? she
says to Siegfried. Don't mind if I do says Siegfried here's to
Brünnhilde (quaffs) magimix has instant effect: do I fancy *you*? he
says what's your sister's name Gunther? Gutrune says he.
Gutrune I am getting good vibes. Grabs her. Will you marry me?
he asks (Gutrune exits indicating assent).

Have you a wife Gunther? No says Gunther but I know who I
want: it's Brünnhilde but she's in a circle of fire and I'm not very
brave so I couldn't get in there. I'll get her for you says Siegfried.
I'll give you Gutrune in exchange says Gunther: let's be blood
brothers says Siegfried. They go through a nauseating routine of
mixing blood and wine and quaffing. How about joining our blood
brotherhood Hagen? they ask. Sorry my blood is of an extremely

rare blood group and will not mix says Hagen. Sullen bastard let him be says Gunther.

OK says Siegfried let's get going. Like a bit of a kip first? says Gunther. No sir says Siegfried on on on. Oho says Hagen as they disappear let the happy lads go wife-hunting so long as they bring back what I want – the ring.

Sc 3 Brünnhilde's rock
In which through the agency of the Tarnhelm magicap Siegfried as Gunther carries Brünnhilde off for a second time and for a different purpose

Who's that arriving? says Brünnhilde. Sounds like one of the old Valkyrie gang thunder and all. Hey Brünnhilde shouts Waltraute wake up it's me. What's up? asks Brünnhilde by the way I'm in love with Siegfried. Trouble at t'mill says Waltraute the governor's lost his marbles. Wotan's stopped sending us corpse-gathering. He took a sabbatical and travelled incognito as A. Wanderer. He came back with his spear broke. He has stacked up wood around Valhalla as if for a Guy Fawkes Night bonfire. He called a staff meeting won't eat won't talk sits there everyone around him waiting for Godot.

I asked him what was bothering him. That ring he said. Brünnhilde has it. Unless she gives it back to those Rhinemaidens we're all for the old heave-ho. Brünnhilde honey give it back please do love. Not on your nelly says Brünnhilde. Are you crazy or something? This ring is the cream in my coffee it's holy sacred love it's the tops it's the Mona Lisa. Valhalla can go to blazes: I keep the ring. Get off. (Waltraute exits in an electric storm.)

Nice evening says Brünnhilde the ring of fire is burning nicely. Whoops! is that Siegfried's horn? Siegfried magicapped appears through the flames as Gunther. Who the hell are you? says Brünnhilde. It's me I'm Gunther the Gibichung says he. You must come and be my wife. God help us how did this creature get past the flames? says she: Wotan you let me down you sod.

Let's go to bed in your cave says he. Stand back! says she this ring will stop you in your tracks. Will it hell says he. Jumps on her. After an ugly struggle wrenches off the ring. Get into that cave says he and we'll put Nothung down the middle of the bed to prevent any hanky-panky. I promised to deliver you to my blood brother a virgin. [Siegfried is, of course, suffering from sexual amnesia: Ed.]

**Act II The bank of the Rhine outside the Gibichung hall
Sc 1 In which Hagen and his singularly unpleasant
dwarf father chat about the ring, its past history and its
future ownership: it will be theirs**

Are you awake Hagen? asks the revolting Albert Alberich. What'ya
want? asks Hagen. You're a clever lad Hagen says Alberich.
Listen: did you know that Wotan and his lot have pretty well
packed it in? Broke his spear or something? Who's going to take
over? asks Hagen. We are says Alberich we nick the ring off this
young bonehead Siegfried and Bob's your uncle. I have the matter
in hand says Hagen. Relax. I will get the ring. But it's mine says
Alberich you wouldn't let your old dad down would you son?
Mind your own business says Hagen.

**Sc 2 In which Siegfried returns to Gibichung Hall and
reports the success of his mission**

Hi Hagen says Siegfried. Hi Siegfried says Hagen how did it go?
OK says Siegfried I fetched out Brünnhilde and passed her on to
Gunther they're coming along behind. C'mon out Gutrune shouts
Hagen Siegfried's here. Everything OK? asks Gutrune did
Gunther get singed at all? He didn't go near the fire says Siegfried
I went in as his ringer thanks to the magicap. Got her out slept
with her – whassat? says Hagen you had sex? Never a tickle says
Siegfried I put this great thing between us [Nothung of course:
Ed.] then early this morning I magicapped the changed Siegfried/
Gunther into Gunther/Siegfried. So that's it and here they come
now I hear them. Fine good say Gutrune and Hagen blow the
foghorn to get tenants together and let's have a double wedding.

**Sc 3 In which the gloomy Hagen makes the tenants
laugh at a joke and Gunther and Brünnhilde arrive**

Alarum! Emergency! Stand to your weapons! shouts Hagen. Here
we are boss is it the mob from up the river again? they ask.
Gunther is coming back with a wife says Hagen. Yeah yeah say the
tenants so are her folks trying to get her off him? We shall kill a
cow, horse, pig, sheep or a cock as a sacrifice today says Hagen –
but no humans. OK OK boss they say so what? A big booze-up
says Hagen. Ho Ho Ho what a good joke Ho Ho say the easily
amused tenants. Here come the bridal pair says Hagen. Nice to see
you back Gunther shout the tenants.

Sc 4 In which Brünnhilde is shocked to find Siegfried planning to marry another woman: she reminds him that they are in German opera parlance man and wife (means they had sex together) and this sets the cat amongst the Gibichung pigeons

Welcome to our place Madam shout the tenants. Listen folks she's a very superior person is my fiancée says Gunther. Hey Siegfried old bloodie how about a double wedding? Is Siegfried here? My God! says Brünnhilde. And with Gutrune? I'm going to marry her says Siegfried. Brünnhilde blacks out: comes to. That's my ring he's wearing she says the one that you Gunther wrenched off me. I never says Gunther. I didn't get this ring off any woman says Siegfried I got it off a dragon. (Tenants signal to each other that the gent is a little funny in the head.) Not so says Hagen Siegfried got that ring off Gunther by trickery (a dastardly lie of course).

This is too much screams Brünnhilde he pinches my ring and makes to marry Gutrune well she's getting soiled goods anyway because Siegfried had a night of sex with me so there! My my gee whizz fancy that say the tenants. Shut up Brünnhilde says Siegfried. That's not true not true at all. We had the sword Nothung between us all night (he only remembers second night when he was Gunther anyway). Liar says she Nothung was hanging above the washbasin (she is recalling their first night of love).

Hey folks this is a serious matter say the tenants. A fiancée of a Gibichungy sleeping around with Volsungs. Come and swear to the truth on my spear says Hagen. I swear I never touched her swears Siegfried. I swear he gave me the full works says Brünnhilde.

Gunther your fiancée needs psychiatric help says Siegfried or maybe that Tarnhelm didn't do its job on some important parts of my body anyway women change their minds at the drop of a hat so let's just carry on with this wedding party. Exits on a high with Gutrune. The tenants follow tongues hanging out for booze.

Sc 5 In which Hagen secretly lusting after the ring plots to kill Siegfried. Brünnhilde tells him how to do it and Gunther is enlisted as an accomplice

This is a real old puzzle says Brünnhilde. I don't know what's come over Siegfried. I'll fight him for you says Hagen. You? says Brünnhilde. Poof! Not a hope I magicked him swordproof. All over? asks Hagen. Well now you come to mention it I didn't magic the rear portion because his style was always face to face. Thanks for the tip-off says Hagen.

Fancy Siegfried cheating on me like that I feel dirty says Gunther. All your fault for going in for that magicap stuff says Brünnhilde you were too chicken to go in there and get me yourself. Only Siegfried's death will make you feel better says Hagen. How about all that blood brother stuff? says Gunther. Never mind that if you killed him you could get your hands on the ring says Hagen. How about Gutrune? says Gunther. Tell her he was gored by a rhinoceros says Hagen. Agreed? Agreed says Gunther. Yes agreed says Brünnhilde.

Act III Sc 1 A valley on the Rhine, with a cliff beetling and Rhine waters visible
In which the Rhinemaidens beg Siegfried to give them back the ring but to no purpose

Nice morning isn't it sing the Rhinemaidens what a smashing sunrise – it would be even better if we still had the gold. Weialala! Isn't that the heroic hornblowing hunter on his way? (It is.) Maybe he'll give us back our gold. Seen a dog fox? asks Siegfried I lost him. Give us that ring on your finger say the girls and maybe we'll tell you. I killed a dragon for that ring says Siegfried worth more than a fox besides the wife wouldn't like it. Gee! Isn't he cute say the girls.

OK girls I'll give it to you says he come here. Before you hand it over they say you should know that there's a curse on it so if you'd kept it you would have been killed today anyway. Don't you bloody threaten me says Siegfried the deal's off. On your own head be it sing the girls you'll be rubbed out today. What tiresome females says Siegfried.

Sc 2 In which Siegfried tells us his life story which we already know and is killed by Hagen

Halloo Siegfried shouts Hagen. Halloo to you says Siegfried. Any luck? asks Hagen. Went after pheasant but finished up with waterfowl and a lost fox gimme a drink says Siegfried. Somebody told me you were psychic with birds says Hagen. Lemme tell you all says Siegfried.

He embarks on lengthy C.V. including: Mime – forging sword

– Nothung put together again – death of dragon – tasted dragon's blood (ugh) – understood birds – helpful bird advised on Rhinegold – took Tarnhelm magicap ring etc. – bird advised Mime a wrong 'un – Mime killed – bird directs to Brünnhilde – walk through fire – wins Brünnhilde.

Here Siegfried is interrupted by ravens: he turns to look at them: Hagen inserts a spear into his back. Hey Hagen what are you at? cry the tenants you're killing that man. Revenge for perjury says Hagen arcanely. Siegfried badly wounded jacks himself up for goodbye message to Brünnhilde: Brünnhilde he says my life my love I went through fire for you Brünnhilde and wakened you with a kiss. I'm coming to you. . . . (Expires.) So now we have an extempore procession to the crematorium accompanied by the great funeral march.

Sc 3 Gibichung Hall and beyond. Night
In which Gutrune learns of Siegfried's death, Hagen kills Gunther in a squabble over the ring, Brünnhilde rides her horse into Siegfried's funeral pyre, Hagen is drowned by the Rhinemaidens and Valhalla goes up in smoke

Siegfried is late back from the hunt says Gutrune. Panics. Hagen and all return. Sorry Gutrune says Hagen I'm afraid Siegfried's dead. A rhinoceros got him. Not so says Gunther it was Hagen what done it. So I did too says Hagen because what he swore on oath on my spear was a lie. By the way I claim that ring in return. Get off you dwarf-begotten bastard says Gunther it's mine. Want to bet? says Hagen. Kills him. As Hagen goes to take the ring from Siegfried's finger the corpse raises its arm scaring the hell out of everyone.

Quiet please listen to me says Brünnhilde the two Gibichungies plotted his death. You were in it too you jealous bitch shouts Gutrune. Hush you poor miserable thing says Brünnhilde he was my lover before he met you. Blast and damn you Hagen for making me give him those forget-all pills says Gutrune she was his true love and I done her wrong.

Pile up a bonfire fit for a hero's cremation and bring on my horse Grane says Brünnhilde. Goodbye Siegfried great hero my lover perfect man the Rhinemaidens have told me all. Listen Wotan you evil man you used Siegfried to rid you of that curse and sure enough it passed on to him so he has destroyed himself and destroyed my life. Now I know everything. The ring I shall give back to the Rhinemaidens (she takes it off Siegfried's finger) and now get off you ravens (they are circling around again) and tell Loge to put the match to Valhalla.

So now I'll light the pyre (does so) and listen to me old Grane – jump right into the flames with me on your back (he jumps in obediently). Fire breaks out all over the stage (as widespread as fire regulations will allow). Tenants cower by the footlights. The Rhine rises rather suddenly and overflows onto the stage putting out the fire. The Rhinemaidens appear. They take the ring from the ashes of the quickly burnt-out bonfire. They return to the Rhine. Hagen dives into the Rhine to get the ring. The Rhinemaidens drown him.

In the distance Valhalla burns up nicely with all the gods visible as they fry until smoke blots them out. All is over and the mighty saga has reached its end. (Whew!)

LOOK OUT FOR

MINUTES FROM START

Prologue (For motto numbers see the Table on page 133.)
A loud brass chord – the chord of doom – opens the action (we heard it when Brünnhilde was woken up). Then we are immediately taken back in time into Rhine music [1] – next a sharp reminder of Fate [19] and the prelude is over.

2: *Welch Licht leuchtet dort?* The three Norns tell the tale, past, present 2 and future. This is calm music, the sort of thing suitable for priests, priestesses and seers. It's more alive than recitatif, in no way stunning, but it reaches its small climax effectively enough. As at the beginning of a marathon film you are prepared to sit through a fairly slow-moving first reel, so here you feel this is a very fair introduction for big things to come. (Fate [19], Valhalla [5], Spear [7], Loge [8].) The rope snaps (Fate [19] again), not a moment too soon. No star.

17 Prelude for Siegfried and Brünnhilde.** Fate 17 [19] is followed by a long recitatif for the lower strings and then two shining new mottos break the surface, the first (which has the same notes

as Horn I but in an entirely different rhythm: Horn II [27]) answered immediately by the second (glorious Brünnhilde [28]: low note – twiddle – high note and three more, making a sweet phrase, this time on a solo clarinet) and the two work together to make a wonderful thing of this second, bigger and better prelude.

The Siegfried/Brünnhilde duet. It would be wrong to say that this duet takes over where the later scenes of *Siegfried* left off, for nothing could top that great climacteric. But the music of this duet is of the same kind and has both a sexual and romantic intensity. It is topside Wagner – and so early in the opera too. The piece goes something as follows:

21: *Zu neuen Taten*

1. Brünnhilde:** I wouldn't properly love   21
you if I didn't let you go and do your heroic business (Brünnhilde [28]). Anyway I'm not really good enough for you. She sings all this to a superior sort of freestyle recitatif and sounds so joyful as to give the lie to the humble line she is taking.

23: *Mehr gabst du*

2. Siegfried:** Don't be cross if I'm not yet very good in bed. The main thing is we love each other madly. This is a poem of happiness and again he does not seem cast down by his poor sexual performance. Introduced by Horn II [27].

26: *Lass' ich, Liebste*

3. Now he gives her the ring and she gives him her horse Grane.** Not a very fair swap   26
because by any standards Grane must be aged and unlikely to show any turn of foot. [But he has no curse attached to him: Ed.] There are changes of rhythm and style here, but it all remains pretty ecstatic with references to the love music at the end of *Valkyrie*, to Siegfried Heroic [20] and Valkyrie [16]. They finish with a bout of saying Hail! to each other, both still on a high. The accompaniment is luscious and the climax terrific. Siegfried rides off on his journey (Horn II [27]).

31

Siegfried's journey down the Rhine.** A rich   31

and varied orchestral *tour d'horizon* starting with Horn II [27] and Brünnhilde [28] and moving out into the big world with Horn I [24] which after some busy traffic gets the concerto treatment, first for horn and then oboe and is developed into a mighty string tune which makes way for – wait for it – the Rhine [1]. Now we are back amongst the Rhinemaidens and we have Rhinegold [3], Gold [2], the Ring itself [4] and a bit of a rumble in the bass which could be Loge's fire music still smouldering away. Anyway the end is portentous (Bad News [d]) and it portends something pretty dire.

Act I Sc 1

So we are back on earth and at rest, indeed inside Hagen's hall where for the next fifteen minutes there is to be nothing but plotting and scheming. Hagen himself is given a rather physical motto – a sweep up then a jump down, twice – unlisted. The story is developed in

o: *Nun hör, Hagen*

Wagner's grown-up vocal style,* that is to say   o the music moves along very close to the sense of the story, sometimes in VSR (Very Superior Recitatif), sometimes picking up a fragment of melody when required) building up into little puffs of excitement. The orchestration is strong, rich and clear and the orchestra is, as usual, the spokesman for the relevant mottos, which include Valkyrie [16], Loge [8], Volsung [h], Horn I [24] and the Ring [4].

After a conspiratorial whisper from Hagen about the nasty drug they are going to inflict on Siegfried, Gutrune says 'I wish I could see Siegfried' and right on cue we hear Curse [11] immediately followed by all of Siegfried's horn

11: *Möcht' ich Siegfried*

calls which break out in a jumble,* but soon,   11 thanks to some heavy work from the strings, Horn I [24] wins and excitement builds as Siegfried is sighted spinning down the Rhine in his punt with a horse. Once again a little unfair to animals, Wagner gives Grane very poor musical recognition (Valkyrie [16]), but by now

Siegfried's horns are busting out all over. An entry fit to make the Queen of Sheba send for her court composer.

Act I Sc 2

16: *Begrüsse froh, O Held*

After the preliminaries (for some arcane reason a whiff of the Curse [11]) Gunther welcomes Siegfried in a good set piece* and Siegfried replies in an equally traditional fashion with a fair bit of Siegfried Heroic [20]. After so much go-as-you-please it is quite a relief to have things steadied up into an old-fashioned operatic exchange.

16

20

But soon we are off again chatting about the Tarnhelm and Gutrune comes in with a new motto (a gentle sighing woodwind phrase: soft and sweet [29]) to offer Siegfried the magic medicine. Here we have the music of witch doctors, spells and curses – sotto voce – until Siegfried looks up and Wham! falls in love with Gutrune.

20

The blood brothers duet. After Siegfried has announced that he will marry Gutrune in two minutes flat (Gutrune [29] and Curse [11]) he gets into finding a wife for Gunther. Why not Brünnhilde? A most suitable choice and I'll get her for you says Siegfried (Loge and fire music [8] and Horn I [24] as developed on the journey). Use the Tarnhelm? Yes, I'll change myself into you Gunther old boy. So let's be blood brothers.* Now we have the disgusting spectacle of two men mixing their blood into a wine cocktail. Whilst this job is being done we have a shower of mottos (Curse [11], Siegfried Heroic [20], Spear [7]).

26: *Blühenden Lebens labendes Blut*

26

(Now a digression. It must be said that in the matter of mottos, from now on it becomes pretty hard to explain Wagner's thought processes. Why does he keep dredging up mottos from the past that seem to have nothing to do with the matter in hand? What the hell is the Spear doing here? Is it because it symbolizes deals? But surely only Wotan's deals. Is it because the whole house of cards is built on deals? Including the blood brother deal being done now? No doubt the Wagnerian scribendos will find an answer to it.)

Anyway, to get back to blood-brothers, they drink the revolting liquid and sing a little blood-brother ditty* in thirds which simply must have been suggested by the palship duet in *Don Carlos*. It's an oddity in Wagner and rather nice (Curse [11] and Spear [7] still around). It's interesting that this duet should have a collegiate, even a Masonic, ring to it. (Hagen disassociates himself from these goings-on with the Ring [4] booming away behind.)

26: Treue trink' ich dem Freund   26

A burst of mad excitement.* Let's go! shouts Siegfried. It's all hustle and bustle. Gutrune can't stop him. So he jumps in a boat and leaves after a visit of twenty minutes, having swigged a forget-all potion, got a new wife, drunk blood, sworn blood-brotherhood and planned an expedition to abduct a lady surrounded by a ring of fire from a mountain top. Even the Harvard Business School would regard this as a productive use of time.

30: Frisch auf die Fahrt!   30

Hagen sings a doomy gloomy farewell. It's all going to end in tears.* Impressive.

35: Hier sitz' ich zur Wacht   35

The intermezzo* to cover the scene change back to the rock is agreeable but scrappy compared to Siegfried's Journey down the Rhine which we have already had. It has an air of mystery (a little thunder in the background) and bristles with mottos – Rhinegold [3], Ring [4], Horn I [24], Siegfried Heroic [20], Spear [7] and finally and gloriously, Brünnhilde [28]. Now the thunder is close.

36   36

Act I Sc 3

Idyll music, thunder, Valkyries [16] and War-Cry [17] open the duet Brünnhilde/Waltraute.*
1. First, some free writing. Brünnhilde tells Waltraute what happened to her. Although the thunder is now very close there is a feeling of mountains and fresh air in the music which

42: So wagtest du   42

moves swiftly from point to point (Valkyrie [16], Siegfried Heroic [20] and, as we get to the matter of how Wotan is going along, Frustration [18]).

2. Waltraute's report on the state of Valhalla is paid out in inches. It is not exciting: packed with mottos, some of which are Frustration [18], Spear [7], Valhalla [5], Ring [4], Rhinegold [3] and Curse [11].

3. But when Brünnhilde asks her what she wants things take wing, nearly all mottos are shaken off and we are into a spell of fresh free music. Brünnhilde's assertion that she is going 54: *Ha! weisst du,* to stick to the ring whatever** is quite splendid 54 *was er mir ist?* (Ring [4]). In a quiet moment it takes us back to the love music at the end of *Valkyrie* – Sigh [0], also Brünnhilde [28].

Now for one of Wagner's great musical/ spectacular *coups de théâtre*. Claps of thunder. 68: *Blitzend* Waltraute disappears in an electric storm.** 68 *Gewölk* The surrounding fire (Loge [8]) goes all funny and creeps nearer. Siegfried's horn! [24]. Fire blazes up (Curse [11]). Siegfried jumps out. Rapture! But it's not Siegfried. Significant chord. Owing to the magicap it's Gunther. Horrors! Who the hell are you? gasps Brünn- hilde. It's as good as the movies. And musically a knockout.

The final scene is all flash! bang! pow! Brünnhilde reacts with horror to the advances of 71: *Wer ist der* Siegfried/Gunther.** Due to the magic of the 71 *Mann* magicap everything is distorted – Siegfried's voice and also the mottos. Only Brünnhilde stays straight (Tarnhelm [10], Horn II [27], Curse [11]). After the noisy scuffle over the ring (she loses) there is an oasis of soft sound, a touch of the Idyll and Brünnhilde's own haunting motto [28]. Soon to be wiped out by the brutish Siegfried/Gunther, instructing his sword (in his natural voice) to act as a chastity barrier between himself and Brünnhilde in case he feels inclined to indulge in any funny stuff before delivering her intact to the real Gunther. A quaint note on which to end an act that has turned the world topsy-turvy. (Frustration [18], Brünnhilde [28], Nothung [15].)

Act II Sc 1

A gloomy prelude based mainly on Hagen's motto (unlisted) is interrupted by the unspeakable Alberich with an onrush of nasty Nibelungen music. He goes on and on about getting the ring back (many sidelong glances at many mottos). Hagen shows his good judgement by treating his father with complete disdain. In this scene we are in the doldrums – but wait: a flush of horns break cover and weave about to greet the dawn as it comes up over the Rhine. This is a pleasure. Suddenly Siegfried's personal horn bursts in [24] as bold as brass and as brisk as can be and we are off into Scene 2.

Act II Sc 2

17: *Euch beiden meld' ich*

A rollicking scene as Gutrune and Siegfried get acquainted. Uneasily she asks him how went the day and he,* as always in *The Ring*, gives her a very full account of what we the audience know already. You ask a silly question, you get a long answer. Gutrune may not be the great and glorious soulmate that Siegfried found in Brünnhilde, but she certainly sounds good for more laughs. The main mottos: Tarnhelm [10], Nothung [15], Loge [8] and Horn I [24]. One of Wagner's jolly scenes and only a little galumphing.

17

Act II Sc 3

20: *Hoiho! Hoihohoho!*

Hagen blows his emergency foghorn several times. It makes a noise in questionable taste but does its job of rousing the tenantry. Wagner now goes horn mad and a variety of horn noises in various horn keys boom out.* The tenants pour in all eager for the fray and singing something between Rufty-Tufty and the chorus from a particularly bloodthirsty oratorio. Hagen tells them it's not war, it's a wedding party. Big joke. The tenants laugh dutifully and chorus on.

20

Two new mottos here: Rufty-Tufty, a skittering dancing figure usually in the bass, unlisted; and We Are the Gibichungies, a brassy swoop down and up in thirds, starting and finishing on the same note [p]. Although this crowd scene goes with a swing and is very welcome at this point, since for most of the preceding fourteen hours we have been gazing at two hominids on an empty stage, it is not one of Wagner's best efforts. If he was going to the expense of having a chorus of thousands brought in for this one item plus the odd shout or two hereafter, he might have given us something more on the lines of the choruses in *Tannhäuser* or *Meistersinger*. This is not value for money. The Sieg Heils! at the end would not have been out of place at the Nuremberg Rally.

Act II Sc 4

Brünnhilde Bouleverséed.

29: *Brünnhild', die hehrste Frau*

The would-be wedding scene opens with the nearest thing to a song* we have had for a long time, accompanied by what, if it were not Wagner, we might call a vamp. After Gunther has set things going we get into the high dramatics of poor Brünnhilde's struggle to cope with this nightmare situation. Mainly exclamatory and high recitatif (with a distort of Valkyrie [16], the Gibichungies [p], Fate [19], a snatch of Brünnhilde [28], the Curse [11] and a little Frustration [18]).

39: *Ha – Dieser war es*

The dam bursts. Brünnhilde can contain herself no longer. *J'accuse* Siegfried of taking the ring off me she sings** in a furious outburst. He done it! Traitor! Now we soar and swoop along with her anger and Siegfried's rebuttal. But the subject changes to the matter of whether or not Siegfried had sex with her and now everyone gets into the act – the stage army, the women and all, and in the general mish-mash the voltage drops (Frustration [18], Nothung [15], Sword [14]).

Now we are treated to the sort of ritual dear

29

39

to myth and ancient lays. This time it's spear-point swearing, the spear-point being a substitute for the Bible, which has not yet reached these parts. Hagen goes first, Siegfried second, then Brünnhilde. The matter at issue is whether when first they met Nothung hung on the wall (bad) or was placed between them in the bed (dangerous, but good, because this will prove Brünnhilde's virginity). Her swearing is easily the best** and as a woman wronged her outbursts of passion ring true and clear amidst all the musical skulduggery around her (Valkyrie [16], Nothung [15]). Siegfried, well out of character, ends the scene by saying Well let's be friends anyway and have a jolly party. But the playout doesn't sound all that jolly, ending as it does with variants of the Gibichungies [p] and a little reminder of the Curse [11].

49: *Helle Wehr!* 49
Heilige Waffe!

Act II Sc 5

The scene opens with Brünnhilde pensive and then rolls on to allow the trio Gunther/Hagen/Brünnhilde to consider how to dispose of Siegfried in what sounds the most surprisingly laid-back and lyrical fashion (Fate [19], Siegfried Heroic [20], Sword [14], Bad News [d] and Brünnhilde [28]). Only when Brünnhilde has a stab of jealousy for Gutrune do things wake up** and the final trio, the three singing together (against Wagner's general ground rules) is glorious indeed. Siegfried shall die! That's one thing settled. And to keep things on a high the playout makes merry with the Gibichung motto [p] as the wedding procession comes on.

68: *Was riet mir* 68
mein Wissen?

Act III Sc 1
0

Horn calls start off the prelude,* Siegfried's first [24] answered by the moody call of the gloomy Gibichungs. Then, serenely, the Rhine music that opened the whole cycle breaks in [1] – and what a relief it is to hear the cool water music again after such a dose of the noisy domestic life of the Gibichungies. The prelude (Rhinegold [3]) runs on into some watery dance music for

0

3: *Frau Sonne*
sendet Lichte

the Rhinemaidens as they sing*** a surprisingly   3
cheerful song about their lost gold (Gold [2],
Rhinegold [3]). A nice new motto here – Happy
Rhinemaidens, lingering phrases in the woodwind in close harmony – unlisted. This is a
delight. It is interrupted by Siegfried's horn [24]
and then his arrival.

7: *Ein Albe führte*
mich ihr

The Rhinemaidens ask Siegfried for the ring
– he refuses.* Bits of the old Horn around [24].   7
This is all done in a spirit of persiflage with
peals of laughter from the girls; not what one
would expect when so serious a matter is at stake
– like the end of the world – but let us be
thankful, for Wagner is here in a wonderfully
unbuttoned mood.

14: *Siegfried! Wir*
weisen dich war

The exchanges become more agitated as the
debate goes on* – you'll be cursed Siegfried say   14
the girls. Pshaw! says Siegfried. OK on your
head be it say the girls, moving delicately into a
synchronized trio and swimming offstage. Great
play is made of the new motto but we have
reminders of Spear [7], Gold [2], Rhinegold [3],
the Ring [4] and Curse [11]. This is lively,
buoyant music. No stodge at all.

Act III Sc 2

After the Hails and Hellos, mostly spoken by the
horns (lots of [24] and [24] developed) and after
the drinking horn stuff (the new motto from the
last scene still around), Siegfried moves into a

24: *Mime heiss ein*
mürrischer Zwerg

musical autobiography,** with appropriate mot-   24
tos, Anvils [9] as he runs through his early days
with Mime, then the forging of Nothung [15],
the death of Fafner [23], the death of Mime, all
with the Forest [25] giving a background to a lot
of the story as the bird trills it out [26]. There is
a break for refreshments: Hagen slyly slips some
anti-amnesiac into Siegfried's drink and when
Siegfried carries on we get to the Brünnhilde bit
(Brünnhilde [28] and Loge [8] and more Bird
[26] and so on) and up to the rock (Trance [22])
and references to the Brünnhilde love music.
Suddenly – two frightfully important ravens

32: *Was hör ich!*

34: *Brünnhilde, heilige Braut!*

40

Act III Sc 3

46: *War das sein Horn?*

interrupt the proceedings.* As Siegfried looks up at them he is speared in the back (Curse [11], Siegfried Heroic [20] and Fate [19]). One can't but think that Wagner muffs this bit. The music, although tense and mildly dramatic, really doesn't seem to rise to the occasion. After all, this is *it*. The death of Siegfried! Or almost, for he yanks himself up on his elbow and delivers his farewell message.* This is introduced by the brass chord of doom and is then delivered in hushed tones. (Siegfried Heroic [20], Brünnhilde [28] and Fate [19].) This farewell piece is calm, peaceful and moving. At last he dies. And now, to assure us that his death is a frightfully important event, we have the mighty Funeral March.*** This stunning piece opens with a chord punched out twice on the brass (insistent, upsetting and to dog us throughout the whole course of the march), which turns out to be a musical retrospect of Siegfried's life. Every motto tells a story, and there are plenty (listed below) but the two that blaze out in their full glory are Sword [14] and Horn II [27]. These are the mottos of a hero and they are given the full treatment. Other funeral marches (Handel's, Chopin's) can be used for quite modest funerals of Class I and Class II VIPs, but this one is too grand even for a Prime Minister and too glorious for a royal. It would have done well for Charlemagne or – perhaps – de Gaulle. As it dies away it leaves one problem behind it – how to get the opera started again. (Prominent mottos besides Sword [14] and Horn II [27] are: Self-Pity [g], Siegfried Heroic [20], Brünnhilde [28], Curse [11] and Ring [4].)

So things do start moving again in a quiet but effective recitatif* by Gutrune as she waits for the return of the hunters. Does she hear Siegfried's horn? No, but *we* do (also Brünnhilde [28] and Fate [19]).

Now it's all go; the hunters return; no

32

34

40

46

Siegfried; he's dead; he's carried in on his shield. Gutrune bursts into an agony of hatred for Gunther and Hagen* (introduced by the two funeral chords): there is high drama as Gunther and Hagen fall out over the ring and get into their swordfight.** Gunther is killed. Siegfried raises his dead hand with the ring on it to music of immense power. It sweeps us along from shock to shock. (And incidentally look out for the tenants' oohs and aahs when Siegfried's dead hand comes up – they send a shiver down the vertebrae.) Mottos: Curse [11], Sword [14] and Destruct [13]. Gutrune sees the light (a bit late), namely that the forget-all magimix that she had given Siegfried made him forget his true love Brünnhilde – the duet between the two is ennobled by a shining lyrical passage from Brünnhilde.** (Mottos: Gutrune [29], Fate [19].)

The finale. In the short intermezzo before Brünnhilde's final spiel we have reminders that she was once a Valkyrie. Now she sings once again with authority,** telling the lads to pile up the logs on Siegfried's funeral pyre and declaring she will ride along with him to wherever it is he is going. (Heaven? Hades? Not Valhalla.) (Loge [8], Siegfried Heroic [20].) She goes on to muse, beautifully and quietly, on Siegfried's nobility. Now she knows why he broke his word. (Heroic love [n], Sword [14], Nothung [15], Fate [19], Curse [11].)

She contemplates the ring, taken from Siegfried's finger, and promises to return it to the Rhinemaidens. She is now into her stride. Noble heroic Brünnhilde music, still poppling with mottos (Rhine [1], Curse [11]).

The climax.*** Brünnhilde tells the ravens to get back to the rock and tell Loge that the time has come for his great act of arson, namely to put a match to all those logs stacked up against Valhalla. Then instructions are sung out in queenly fashion, the music surging and billowing

50: *Siegfried, Siegfried erschlagen!*
52: *Nicht klage wider mich!*
55: *Armselige, schweig!*
57: *Starke Scheite schichten mir dort*
68: *Fliegt heim ihr Raben!*

beneath with mottos now a living part of the noble stream of sound (introduced by Spear [7] and leading to Loge [8] and Destruct [13]). Grane appears and Brünnhilde tells the poor beast its next and final job is to leap into the fire. Now Ecstasy [21] (unheard since Act III of *Valkyrie*) rises up and stuns us with its sheer loveliness. Brünnhilde, in a blaze of glory, jumps onto Grane and rides into the fire, and that for her is pretty well it. (Loge [8], Valkyrie music [16] and [17], Ecstasy [21] and Siegfried Heroic [20].)

72   The playout.*** Even the grandeur of   72 Brünnhilde's exit is topped by this mighty final symphony. This is Wagner at the top of his bent with all the stops out and with a compendium of mottos to complete the story: Valkyrie [16], Loge [8], Sleep [i], Rhinegold [3], Rhine [1], Curse [11], Valhalla [5], Siegfried Heroic [20] and, of course, Ecstasy [21]. Even if the stage effects can't rise to the occasion (they never can), nothing can dim the glory of this knockout finale. Finally Ecstasy takes over and the mighty *Ring* dies away in a rare moment of sweetness and beauty. Thank goodness for Brünnhilde, say we. She may not have saved the day for the gods but she has made the night for us.

NOTES and NEWS AND GOSSIP See **The Birth of** *The Ring* page 215

COMMENT See also **The Ring – A General Hello** page 123

Although *Götterdämmerung* is the longest of the four legs of *The Ring*, it has the fewest longueurs. The Norns at the start are not madly exciting. We could well do without all that stuff about the World ash tree. Also the scene between Alberich, dwarf father, and Hagen, human son, both of them deeply repugnant figures, is no fun. But the re-caps and now-read-ons are no longer a bore. Brünnhilde bringing Waltraute up-to-date and Siegfried telling the by now well-worn tale of his life, although dramatically as tiresome as ever, are both musically rather splendid. But the main thing about *Götterdämmerung* is that the good bits far, far outweigh the mediocre. The early Siegfried/Brünnhilde duet takes us back into the heady upper air of the last scene in *Siegfried*, the scene between Siegfried and the Rhinemaidens is full of delights, the Gibichungs, especially Gutrune, have surprisingly civilized music, no grunts and uncouth tuba noises here; the two orchestral pieces, the Journey and the Funeral March, both come off a million dollars and the finale – well – the finale is one of Wagner's greatest achievements. It gains its strength dramatically from the heroic nobility of Brünnhilde. Here we have music not, as so often in *The Ring*, sung by or about people for whom we do not care a fig, but by a woman we have come to love and venerate. By now Brünnhilde is a true heroine. The final stretch of *The Ring*, from Brünnhilde's message to the ravens to the end, and the orchestral symphony that follows generate opera power of a kind we have never known before. It is as if the opera, which had up till now been driven by steam, had suddenly discovered how to use atomic energy. Well, perhaps not quite like that, but Wagner would be pleased with the comparison.

THE BIRTH OF *THE RING*

The Ring	Four operas, **Rhinegold, Valkyrie, Siegfried** and **Götterdämmerung**. The chief work of Wagner's life, for the pattern of composition see below
First nights	
Rhinegold	Königlich Hof- und National Theater, Munich, 22 September 1869
Valkyrie	As above, 26 June 1870
Siegfried	Festspielhaus, Bayreuth, 16 August 1876
Götterdämmerung	As above, 17 August 1876
	First performance of **The Ring** as a complete cycle: 13, 14, 16, 17 August 1876 at the Festspielhaus, Bayreuth
Reception	Always mixed: see below
Libretto	Wagner
Sources	See below

It took Wagner 26 years to complete *The Ring* from first draft to putting the final touches to *Götterdämmerung*. He wasn't a slow worker, he just kept getting involved in other operas. His first idea was for a single opera, *The Death of Siegfried*. But as he got hooked on the Sagas the size of the story ballooned up. He realized there would have to be too much now-read-on to make the thing dramatic, and if Wagner reached this conclusion then it must indeed have been true. So he decided on two operas, *Siegfried's Death* and *Young Siegfried*. Then these two got a bit crowded so he split the *Death* into two by adding *Götterdämmerung* and put some of the now-read-on stuff into a prologue, *Rhinegold*, which he tiresomely and insistently called 'a preliminary evening'. The four pieces in approximately their present form were in draft script by the end of 1848.

The main sources for the gloomy tale were the Icelandic sagas. These were not at all ancient, being written about a hundred years after our own Norman Conquest. Siegfried etc. were remembered historical characters, like our Alfred and the cakes, but even more unfortunate. They also supplied some of the Who's Who of the gods, Wotan = Odin, and so on. Another source were some German–Nordic poems, no doubt equally brutish. When one reflects that only a couple of hundred years later the witty and sophisticated Chaucer was writing stuff that would have rated a fourteenth-century *New Yorker* we can be thankful we lived in warmer climes.

Wagner set about writing the librettos for *The Ring* in reverse order, *Götterdämmerung* first, *Rhinegold* last. But he took his eye off the ball to write *Tristan*, finished in 1857, and *Meistersinger* ten years later, two walloping great works that finally and decisively put him to No. 1 in the German opera ratings and equal No. 1 to Verdi in the international league.

Wagner's method of working was first to write a prose version of the story. He then translated this into his own kind of poetry – scansion, alliteration, high-flown words, but no rhymes. Those in a position to judge, most of them pro-Wagner, will reluctantly admit that this is not great poetry, so we are probably right in thinking that *qua* poetry it is pretty dreadful. (Surprisingly, this was perhaps the only area where Wagner was not vain: he never claimed to be a great poet, so why did he take such enormous pains to give second-rate words such careful treatment when setting them to first-rate music?) He then went on to a sketch score on three staves – one for the voice and two for the orchestra. Sometimes he went to a second sketch score, sometimes straight to the full score. Then a bit of fiddling around and into rehearsal.

Wagner had practically no income and spent a lot of money and so required sponsorship to keep the wheels turning. He found this in a small way from a number of female fans and in a big way from a young man of eighteen who was potty about his music and was, fortunately for Wagner, a king and could therefore divert state money, regardless of the wishes of the taxpayers, into Richard Wagner Enterprises. So it was that under the admiring eye of King Ludwig of Bavaria *Rhinegold* and *Valkyrie* were premiered in the King's Theatre Munich in 1869 and 1870. Bits of the unfinished works had been performed at a concert in Vienna some seven years earlier and this had already got the adrenalin running in musico and critical circles. This first full helping of *The Ring* fuelled the civil war that was to rage amongst musicians for a quarter of a century after Wagner's death. Those against were led by one Hanslick, a leading Viennese music critic, and those for by Wagner. Three of Hanslick's main planks were: Wagner was pushing music beyond the bounds of what music should properly be asked to do (wrong), Wagner paid far too much attention to the setting of the work – music should come first, words second (right) – and Wagner was wrong to be lurching around in the area of myth and legend: opera should be about people (half right). And many other things too, for as a great classicist Hanslick found Wagner desperately untidy. So did the Wagnerites and anti-Wagnerites rage against each other until the war began to peter out about the middle of this century.

Wagner had many theories about how to write music for opera. He was extremely strong on theories and plucked ideas from all over the place and especially from Aeschylus and Schopenhauer and put them into his operatic magimix formula.

Some of the novelties were:

1. Motivic integration. The whole idea of musical mottos telling you what to think while you listen. Cues without words. Plenty about this on other pages.

2. Musico-poetic synthesis (!). Making the words and music fuse into a single experience. Further and better particulars on pages 128–9.

3. Tonal structure. The overall strategy of key relationships and the (to us) rather crazy emphasis on the association of a musical idea (often a motto) with a particular key. Scribes will report with triumph that he brings back motto *xyz* IN THE ORIGINAL KEY. So bully for him.

Wagner the theoretician had the unusual capacity to put his theories into practice. He certainly made it hard for himself, but after some pretty dour early stuff (the dwarf bits of *Rhinegold*, *Valkyrie* Act I) and after *Tristan*, his learning curve speeded up and in the music of *Siegfried* (second half) and the later additions to *Götterdämmerung* he is really motoring with all the computer controls showing positive. But whether or not this huge apparatus of musical technology improved or impeded his performance as an opera composer, we shall never know.

It was Wagner's dream to have a Festival Theatre designed by him to perform his works. This would ensure that they were 100% proof. Written by Wagner, composed by Wagner, cast by Wagner, produced by Wagner, performed in a Wagner-designed theatre, where the programme notes and even the notices in the gents' advising clients to adjust their dress before leaving, would be written by Wagner himself. Amazingly enough he delegated the musical direction of the first full cycle to Hans Richter but we can be sure there was some pretty imperious back-seat driving.

At first he tried to site the Wagnerfestspielhaus in Munich but Ludwig was getting such a hard time from his civil servants (most of whom were probably crypto-Hanslickers) for spending money on a megalomaniac composer that he had to switch to the Glyndebourne concept and set up a Festspielcountrykindofhaus at Bayreuth. To finance it he opened a fund to which all big-hearted supporters of the arts (i.e. of Wagner) were invited to contribute. It flopped, and the opening *Ring* cycle had to be postponed. Once again the Wagner-crazy King Ludwig picked up the tab. (You can imagine the scene when this news reached the permanent secretary to the Treasury.)

The two Munich productions had passed off reasonably well. The house had a firm management and Wagner, as an old opera house pro, respected the musical standards and the technical team. But the rehearsals for the full cycle at Bayreuth must have been murder. By nature Wagner was a dictator and at Bayreuth he was also a god. Added to this, he was now into an advanced stage of megalomania, and who would like to have been the person responsible for the anvil splitting in half while Siegfried's sword was still up in the air (which did happen)? Wagner must have come to realize that his vision of *The Ring*'s scenic effects was not going to come off and – worse still – could never come off. Sitting in his study, he was complete master of words and music, but when it came to opera's third estate – the *mise en scène* – he could not by sheer brainpower make flats, backdrops, gaslight and stagehands do magic things. This must have been a terrible blow to him, like when he found he couldn't walk on water either.

So the Bayreuth theatre was built, the full cycle of *The Ring* performed, the dream realized, and Wagner didn't like it much. He thought the sets looked crummy and Richter took the gloomier bits too fast, The Ride of the Valkyries too slow.

But the first full cycle of *The Ring* was a sensation. It had made its mark and during the 1890s it was given in Vienna, London and New York and, liked or loathed, it was universally recognized as the Everest amongst operas that it is.

Since then it is staged from time to time when the major houses can afford it and, whereas the announcement of other operas may be news, a production of *The Ring* is still a headline event.

It is impossible to grade this Xtraordinary and Xceptional work as if it were an ordinary opera so let us therefore just give it an X.

Parsifal

Holy melodrama

The one where a simple-minded teenager by shooting a swan gets
involved with a religious sect whose king is permanently wounded
and whose official messenger is a convertible woman, sometimes
witch, sometimes houri.

CAST

Titurel, semi-retired king, father of Amfortas	Bass
Amfortas, acting ruler of the Kingdom of the Grail	Baritone
Gurnemanz, a senior Knight of the Grail	Bass
Kundry, a woman under a spell	Mezzo
Klingsor, failed knight of the Grail, now evil	Bass
Parsifal, a foolish boy	Tenor

Knights of the Grail (tenors and basses), **Squires**
(some trebles), **Flower Maidens** (sopranos and
mezzos), voices from above

3 acts: running time 4 hrs 40 mins

BEFORE WE BEGIN

Some Angels, we hope with due authorization, gave to King
Titurel the Grail, the cup from which Jesus had drunk at the Last
Supper, and the Spear, which had pierced His side on the cross.
The motive for this transaction is not known, but the Angels
certainly thought they had put the things in safe hands. Alas no.
Titurel recruited a body of knights to guard the castle where the
relics were sited but one applicant for the job, Klingsor, was
blackballed because he failed to pass the safe sex test. Indeed, his
sexual history showed him to be quite unfit to consort with
knights who were so pure in mind they had never had it off with
anyone, ever. Klingsor foolishly castrated himself, thinking that
would lessen his sex drive and get him accepted. But no, the
blackball stood. In a fury he set up a lavish brothel close by
Titurel's place in the guise of a castle with the park full of hookers,
who in order to spare the blushes of the Bayreuth set were called
Flower Maidens. By these means he hoped to de-purify Titurel's
knights one by one, get them fired and, when there were none left,
to seize the Grail; though why such a loose-living chap should
want a grail, even when castrated, is a mystery. So many of

Titurel's knights slipped off for a short time at Klingsor's open-air massage parlour that his operational strength fell dangerously low. He therefore sent his son Amfortas to close down Klingsor's house who unfortunately fell for the chief hooker, one Kundry, and Klingsor took the holy Spear off him while he had his trousers down. He then gave him a nasty wound with it just below his rib cage which went septic and for lack of penicillin which had not yet been invented, would not heal. Kundry while continuing as a hooker by night lived a double life, becoming by day a sort of down-at-heel witch who acted as a runner for the Grail knights whose staff-vetting procedures were poor. Now read on.

STORY

Act I Sc 1 The grounds of Titurel's castle
In which Kundry rides in with some medicine for the wounded King Amfortas who graciously receives it on the way to his bath

We are in the land of myth vaguely located in Spain and the time is AD but not much. Hey lads get up and pray says Gurnemanz to two young sleeping sentries and good day to you he adds to a couple of stray knights how's HRH Amfortas this morning? Much the same say the knights temperature 101° pulse normal wound still suppurating. He's on his way to his morning ablutions. There's only one cure for him says Gurnemanz and I'm not telling at this stage for fear of spoiling the plot.

A witch is seen riding fast. She rushes in. Here's some Friars' Balsam for Amfortas she says: it's the last bottle left she says nothing like it. Enter Amfortas groaning on a litter. God what a terrible night says he. Sorry that new prescription from Professor Gawain didn't work says a knight he's gone off by the way. AWOL? says Amfortas. Probably sneaked off into Klingsor's whorehouse. None of these damn medicos are any good I just have to wait for the arrival of the holy fool. Remember I told you that I got this holy fax saying only some innocent fool who had come to see the light through some terrible experience could cure me. But meanwhile says Gurnemanz try some of this Friars' Balsam. Kundry got it for you. Thanks Kundry says Amfortas (exits).

Ho ho look at Kundry nasty dirty brutish thing say the squires. Leave her alone says Gurnemanz she does a good job for us and has the misfortune to be under a curse. By the way Kundry where

were you the day we lost the Spear? (Kundry looks at the ground.)
Why not send her to get it now? say the squires. That would be
against the Grail rules section 17B says Gurnemanz mysteriously.
How well I remember the day Klingsor nicked it off Amfortas
while he was bonking. A disastrous bonk that was. Tell us more
say the squires. Gurnemanz tells them a whole heap more about
the blackballing of Klingsor etc. and also that when the wounded
Amfortas got back to the Grail Hall and was praying like crazy the
Grail spoke and read out to him the fax about waiting for a holy
fool (and the cleaners found the hard copy on the floor next
morning).

Act I Sc 2 The same
In which a swan is shot and Parsifal discovered to be of
subnormal intelligence

A dead swan falls from the sky amongst some squires. Who done
this dastardly act? they cry. Some knights enter giving Parsifal the
bum's rush. He done it they cry this big loony done it with his
bow and arrow. You done this? asks Gurnemanz. Yeah it was a
great shot he was coming really high says Parsifal. You feel no
shame murdering a beautiful animal? says Gurnemanz the birds
and the beasts have as much right to this forest as do you.

He goes on to give him an animal rights lecture and ends by
asking him how could you do such a thing? Dunno says Parsifal.
Who's your father? asks Gurnemanz. Dunno says Parsifal. Where
are you from? Who do you work for? What school did you go to?
University? What's your blood group? asks Gurnemanz. Dunno
dunno dunno dunno says Parsifal. What's your name then? asks
Gurnemanz. Dunno. Lordy Lordy we have a real thickie here says
Gurnemanz and maybe one for the men in white coats. Look to it
lads and give this swan a decent Christian burial (they knock up a
small coffin and reverently bear the swan to its final resting place).

So what *do* you know? Gurnemanz asks Parsifal. How to make
bows and arrows and I know I had a mum called Gloomy Kate.
Enter Kundry. I can tell you more says Kundry: his dad was killed
in battle before he was born. And one day I saw soldiers says
Parsifal. And he kills giants and poachers and any other wicked
person with his bare hands says Kundry. What's wicked? says
Parsifal. This poor loony certainly should be inside says Gurnemanz. And your mum took it very badly that you ran off and left
her says Kundry. Parsifal leaps at Kundry's throat. O God and a

violent one too says Gurnemanz as he separates them.

I think I'll take a nap says Kundry (disappears into the bushes). You come with me son says Gurnemanz the Grail might do you a power of good. What's Grail? asks Parsifal as they start trudging along a moving walkway while scenery rolls past (if it's a traditional production) until they are in the Grail Hall.

Act I Sc 3 The Grail Hall in Titurel's castle
In which Parsifal is subjected to Holy Communion apparently to no effect but we are tipped off that he is going to be Amfortas's saviour

An all-male Holy Communion is being celebrated by boys youths acolytes squires knights etc. You do the honours Amfortas says Titurel. No you do it Dad says Amfortas my ribs are killing me and I think all this stuff about Christ's blood plus my guilt is giving me a nervous breakdown. O my God it's started bleeding again. He passes out. Whilst Amfortas is in dreamland the boys sing about the promised coming of the converted fool though it's hard to see how that could have worked its way into the Liturgy. Amfortas did you hear me? says Titurel. Amfortas comes to and jacks himself up and does the priest's office for the whole stageful of choristers extras etc. The hall empties and Gurnemanz goes up to Parsifal and asks well how did that grab you? Dunno says Parsifal. OK you loony says Gurnemanz and – stand by folks for the only attempt at a joke in *Parsifal* – since you are such a gander get out there and look for a goose. Heavenly voices are heard by us – maybe not by anyone else – singing That's the boy! that's the converted fool elect! watch that man!

Act II Sc 1 On the ramparts of Klingsor's magic castle
In which Klingsor summons Kundry to his castle to seduce Parsifal who kills a number of Klingsor's security police in forcing an entry

Klingsor is sitting looking in his magiscope: aha I see this loony is on his way he says. Wake up Kundry you idle bitch report for duty. Now! At once! Kundry appears in a haze of blue light. You been working for that Grail mob again? asks Klingsor. Kundry screams very loud and writhes too. Yes she says. So you like to think the good you do for them there makes up for the harm you do them when you are with us here says Klingsor. A likely story.

OK get your war paint on. No! No! spare me wails Kundry. Not likely says Klingsor I got you well magicked into my power. And yet you used to sleep around yourself says Kundry. Belt up! says Klingsor I don't want any of that stuff. You get on with your job of seducing your way through those Grailers so I can get my hands on the Grail. That Parsifal's nearly here now get into your tart's togs quick. Must I? asks Kundry. For Chrissake give over says Klingsor he's a sexy chap you'll enjoy it.

My God there's Parsifal attacking my chaps – there's Jimmy Ferris gone – now he's got his sword through Claude – there's Jack Beauchamp's arm off. An unforced error there – oops! right through Charlie's thigh on the backhand – they're leaving the court – game set and match Parsifal. Are you ready Kundry? As for you my lad one bedroom bout with her and you'll be magicked into my power. He presses the garden release button and the castle shoots to the back of the stage. A garden springs up in front.

Act II Sc 2 Klingsor's garden
In which Klingsor's hostesses make minor attempts on Parsifal's virtue and Kundry launches a full-scale seduction but all fail in the face of the impenetrable stupidity of our hero

Klingsor's full establishment of hostesses come in whingeing about the death and mayhem caused amongst their playmates by Parsifal. Jimmy Ferris was the biggest tipper in the business says one. Charlie won't be able to do much with only one thigh says another. Some of them will need weeks in hospital before they can perform again says a third. Who done it? they all ask: who is this murderous bastard?

Parsifal jumps over the fence. It's him they cry. Why did you do it? In order to get to you says Parsifal I had to clear the way somehow. You killed our men. Who'll be our playmates now? they ask. I will says Parsifal. O goody say the girls we're not greedy it's only fifty dollars for half an hour. I saw him first says one he's mine. Bollocks says another he took my card let's have some harmless foreplay and dance a-ring a-ring of roses before anything else happens says a fly one.

They dance but the girls start pushing shoving and kicking each other in the groin trying to get their hands on Parsifal. Stop it he shouts and pushes them off. An eerie voice rings out: Parsifal! it says P..A..R..S..I..F..A..L. Whosat? says Parsifal. Stay here says the voice. The girls run off. Are you speaking to me? says Parsifal. Yes says Kundry (for it is she – now transformed for seduction duties) your Pa called you Parsley before he died and your Ma called you that parsley fool but things got mixed up in the word processor and . . . OK OK OK says Parsifal.

Whew! you look sexy are those the things they call suspenders? Do you live here? No I came a long way just to see you says she. I knew you when you were a kid living with your mum Gloomy Kate. She thought the world of you and died of sorrow when you walked out on her. Oh my God! I never thought of that! I killed my mother! I am guilty guilty guilty! cries Parsifal. Never mind I bring you this message from your Mum says Kundry and gives him a long sexy kiss. Parsifal reels back. Help! Amfortas! he says save me from sin which this must surely be because of the funny feeling I have in my trousers. I must think of the Grail like mad.

He has a fit and when he comes to he goes on I should not be consorting with a high-class tart in this garden. I am guilty guilty guilty . . . and he goes off again. Hey Parsifal can't you keep your mind on the business in hand says Kundry. You whore says Parsifal you must be the one who got Amfortas into trouble. Get off! Get out! Get lost! If you're off sex and on to redemption says Kundry what about me? You know I'm under a curse because I made a joke in front of Jesus about his Father and in his infinite compassion he is now giving me hell.

I have an idea if we had a nice time together that might just lift the curse. No it wouldn't says Parsifal you stand a much better chance if I follow the holy option. If one kiss gave you such a lift says Kundry just think what the full personal service could do. Leave it to me says Parsifal I will fix your redemption without any full personal service. Just show me the way to go home – the way to Amfortas. Never! Not on your life! says Kundry he's a wimp I'll get after you with that self-same Spear if you start trying to help that weasel. Come on Parsifal just a short time and with your clothes on if you like . . . Get thee behind me evil woman says Parsifal. Hi! Klingsor jumps out holding the Spear. This Spear will stop you in your tracks my boy says Klingsor. But no Parsifal seizes the Spear and makes the sign of the Cross with it. This activates a destruct button within the castle which promptly falls down in ruins.

Act III Sc 1 In the grounds of Titurel's castle. Early
morning. Some years later
In which Kundry goes into domestic service and Parsifal
turns up in a dark suit

Kundry lies groaning in a bush. Gurnemanz pulls her out.
Springtime Kundry he says wake up. But there's not much
messenger work now owing to the recession. How about a cleaning
lady? asks Kundry could I do for you for instance Mr Gurnemanz?
OK says he – who's that coming onstage in black armour? (It's
Parsifal of course.) Hey you do know this is a no-armaments area?
And that it's Good Friday which is a no-armaments day? (Parsifal
strips off.) My God it's that loony what shot the swan! and he's
got the Spear! says Gurnemanz.

Nice to see you again says Parsifal. I wanted to help that nice
Amfortas but I got lost for about ten years. I rather think there
was a curse on me says Parsifal. I now see you are the converted
fool who is to be our saviour says Gurnemanz: you've arrived in
the nick of time for things are pretty bad in the Grailhouse.
Titurel dead Amfortas refusing to do his bit with the Grail low
morale generally grafitti on the castle walls also mass visitations to
the massage parlour. My God it's all my fault says Parsifal if I'd
got to Amfortas right away all this could have been avoided I'm
guilty guilty guilty and he's off again. Never too late to mend says
Gurnemanz we can get along there and sort things out shortly.

Would you please purify me first? asks Parsifal. My feet are a
bit smelly after ten years of wandering. Certainly says Gurnemanz.
Kundry! The gentleman's feet. I'll do your head says Gurnemanz.
Parsifal sprinkles holy water on to Kundry as she wipes the engine
oil off his feet. She is thus released from her curse. Nice day for a
Good Friday says Parsifal. I see the birds and the bees are all at
work. Yes that's what Good Friday's all about says Gurnemanz.
Parsifal kisses Kundry on the head to make quite sure she's curse-
free. Gurnemanz puts a spare set of Grail-knight's ermines onto
Parsifal. Avanti! says Gurnemanz and they trudge off into Scene 2.
Probably past the same forests rocks etc. as in Act I for few houses
can afford two such huge panorama cloths.

Act III Sc 2 The Grail Hall
In which Titurel is taken to his grave, Amfortas is cured
and a pigeon flies over Parsifal

By a lucky stroke of timing Gurnemanz and Parsifal arrive just as a procession of knights comes in carrying the body of Titurel fronted by the Grail. This will be your last Communion old boy they say. They open the coffin in front of Amfortas and there is a brief ululation by one and all at the sight of the body. True to form Amfortas starts whingeing noisily about wanting to die too. Serve the sacrament Amfortas shout the knights: go on. Do it. It's your job. It's what you're paid for. Can't do it says Amfortas look at my wound it's bleeding (he rather disgustingly shows it) besides I have this psychological block. Kill me please do but no serving of the sacrament.

Parsifal steps up and touches Amfortas's wound with the Spear. I think this might help your problem he says (and it does): this is the Spear he adds I've brought it back. (Sensation.) Uncover the Grail please he says. He kneels down before it. Kundry lies down at his feet. She expires. The Grail begins to give off sparks. It's a miracle that's what it is say all the knights etc. A pigeon flies in and hovers over Parsifal's head. Clearly everyone including God thinks Parsifal has done a good job.

PARSIFAL MOTTOS

Number	Name	Description
1	Sacrament	First item in the prelude. Slow, solemn, aimless.
2	Grail	Alias the Dresden Amen. Upward phrase and A-MEN.
3	Faithful	O come all ye faithful – but not quite. First heard as a clarion call repeated three times.
4	Spear	The end of Sacrament [1]. Three shorts run up to a long and it trails away.
5	Kundry	Downward sweep in the strings from very high to very low – four octaves.
6	Amfortas	Two slow opening notes with a long tail behind them.
7	Klingsor	A fleeting figure up and down sloped like the arch of a bow.
8	Innocence	Slow and hymn-like, much longer than most.

| 9 | Parsifal | Soft horns in thirds, bouncing gently upwards. |
| 10 | Bells | Not quite the first four notes of Big Ben. |

LOOK OUT FOR

MINUTES FROM START

Prelude

0 — The prelude is intensely serious but lacking in charm. It begins with a parade of mottos as follows: Sacrament [1], Grail [2], Faithful [3]. Then Grail [2] again. Then some powerful stuff building up (Faithful [3]) in sequences. The rest of the prelude pushes around these mottos in a stop—start fashion until we reach a new one, Spear [4] – the end of Sacrament [1]. We wait for the thing to come together and to give us some nice ongoing music but it never does. Greatly admired by many good judges but no star from this guide.   0

Act I Sc 1

Gurnemanz wakes the two squires. All pray. Grail [2] and Faithful [3]. Two knights appear, outriders of Amfortas's bathing party. Mostly recitatif but then some arioso trying to get out. A sluggish start. Mainly Hellos and How is hes? No star.

Kundry is spotted by one of the squires, surprisingly a soprano (arranged for choral duty? or else very young?) and Kundry arrives in a fluster of strings. We hear that her horse is not flying through the air today but crawling (very odd because the fiddles are certainly giving us fly-music not crawl-music and it is not all that common for a horse to crawl). Anyway Kundry comes in to her motto [5]. She gives Gurnemanz the Friars' Balsam and he greets Amfortas on arrival. Quite nice exchanges. Things are looking up but still no star.

21: *Recht so! Habt Dank* — Amfortas to the rescue.* As he gives the bulletin on his overnight health we hear his motto deep in the strings [6] (we heard it first at   21

the beginning of the act) and he sings splendidly
for so sick a man, calm sweet music in three
stanzas, although in the second he has a moment
of bad temper on hearing that Gawain has gone
AWOL. He is looking forward to his morning
ablutions.

27   As the invalid's procession moves on there is
a short orchestral symphony* passing Amfortas   27
[6] from instrument to instrument in the most
beguiling fashion.

The squires start to pick on Kundry but
Gurnemanz, in a strong bid to become a Wotan
for Christ, starts to tell us about her extremely
unusual past life and then goes on to tell the tale
of the Grail.

29: Hm! Schuf sie   1.* Kundry is a good woman. Provides a   29
euch Schaden je?   reliable messenger service. May be under a
curse. May have been reincarnated. Old Titurel
first found her lying about in the bushes. Where
were you Kundry the day we lost the Spear?
(Kundry looks at the ground.) This is bold
recitatif with some fragmentary tunes. Bits of
Sacrament [1], Kundry [5] and Faithful [3].

36: Das ist ein   2.* Why not send her to get the Spear now,   36
andres   ask the lads. No that wouldn't do. It's forbid-
den, Amfortas had it nicked off him by a woman
– well, sort of a whore – I was there. Tell us
more say the squires. A lot of Spear [4] and stuff
distantly derived from Sacrament [1].

40: Titurel, der   3.** Let's start at the beginning [after ten   40
fromme Held   minutes! Ed.] Titurel was given charge of the
Grail and Spear [4] also Grail [2] and Sacrament
[1]. He knew Klingsor who applied for membership of the Grail club. Much as 2. above.

44: Klingsorn, wie   4.** Klingsor was blackballed! Change of   44
hart ihn Müh'   gear. The easy-going narrative gets rumbustious. We have a new motto, Klingsor [7], first
heard on a clarinet doubling a bassoon – a
spooky sound. After the agitato about Klingsor
(with a bit of the sexy music to come) things
settle down as the aged Titurel hands over to his
son Amfortas. And you know what happened to

him. Derivatives of Sacrament [1]: Grail [2] pretty well its old self.

48: *Vor dem verwaisten Heiligtum*

5.** To get the Spear back Amfortas was told by some angelic means that only a fool (with certain other qualifications) could get it back. Solemn, quieter, almost sotto voce. Now the motto of simple fools, Innocence [8], is sung twice first by Gurnemanz and then by the prefects. Trembling strings, soft brasses and the apparatus of hush. (Grail [2].)

Throughout this twenty-minute account of past history the vocal line gives no great pleasure. Gurnemanz is telling us the plot, not singing about it. It is in fact a marathon recitatif with scraps of melody for the voice but accompanied by gloriously rich orchestral backing. Although a shower of fresh ideas lies thick on the ground the texture is not so dense as in the earlier Wagners. There are lots of striking phrases floating around which sound as if they are important new mottos, but they aren't. Many are distant relatives of bits of Sacrament [1] and of Grail [2]. The woodwind has a big piece of the action. The interjections from the listening prefects (most of whose voices have broken – what a relief) come as welcome breaks.

Act I Sc 2

Now it's all go. A swan! Dead! Who done it? Parsifal done it. (Knights and squires solus and in chorus.) This gives Gurnemanz an opportunity for a short Party Political Broadcast** on behalf of the World Wildlife Fund. The thought of the birds and the beasts unleashes some of Wagner's loveliest nature music, as did the forest in *Siegfried*. This is something really different, fresh, outdoor and not in the least holy. But after he has spoken sharply to Parsifal we have holy lift-off again with the Parsifal motto [9].

53: *Du konntest morden*

56: *Wo bist du her?*

Gurnemanz quizzes Parsifal.** Gentle probing and innocent replies from our Candide.

There is something strangely touching about these exchanges which happen over a sweet accompaniment. (Amfortas [6] and Parsifal [9].)

60: *Ja! Und einst am Waldessaume vorbei*

Getting to know our hero. Parsifal tells us some of the things he *does* remember.* He saw a troop of soldiers and knocked off the odd robber and giant. We have a jolly musical ride in the background and then some brisk adventurous music. After which the motivation of the scene is hard to follow, especially when Parsifal assaults Kundry for telling him of his mother's death and indeed his general mode of behaviour is incomprehensible. But Gurnemanz thinks he may be spotting a champ in our Candide. Musically scrappy, but always on the go (Parsifal [9], Kundry [5], Grail [2] and Klingsor [7]).   60

Gurnemanz marches Parsifal through caves and rocks to the Grail Hall [2].

Act I Sc 3

67

This transformation scene* is pleasant enough but not on the same scale as the great transformers in *The Ring*. Wagner seems inhibited by an excess of holiness and the great hall steals in in a discreet fashion not in any way dramatic. No bang, no wallop but quite a sizeable climax built out of Amfortas [6], Grail [2] and Bells [10], a new motto (not quite the first four notes of Big Ben, with a hitchkick on the first note when played on the strings or the timps, but losing it when the bells become real). The male chorus   67

73: *Zum letzten Liebesmahle*

that follows* is sung almost entirely against a combination of Bells [10], banged out on the timps, and Grail [2] in counterpoint above. This goes on so long as to make you think there is a spectral stage army marking time in the wings. The last of the choruses (the boys alone) makes some play with Faithful [3]. The choruses are all very decent and they come off better on stage with the holy sets and props than they do in the study where they sound a little dim.   73

The old Titurel tells Amfortas to serve Communion. Amfortas agonizes for seven minutes and then faints. Again it is hard to find satisfaction with the words (there is a lot about holy blood) and the vocal part is much what we have become inured to. But the orchestral scene is full of interest** and of beauty. (A lot of 82 Amfortas [6] now so developed as to be quite unlike its old self, and of the inevitable Sacrament [1] and Grail [2].)

82: *Nein! Lasst ihn unenthüllt!*

We are now into something like a full-dress communion service conducted partly by divine agencies and partly by humans. One divine stroke is to shine a ray of light onto the Grail, like Tinkerbell in *Peter Pan* (but the Grail doesn't move). The introductory music is melodramatic – Wagner at his phoney holiest – it then passes through some standard religious voluntary stuff (Sacrament [1], Grail [2], Bells [10]) to a surprise – the college song of Grailers,* which breaks in, sung with gusto first 101 by the knights on one side then by the knights on the other side then by all the knights together and it goes with as much of a swing as the Eton Boating Song. This unholiest of tunes comes as blessed relief. The words are of course still part of the service so what we have here is the opposite of the rugger song which sets bawdy words to Hymns Ancient and Modern. Here we have holy words to Grailhouse Rock. But it lapses back into the holiness of Grail [2] with treble voices and high fiddles. Faithful [3]. And a bit of Amfortas [5] and Innocence [8] still clinging on. This is a processional, and very effective it is, right up to Bells [10] dying away at the end.

101: *Nehmet vom Brot*

Act II Sc 1

0

The opening orchestral piece* is a mildly 0 effective rush-around mainly by the strings telling us that evil men are afoot (Klingsor [7] and Kundry [5]).

Klingsor is looking in his magic mirror and knows all. Parsifal is approaching (Innocence

[8]). Klingsor calls Kundry. She awakes dramatically.

There is some cross-talk between Klingsor and Kundry which doesn't advance the plot and is probably the musical low point of the opera. But hark! Parsifal's call rings out [9]. Action! Klingsor race-reads to rousing battle music based on Parsifal [9] and Innocence [8]).* His knights get knocked out one by one. Klingsor magics his castle into a pleasure-garden.

14: *Ho! Ihr Wächter!*

Act II Sc 2

This surprises Parsifal, especially when a lot of hostesses run out of the bushes. The music is superior theatre-music. Now we have something very close to the Act II ballet of the old French opera – a complete change of mood, light tuneful music and lots of girls, only they don't dance.

1. The girls are sad. They have no playmates, Parsifal has killed them all. Sad music, not too sad, close harmony singing, no mottos.

2. They parley with Parsifal. Is he friend or foe? Pert dialogue, music cheering up.

3. Friend! Fluttery cheerful music, dead playmates forgotten, leading to –

4. Sexual harassment of Parsifal in waltz time.** This is enchanting. No holy blood around, no holy anything, everything quite quite human and a rattling good tune too. And Klingsor's hookers all sound like the sweetest of young things. But they quarrel over Parsifal and, alas! we are back to four in a bar.

22: *Komm, Komm, holder Knabe!*

Now we strike gold. We hear Kundry offstage calling 'Parsifal'. Her voice floats in asking Parsifal to stay and the girls to go, which they do with a final flutter and giggle.

1. Kundry appears (Innocence [8]) and gently tells Parsifal about his father and more especially his mother,*** how she doted on him and how she pined for him and died when he left her. This is Wagner spinning a web of stunning beauty. No mottos, but a recurrent ear-catching

31: *Dich nannt' ich*

14

22

31

phrase that starts each fresh section (long higher
note smoothly down to the second, a beautiful
and enlarged cuckoo call). As she tells him of his
mother's grief the smooth flow is interrupted by
the Frustration motto imported from *The Ring*
(a buzz like a bee – unlisted). But up till then,
dreamy.

2. Parsifal is really cut up to think of what he
did to his mother. Kundry seizes this mother
thing as an aid to seduction** and moves
decisively into the sexual assault. Then the kiss.
Wagner muffs this one. It is not as big an event
as it should be. (It has the 'Tristan chord'
embedded in it: there is also some clever work
with Sacrament [1].) But Kundry's wily
approach still holds the dreamy magic of 1.
above. Look out especially for the fancy patterns
from the solo woodwind.

3. Parsifal jumps back like a startled mustang.* He rejects her. At first tumultuous, then
noble and holy (Grail [2] and Sacrament [1]).
Kundry is really surprised but goes on trying to
seduce him (aided by a reprehensible solo
violin). Parsifal re-enacts Amfortas's seduction
and rejects her even more firmly, using fairly
strong language.

4. Kundry tells Parsifal of her hard life and
the reason for it.* (Quite a lot of the borrowed
Frustration.) Lower voltage, sad, halting. A
shriek of shame when she gets to the bit about
her laughing at God. She just can't seem to get
holy again (Grail [2]). Can Parsifal bail her out?
What about just a bit of short-time sex?

5. I can only save you by being a goody says
Parsifal in a short lecturette on the nature of
salvation.** Powerful, free-ranging stuff. Kundry suggests that a full personal service now
would be very helpful to Parsifal's career. She is
now getting desperate and the music has lost all
its early control, it goes into waltz time. They
get into a ding-dong. Parsifal wants to find
Amfortas, Kundry still wants Parsifal. Quite

41: *War dir fremd
noch der Schmerz*

45: *Amfortas!*

53: *Grausamer!*

60: *Auf Ewigkeit
wärst du verdammt*

41

45

53

60

66: *Hilfe! Hilfe!*
Herbei!

hectic. Kundry calls to the boss for help.* She is   66
now hysterical and the music is surging about
like the Dutchman's sea, but not so well
ordered. Klingsor throws the Spear to a sweep
on the harp. It hits holy air above Parsifal's head
and stops dead. Grail [2]. Parsifal hauls it down
and is triumphant. He is also full of magic and
uses it to destroy the Klingsor residence and
policies. Bang! Crash! Crumble! Deeply
descending bass. Exit.

Act III Sc 1

0

The prelude* in its wild chromatic meanderings   0
is telling us that Parsifal has wandered for a long
time (but with the Grail [2] in mind). It is a nice
mild piece, not ambitious.

It takes Gurnemanz some time to drag
Kundry out of a bush (Kundry [5]). He finds
her much improved and suitable for domestic
service. This is mostly quasi-recitatif and pretty
ornery music-to-suit-the-action.

A black knight comes on (Parsifal [9] in the
minor mode: he's tired). He is fully armed. It's
Parsifal! Gurnemanz tells him it's not the thing
to wear full battle order on Good Friday.
Parsifal strips off. Gurnemanz recognizes him,
and his Spear. The first half of this scene moves
haltingly from line to line of thinly accompanied
recitatif. Sometimes it seems as if it would peter
out altogether. Certainly it would win any
operatic slow-bicycle race. But after recognition
the music flashes out in one of those spellbind-
ing patches of slow wonder that are one of

17: *Erkennst du*   Wagner's trademarks.* Mottos abound (Parsifal   17
ihn?   [9], Spear [4], Amfortas [6], Grail [2]).

The wheels begin to turn. Parsifal gives a
spirited account of his wanderings and in the
next half hour we are to see his progress from
roving lunatic to king.

22: *Zu ihm, des*   1. Parsifal's report* flows freely and with a   22
tiefe Klagen   strong pulse. Mottos: Innocence [8], Grail [2].

2. Now it's Gurnemanz's turn to give his
sitrep, and pretty gloomy it is – but easy on the

24: *O Gnade!*
Höchstes Heil!

36: *Du wuschest*
mir die Füsse

42

52

Act III Sc 2

ear.* Before his opening phrase we have a long   24
sweet melody extracted from Sacrament [1] and
towards the end we hear the music of the
prelude to this act. (A derivative of Sacrament
[1] is worked pretty heavily and there is a
smidgen of Bells [10].) Parsifal replies that he's
frightfully sorry to have caused so much grief.

3. The rituals. The washing of the feet,
anointing of the head, etc. Six minutes of
magic.*** The music is gentle, caressing. A   36
sense of Parsifal's simplicity and goodness
reaches through to us, perhaps for the first and
only time. Gurnemanz tells Parsifal he will meet
Amfortas (Parsifal [9]). As Kundry deals with
Parsifal's feet we have a reminder of the Flower-
girls music. (Does Parsifal recognize Kundry as
the Other Woman and do evil thoughts cross his
mind just for a moment?) Gently and tenderly
with a cushion of soft sound we get to the
crowning and now we have Parsifal [9] triumphant and Grail [2] very triumphant indeed to
end the ceremony.

4. The Good Friday music*** heralded in by   42
Faithful [3]. Then a fresh piece with no mottos
(to start with anyway). It is calm and melodious
with woodwind solos swinging out very agreeably. Parsifal nearly spoils it all by harking back
to the gloom of the Crucifixion but Gurnemanz
brings happiness back. According to him all the
birds, beasts and flowers are well briefed in the
story of the Resurrection. This lovely piece has a
reference to Grail [2], otherwise it is pretty well
its own man. Parsifal adds a pretty coda.

Time to get moving says Gurnemanz and the
long march* begins to Bells [10] and a stalk-   52
about figure in the bass which this time builds to
an ear-splitting climax as they reach the Grail
Hall.

The two processions of singing knights start off
sounding like any old anthem for two choirs but
the texture is artfully thickened and once Bells

60: *Ach, zum letzten Mal!*

[10] comes back in on the timps we are won over.* It's a good piece and a perfect preparation for Amfortas's miserable solo. 60

Amfortas's miserable solo. He really is very unhappy and in great pain. Snatches of melody but a glum piece on the whole that fails to arouse much sympathy until the very last few bars which do strike a chord (a touch of Sacrament [1]). The knights get stroppy. Amfortas stands firm (variants of Amfortas [6]). Parsifal interposes (Grail [2], Amfortas [6]). Heals Amfortas (Parsifal [9], Innocence [8] and Spear [4]). Takes the Grail (Faithful [3]). Kundry drops dead. Tinkerbell again. A pigeon appears above his head. This pantomime is accompanied by glowing ethereal music, of

75: *Höchsten Heiles Wunder!*

which the last chorus** and the closing sym- 75 phony are of great beauty and we have farewell references to Innocence [8], Sacrament [1], Faithful [3] and Grail [2].

NOTES

Parsifal   Wagner's thirteenth and last opera
First night   Festspielhaus, Bayreuth, 26 July 1882
Reception   Awed
Libretto   Wagner
Source   Mediaeval poems *Titurel* and *Parzival* by Wolfram von Eschenbach

NEWS AND GOSSIP

Like most of Wagner's operas, *Parsifal* was a long time in the making. First thoughts are recorded as early as 1845, the first prose sketch was completed in 1857, the libretto by 1877 and the score by 1880 – thirty-five years from the immaculate conception to the reverential delivery, during which time it must be remembered he wrote six other operas including the monster *Ring*. *Parsifal* was aimed to be the opening event for Wagner's custom-built opera house at Bayreuth. Only a major religious–cum–artistic event would be big enough to open the Festspielhaus and only the new house would be good enough for *Parsifal*. It was a PR man's dream and Wagner, always ready with a snappy slogan, labelled

Parsifal a Bühnenweifestspiel, or a Play Specially Composed For The Consecration of The Theatre. Early in 1882 the whole of Bayreuth entered into a period of advent and the rehearsals took place in an atmosphere of holy anticipation. The event itself was greeted with the usual angry debate but this time it was not so much about the music as about the propriety of going through what was pretty well a full-dress communion service on the stage of a theatre, even a consecrated Festspielhaus. Megalomaniac to the last, Wagner put an embargo on any performance of *Parsifal* anywhere other than Bayreuth, and then died. His dutiful widow Cosima kept this embargo in force until the copyright ran out in 1913. Although it was challenged by one or two operatic productions, and was cheekily put on at the Met in 1903, the embargo held pretty well. King Ludwig was permitted the treat of a couple of private showings in Munich, but for the Wagner fan who just had to see *Parsifal* it was Bayreuth or nothing. *Parsifal*'s most prosperous decade was probably the 1920s when every major opera house had to put it on. Since then it has settled down near the bottom of the Wagner popularity ratings and this can be explained by the current level of interest in grails and the fact that the Italians absolutely hate it. The Good Friday music is played quite a lot on radio stations on Good Friday.

COMMENT

Even today there are probably some devout Christians who can find in *Parsifal* a sublime experience, but for most of us it is a bit of a pill. It is not so much that we resent Wagner's hypocrisy in lecturing us on the virtues of innocence and purity of heart – as if Robert Maxwell had written a book on business ethics – it is because it is so staggeringly pretentious. Wagner sets himself up as a sort of musical Pope who has produced a work pretty well as important as the Crucifixion itself. He expects us to speak about *Parsifal* in hushed tones and to take our shoes off before we go in to hear it. Many clever and serious writers have spoken of Wagner as a seer and visionary who foresaw all the discoveries of those important Viennese doctors who were to tell us about sex-dreams, mother fixation, the ego, the id and things like that. This may well be true, but those of us who have a sturdy view of European culture find Wagner's claim to have put together bits of Schopenhauer's philosophy with bits of Buddhism, pagan myth and Christian doctrine, pretty irrelevant to the fact that the finished work is a bundle of pretentious nonsense tinged with morbid sentimentality. Even devout Christians were a bit sickened by the banal symbolism of the Amfortas/Christ Kundry/Mary Magdalene relationship when the opera first appeared.

So how does this simply awful libretto affect the music? Unfortunately quite a lot, because the music, however beautiful, and a lot of it is very beautiful, cannot entirely escape its association with the words. The assumption that you are in the presence of great holiness makes even the preludes to Acts I and III overblown and at the moments of extreme holiness (the voices in the dome of the Grail Hall) the pantomime on the stage makes the music sound ludicrous. By far the most enjoyable act is the naughty one, Act II, both the Flower Maidens with their unholy waltz and the seduction scene with Kundry first telling Parsifal of his boyhood (in one of the most beautiful passages in the opera) and then trying to seduce him (how one wishes she had made it: this indeed might have saved him from being such an insufferable prick). Time and again we have a long solo passage (as in Gurnemanz's narration in Act I) where the vocal part, although it may be doing wonderful things in reflecting the sense of the words, doesn't have much musical interest but the orchestra behind it is playing away in the most heavenly fashion. The scoring is rich and the mood mostly relaxed and gentle. Even in the Act I and Act III transformation scenes Wagner didn't go for the huge effects he had pulled off so brilliantly in *The Ring*. There is, however, a lingering smell of incense over even the most rumbustious music in both acts. The one occasion when this is (surprisingly) shaken off is at a very holy moment at the end of Act I when the knights break into Grailhouse Rock as they sit down to supper. This is very jolly.

There is ten minutes of magic in Act III where Gurnemanz and Kundry give Parsifal his wash and brush-up before his entry into the Grail Hall. For once we feel that these are three people with normal human feelings and not just Wagner's creatures acting as mouthpieces. The Good Friday music is not a bit holy and wonderfully refreshing – as good as any of Wagner's nature music, which is saying a lot, for as we know from *The Ring*, this strange man had a real feeling for mountains, forests and rivers.

Wagner's use of mottos has gone a stage further even than in *Tristan*. They are now associated with ideas and moods more than with things and people. People still have them, but Parsifal's motto, which is used more than any other, is still a rare bird compared with Siegfried's in *The Ring*, which comes pumping out every few minutes, and the mottos for the other characters hardly recur at all. By far the most heavily worked motto is the Grail (2) which crops up whenever the conversation moves grailwards and which has a field day when the spotlight is on the Grail itself. As in *Tristan*, the opening phrases of the prelude become a sort of quarry from which a lot of subsequent material is extracted. But often it is so worked and processed on the way that only a motto bloodhound would want to trail it back to its origins. *Parsifal* has one great musical plus. Wagner's orchestration, always brilliant, here moves into its final and rather wonderful phase. It is rich and at the same time clear, reflective, mellow and at ease with itself, producing lovely effects without seeming to try. As ever, he favours the wind band above the strings as spokesmen for his messages, but there is more equality in the treatment of the orchestra than in the earlier works and in *The Ring*.

The odour of sanctity which hangs around *Parsifal* is not always one of frankincense and myrrh. For one thing he has this ghoulish fascination with blood generally, and especially with the blood of Christ. Those of us who recoil even from the idea of being blood donors and have difficulty, as wine lovers, in accepting the idea of Christ's blood being turned into wine, can take a certain amount in the cause of opera, but this is surely too much:

> I feel the fount of divine blood
> Pour into my heart
> The ebb of my own sinful blood
> In mad tumult
> Must surge back into me
> To gush in wild terror
> Into the world of sinful passion
> It now rushes out
> Here through my wound like His
> Struck by a blow from that same spear

This, surely, is pretty disgusting and when coupled with Tristan's similar performance in tearing a wound open on stage, it must be more than a coincidence that the word 'blood' appears with such distasteful frequency.

But perhaps there are still a few for whom *Parsifal* is pure gold, as it was for the great and good Gustav Kobbé, who wrote of the Grail music after the first performance in Bayreuth: 'For spirituality it is unsurpassed. It is an absolutely perfect example of

religious music . . . without the slightest worldly taint.' Even today
Barry Millington, a famous Wagner scribe, though using longer
words, still seems to like it pretty well. He says: 'The juxtaposition
of sublimity with richly ambivalent symbolism and an underlying
ideology disturbing in its implications creates a work of unique
expressive power and endless fascination.' So that's it really. An
alpha.

Wagner's Creative Path

Year	Age	Location	Event	Opera Premieres
1813	–	Leipzig	Born.	
1832/3	19/20	Leipzig	Composes keyboard and orchestral works. Two early operas abandoned.	
1833/4	20/21	Wurtzburg	Chorus master at the local (pretty tacky) theatre. Writes *Die Feen*. No takers.	
1834	21	North Germany	Writes essays on musical topics. Joins a group of radical intellectual writers. Tags on to a travelling opera company.	
1836	23		Marries Minna. Writes *Das Liebesverbot*. Disastrous premiere.	*Das Liebesverbot*, Magdeburg
1837	24	Riga	Director of the local theatre.	
1838	25	Riga	Tentative thoughts about many operas. Writes a libretto for the Arabian Nights. Abandons it. Settles down to *Rienzi*.	
1839	26	Paris	Escape to Paris.	
1839/42	26/29	Paris	Works on *Rienzi* and *The Flying Dutchman* in tandem. Helped by Meyerbeer.	
1840	27	Paris	*Rienzi*, completed.	
1842	29	Paris	Starts work on *Tannhäuser*. *Rienzi* a hit.	*Rienzi*, Dresden
1843	30	Dresden	Deputy music director of the Dresden Hoftheater. Composes occasional music for the court. *Dutchman* not a hit.	*Flying Dutchman*, Dresden
1843/6	30/33	Dresden	Assembles a vast library of philosophy, history, mythology.	

Year	Age	Location	Event	Opera Premieres
			Encounters the stories of *Meistersinger, Lohengrin, Siegfried* and *Parsifal*. Works on *Lohengrin*.	
1845	32	Dresden	Prose draft of *Meistersinger* completed. *Tannhäuser* a mixed success.	*Tannhäuser*, Dresden
1846/48	33/35	Dresden	Works on prose drafts of parts of *The Ring*.	
1846	35	Dresden	Actively supports the Revolution of 1848.	
1849	36	Dresden	Takes part in the Dresden insurrection which fails. Flees to Switzerland.	
1849/53	36/40	Zurich	Develops his theories on opera as an art form. Also art generally. Publishes many books, essays, treatises etc. Composition at a standstill since *Lohengrin* (six years). Fed up with Minna. Unhappy, suicidal.	
1850	37		Liszt conducts *Lohengrin* premiere. The musical world impressed.	*Lohengrin*, Weimar
1853	40		Completes the poem of *The Ring* and publishes it privately. Enamoured by Schopenhauer's philosophy starts composition of *Rhinegold, Valkyrie* and *Siegfried*.	
1854	41	Zurich	Bailed out of debts by Wesendonck. *Rhinegold* completed.	
1856/57	44		*Valkyrie* completed. Abandons work on *Siegfried* and sets to on *Tristan* inspired by love of Mathilde Wesendonck. Minna insufferable. Goes to Venice without her.	

Year	Age	Location	Event	Opera Premieres
1859	46	Venice/ Lucerne	*Tristan* completed.	
1860	47	Paris	Conducts concerts of his own work.	
1861	48	Paris	Disastrous production of *Tannhäuser* at the Paris Opéra.	
1862	49	Mainz	Works on *Meistersinger*.	
1863	50	Vienna	Flees from Mainz to escape debtors.	
1864	51	Munich	Finds his ultimate angel – King Ludwig of Bavaria.	
1865	52	Lucerne/ Munich	Takes up with Cosima. *Tristan* received with acclaim and hostility.	*Tristan*, Munich
1867	54		*Meistersinger* completed.	
1868	55	Munich	*Meistersinger* an unqualified triumph – at last.	*Meistersinger*, Munich
1869	56		The musical world divided but impressed by *Rhinegold*.	*Rhinegold*, Munich
1870	57		Marries Cosima – at last. *Valkyrie* intensifies factional reaction to Wagner.	*Valkyrie*, Munich
1871	58	Bayreuth	*Siegfried* completed.	
1874	61		*Göttedämmerung* completed.	
1876	63		First complete *Ring* cycle recognized as a world event.	*Siegfried*, *Götterdämmerung*, Bayreuth
1876/80	63/67		Publishes numerous essays attempting to regenerate the human race by means, amongst other things, of ethnic cleansing of the arts and vegetarianism. Much taken by the philosophy of Nietzsche. Works on *Parsifal*, completed 1881.	

Year	Age	Location	Event	Opera Premieres
1882	69	Bayreuth	*Parsifal* received with awe, ecstasy and incomprehension. Some heart attacks.	*Parsifal*, Bayreuth
1883	70		Death in Venice.